¶ La vida de Lazarillo de
Tormes/ y de sus fortunas: y
aduersidades. Nueuamente impressa,
corregida, y de nueuo añadi-
da enesta segūda im-
pression. ·

Uendense en Alcala de Henares, en
casa de Salzedo Librero. Año
de. M. D. LIIII.

Title page of *Lazarillo de Tormes* printed at Alcalá de Henares in 1554,
one of three first editions of the original modern novel. Lazarus is point-
ing to the blind man as the master who illuminated him and put him on
the step to social success, evidence that the anonymous author's irony
was understood by early readers.

Actual size: 3½″ × 5¾″             (Courtesy of the British Museum)

*The Myth of the Picaro*

# The Myth of the Picaro

Continuity and Transformation
of the Picaresque Novel
1554–1954

*by*

*Alexander Blackburn*

THE UNIVERSITY OF NORTH CAROLINA PRESS
CHAPEL HILL

Library of Congress Cataloging in Publication Data

Blackburn, Alexander.
    The myth of the picaro.

    Bibliography: p.
    Includes index.
    1.  Picaresque literature—History and
criticism.    I.  Title.
PN3428.B53        809.3'3        78-23605
ISBN 0-8078-1334-6

Tris's

# Contents

# Foreword

*The Myth of the Picaro* is a comparative, critical study of the picaresque novel through history as well as a study of its influence upon the nature and origins of modern fiction. In describing picaresque myth, I have sought a particular narrative structure within novels selected from various literatures over four centuries and have used for the first time the resources of myth criticism as well as the methods of intellectual history. The theory of a picaresque myth was advanced by Claudio Guillén in 1961 and again by Fernando Lázaro Carreter in 1972, but, to the best of my knowledge, has remained unexplored. Consequently, I have departed, sometimes radically, from traditional views of the picaresque novel outside Spain. Recent book-length studies such as Robert Alter's *Rogue's Progress* and Alexander Parker's *Literature and the Delinquent* are either unsystematic or still burdened by the sociological approach popularized by Frank Chandler's *Literature of Roguery* seventy years ago. To clarify picaresque tradition from its beginnings in Spain to the present, a fresh approach has been needed. Not only have I reexamined the problem of the picaresque novel in England, but also, largely for the first time, I have considered picaresque tradition in the literature of the United States.

Throughout this study I have used the word picaro without accent or italics. Picaroon seems an awkward and pejorative Anglicism lacking the iconographic quality with which the familiar word picaro may be invested. Furthermore, the usual definition of *picaro* as "rogue" has contributed its share of critical confusion to studies of the picaresque novel, especially outside Spain.

[ix]

## Foreword

Portions of this study first appeared in 1963 as a doctoral thesis submitted to the Faculty of English of the University of Cambridge. For the wisdom, patience, and tolerance of my professors—David Daiches and Raymond Williams, who supervised, Ian Watt and Matthew Hodgart, who examined—I record a long-standing debt of gratitude. The encouragement of Dr. Douglas McKay of the University of Colorado at Colorado Springs led me to elaborate upon the earlier work. To Lambert Davis and colleagues of The University of North Carolina Press, I am indebted for many valuable suggestions. For permission to quote from my article, "A Writer's Quest for Knowledge," *The Colorado Quarterly* 24 (1975): 67–81, I am grateful to the editor.

Finally, I would like to give especial thanks to my wife, Dr. Inés Dölz-Blackburn, for sharing with me some of the labors of revision as well as her scholar's knowledge of Hispanic culture.

*The Myth of the Picaro*

# I

# Introduction

Since the birth of the modern novel more than four hundred years ago, the myth of the picaro has been a continuous part of fiction, though often in modified form and frequently as an implied polarity to the literature of unity and love. The major literary genre of modern centuries thus not only has a recognizable birth but also has always contained within itself both the distant, undifferentiated human past and a creative present that continues to tell a story of social disorder and psychic disintegration.

The origin of most literary forms remains obscured in antiquity. We conjecture possibilities from magnificent survivors. What epics came before *Gilgamesh* and *The Iliad*, what tragedies before *Job* and *Prometheus*, are known to us as but shadows, but even were they solidly known, that knowledge would not lead to an understanding of the modern novel. Homer was not first to sing tales, nor Aeschylus to write plays, nor the author or authors of Genesis to compose Creation poems. Man's power of imagination is so great that we may presume the existence of many a mute, inglorious Milton before Babylon. Yet even if our knowledge were to expand to make known the entire course of culture, there will still be a mystery, for the story of literature has its ubi sunt.

The first novelists created their readers, and we are still among them. Although, as a literary form, the novel is notoriously mixed with folk tales and history, epic and romance, drama, lyric, sermons, letters, biographies, and so forth, although there is no single Platonic form by which novelistic fiction may be measured, although, in short, no one is absolutely sure what a novel is beyond its being a prose narrative of length and of realistic import, there is nonetheless a historical moment when the novel—call it a modern novel, a conscious art of narration—differentiates itself from all the literature preceding it and gives similar shape thereafter to literary creations.

That moment, beyond any doubt, occurred in Spain in the first half of the sixteenth century. For a long time, of course, there have been American and European scholars who could not or would not peek over the Pyrenees. Consequently, literary nationalism has made some heavy weather concerning the rise of the novel. A prevalent belief, for example, is that the first *real* novels are English of the eighteenth century. According to this belief, Spanish novels are subgeneric primitives like *Lazarillo de Tormes* or embarrassing monuments like *Don Quixote*. However generously their art or tradition are acclaimed, Spanish novels have usually received, outside Spain, less than their due recognition as the first modern novels. Of course, the heyday of printing technology and, more important, of the European bourgeoisie, both significant for the rise of the novel, occurred in the eighteenth century. But it does not follow that the novel is exclusively an art form devoted to the middle class and rooted in capitalist economics. Nor does it follow that the "great tradition" of the English novel is then "the" greatest, greater than the Spanish, the French, the German, certainly greater than the American, and only overshadowed, apparently by an act of God, by the Russian. To be sure, the English novelists from Defoe to Dickens to Conrad and Lawrence, including the Irishman Joyce and the American James, form a tradition of the great, but the critical attempt to equate the English novel with *the* novel suffers from a lack of focus. To place the novel's authentic origin in Spain in the sixteenth century does, I hope, extend our awareness of a subtle literary art.

Surveying the origin of novelistic fiction, we begin to see nuclear themes that for their elucidation require the resources of myth criticism. Yet, perhaps fortunately, there is no generally agreed-upon definition to apply to all instances of myth in art and literature. As Francis Fergusson writes, "One of the most striking properties of myths is that they generate new forms . . .

in the imaginations of those who try to grasp them."[1] Hence we cannot lay hands on a single myth prior to its imaginative embodiments. For Plato, the first known user of the term, *mythologia* meant no more than the telling of stories. Indeed, for many, myth means stories that are Greek—something like the Greek tales of Theseus and the Minotaur, or Odysseus and the Cyclops, or Oedipus and Jocasta. Yet, classicist G. S. Kirk warns, "The truth is that Greek myths provide no better an instance of what myths quintessentially are than any other extensive cultural set." Although we may have been brought up to regard Greek myths "as composing a paradigmatic system that can be used as a central point of reference for the whole study of mythology,"[2] anthropologists and ethnologists have recorded different sets of myths from other cultures, some of them possessed of qualities without Greek parallel. Myth, then, may mean a story from any number of cultures including—to anticipate my argument—the culture of the recent West.

If myth is not confined to a particular cultural set, neither is it a category restricted to particular kinds of tales. A myth does not have to be about gods and men, about centaurs, titans, or Moby Dicks. A myth does not have to be about popular fantasies and superstitions, nor does it have to be related to rituals, although undoubtedly some of the oldest myths reveal such connections. For example, in the myth of the Divine King who was killed annually and was reborn in the person of his successor, a six-thousand-year-old Near Eastern ritual for ensuring the well-being of the community has vast literary and religious implications. But an ever-living, ever-dying god, a Christ figure, "hero of a thousand faces," gives form and meaning only to some stories, not to all. Furthermore, myth and religion are not necessarily twin aspects or parallel manifestations of the same psychic condition, although certainly some myths such as the story of Tristan and Iseult do convey religion's intensity of feeling of the immanent and transcendent divine mystery. Finally, myths are more than folk tales with their reflection of simple social situations, their fantasy and freely developing, often crude narrative designs.

Myths, in short, are both sacred and secular tales that yet may have a serious underlying purpose or, as Kirk calls it, an "imaginative or introspective urge."[3]

In this study I am concerned with myth in two senses: first as a timeless and placeless universal story, second but primarily as a creative narrative structure. In the first sense, already too well known from Freud's and Jung's studies of the parallelism of dream and myth to require demonstration, myth is an elementary idea or archetype continuous with the whole history of man and thus capable of developing spontaneously, along traditional lines, wherever mankind lives, dreaming. Obviously, any theory about the spiritual unity of the human race, what James Joyce calls "the grave and constant in human experience,"[4] may arrest and free the mind at its depths. The mythological archetype, cutting across boundaries of time and culture, functions to awake the sleeping consciousness to the profound mystery and order of the universe. As John B. Vickery declares in his introduction to *Myth and Literature*, "The ability of literature to move us is profoundly due to its mythic quality, to its possession of *mana*, the *numinous*, or the mystery in the face of which we feel an awed delight or terror at the world of man. The real function of literature in human affairs is to continue myth's ancient and basic endeavor to create a meaningful place for man in a world oblivious to his presence." The myth critic, he explains, "isolates latent elements, which, like those of dreams, possess the force that vitalizes the manifest pattern."[5]

The archetype of the first sense of the myth in the picaresque novels is the trickster, as I shall show. To identify a veiled source of vitality, buried roots reaching down into deepest springs of being, however, scarcely discriminates between mythic and aesthetic dimensions. To consider a work a repository of some mythological archetype may violate the integrity of that work as literature. Therefore the myth critic must prepare analysis of structure. Each work is treated as individually and culturally unique, of its moment, reflecting its own time. At one level, a historical approach is called for. At another level, myth criticism comes into play by determining the underlying structure of a basic narrative, recognizing not just a more or less static arche-

[6]

type (such as trickster) but the dynamic "creative mythology" (as Joseph Campbell calls it) of the individual work. An author may not have been consciously aware of the underlying structure. For example, the use of myth by writers of the Middle Ages seems to have been unconscious in the great majority of instances, so that a journey-quest pattern in, say, *Sir Gawain and the Green Knight* surfaces because of an allegorical method of emotional exploration rather than as the conscious symbolic method of a Joyce, Eliot, and Yeats.[6] Whatever the degree of an author's consciousness of a mythic structure, the critic who discerns myth functioning at the narrative core may be able to illuminate the work of art as art, not removing our gaze from a temporal creation but bringing us to closer perception of imaginative forces acting in it.

Thus, I will argue, the idea of the picaresque novels is not exhausted by reference to trickster myth, interesting as that is as an account both of spontaneous transmission and of the attractiveness, to authors and readers, of an otherwise austere kind of story. The other, deep-down myth of the picaro, a myth containing continuity and transformation through various works and cultures for four centuries, is to be sought in narrative structures rather than in apparent content.

I am not proposing an absolute guide for identifying and defining a picaresque novel. The very existence of a literary genre such as the picaresque presupposes certain recognizable characteristics of content and technique. Let the hero be an orphan, let him relate his adventures in a more or less sardonic manner, let him wander into delinquency, and so forth—and we are orbiting in the picaresque galaxy. For genre, that may be enough, or almost. What seems to be needed is some distinction between genre and myth. That is, if picaresque *genre* may be viewed as traditional model or conventional pattern, then let us view picaresque *myth*, as Claudio Guillén declares, "as an essential situation or significant structure derived from the novels themselves."[7] Whereas both genre and myth assume continuities, those of genre are more concerned with technical characteristics, those of myth more concerned with cultural characteristics. Thus, technically considered according to genre, the picaresque novel has its central tradition in certain Spanish narratives but thereafter becomes a subgenre of the modern novel, a tributary of increasingly casual impact and significance. Although useful, the genre approach finally leaves readers and critics sprawling before the probable truth of the proposition that picarism is the contemporary, post–World War II ethos of Western culture. From genre we turn to myth, and suddenly the myth of the picaro expresses and shapes, through the participation of readers who understand themselves in a correlative way, a story that is culturally conspicuous, however infrequently or incompletely imitated.

At no period of literary history is the principle of the integrity of the individual work more demanding of the critic than in the West since the middle of the twelfth century. For the recent West, as opposed to the primitive, Oriental, and early Occidental worlds, has been a period where, in Joseph Campbell's words,

an accelerating disintegration has been undoing the formidable orthodox tradition . . . and with its fall, the released creative powers of a great company of towering individuals have broken forth: so that not one, or even two or three, but a galaxy of mythologies—as many, one might say, as the multitude of its geniuses—must be taken into account in any study of the spectacle of our own titanic age. . . . [In] the fields of literature, secular philosophy, and the arts, a totally new type of non-theological revelation, of great scope, great depth, and infinite variety, has become the actual spiritual guide and structuring force of the civilization.[8]

On this overriding cultural fact of modern centuries, the displacement of traditional authority by individual experience, Campbell's words in *Creative Mythology* deserve still further quotation:

In the context of a traditional mythology, the symbols are presented in socially maintained rites, through which the individual is required to experience, or will pretend to have experienced, certain insights, sentiments, and commitments. In what I am calling "creative" mythology, on the other hand, this order is reversed: the individual has had an experience of his own—of order, horror, beauty, or even mere exhilaration—which he seeks to communicate through signs; and if his realization has been of a certain depth and import, his communication will have the value and force of living myth—for those, that is to say, who receive and respond to it of themselves, with recognition, uncoerced.[9]

The presence of a creative mythology in the new literary form of the novel in sixteenth-century Spain is accordingly to be expected. Only a profound spiritual reorientation such as that described by Campbell can account for the emergence of new nuclear themes in the picaresque, themes of individual alienation from and loneliness within a coercive and chaotic social order.

The novel-making human spirit of the sixteenth century and thereafter perceives the highest objective truth ultimately in the form of its own experiential activity, rather than in the deterministic reality of orthodox belief. But what kind of experience of the human spirit in the sixteenth century is meant? There is a historical correlative to the fictive experience rendered in certain Spanish novels of picaresque kind. This historical correlative is found in the biography of Fernando de Rojas (1476?–1541), author of *La Celestina* (1499), a novelistic drama that in art of characterization through mutual interaction is equal to comparison to a Shakespearean play of a century later. A sketch of Rojas's life leads to an understanding of the first novels, their design and tone, for which the student of fiction stands indebted to Stephen Gilman's recent publication, *The Spain of Fernando de Rojas: The Intellectual and Social Landscape of "La Celestina."*[10]

Rojas was a Renaissance man but also what was called in Spain a *converso*, a Christian of Jewish origin—a person who might have abandoned one faith without gaining another, a potentially lost soul skeptical of traditional dogma and morality. He was a member of a caste subject to intense scorn and suspicion, forced into a marginal position within his world, and reacting to persecution in a number of characteristic ways, among them cultivation of irony. The *converso* situation held the possibility of a counterculture or community of those experienced or conditioned enough to relish the hidden import of the ironist's language. While the category of *converso* must be used cautiously, because the forcibly converted Jews were just as Spanish as were the Old Christians, the circumstances in which lived and wrote a Rojas, whose father and father-in-law were both condemned by the Inquisition, cannot be ignored. Between 1485 and 1501 in Toledo alone over seven thousand *converso* artisans, professional men, merchants, and city officials were permanently dishonored (publicly reconciled, jailed, or executed) by the Inquisition; and there is documentary evidence that when Rojas was perhaps twelve years old his father was arrested, imprisoned, tried, found guilty, and in all likelihood executed by fire in an auto-de-fé. Rojas graduated in law at Salamanca between 1497 and 1500 and thereafter, like many a *converso*, gained at least an outward form of respectability. But he was, one deduces with certainty, an artist acutely aware of his inner apartness from the society in which he grew up and, precariously, survived. His life and art constitute a mode of escape from desperation.

The facts of Rojas's life reveal certain spiritual conditions that could give rise to the picaresque novel. Time and again the *converso* paradox of being at the center of society and also on its margin gives thematic form to early modern novels as it does to *La Celestina*.[11]

Of course, I am talking of a historical correlative, not theorizing about racial or ethnic origins for the Spanish novels. That Shakespeare wrote passionate sonnets to and for a young man tells us absolutely nothing about the art of *Hamlet*; for all we know, Shakespeare perpetrated a hoax and was turning sonnet tradition on its head. By loose analogy, we do not need the kind of logic that goes like this: some Spanish novelists were New Christians, therefore some modern novelists of Jewish background such as Franz Kafka and Saul Bellow are to be domesticated in picaresque tradition. Nevertheless, there is an important point to the scholarship linking the *converso* situation to the Spanish novelists. The point is not that some writers may have been related to the caste, for example, Rojas and Francisco Delicado (*La Lozana andaluza*, 1528) and Mateo Alemán (*Guzmán de Alfarache*, 1599, 1604). It would be foolish to presume that such facts and probabilities explain or categorize the art of fiction and absurd to believe that the power of imagination can be described as anything but human. The point is that such facts and probabilities help to depict a spiritual reality having to do with actual historical experience: Rojas and the first novelists, especially though not necessarily because of the *converso* situation, lived as marginal men in a world bearing fearful resemblance to our own

Orwellian one of Big Brother, Newspeak, Thought Police, and Doublethink. As marginal men, they were "condemned to live in two worlds" and compelled "to assume in relation to the worlds . . . the role of a cosmopolitan and stranger."[12] Dwelling in the shadow of the Inquisition, they suffered extreme tension and instability. "Suspicious of each other," as Gilman describes them, "suspected by everybody else, the *conversos* lived in a world in which no human relationship could be counted on, in which a single unpremeditated sentence could bring unutterable and unbearable torture . . . a world in which one had constantly to observe oneself from an alien point of view, that of the watchers from without . . . a world of simulation and camouflage interrupted by outbursts of irrepressible authenticity." Such a world, as readers of the Shakespearean masquerade are aware, was in general the rigid role-playing one of the Renaissance, but for the *conversos* such social games were an excruciating threat to personal identity. They could, as defense, attempt to merge with the crowd, create a "nonlife" through standardized phrases of piety and ritual gestures, and give lying autobiographical accounts based upon "rigid masking of the inner self, calculated conformity, [and] unremitting self-observation."[13] In society one could never be oneself, and yet the social core was so rotten that one was conforming to the very image of corruption. The poisoned worlds of *Hamlet*, *Troilus and Cressida*, and *The Duchess of Malfi* are prefigured in sixteenth-century Spain, where everyone could be called to account, that is, make a confession in prose, and where outrageous fortune was a euphemism for the Inquisition.

This Spain of Fernando de Rojas is the world as actually rendered in the classic picaresque novels, the protagonists of which —the picaros—are just such anguished souls who conform to a rotten society and mask their inner selves. *La Celestina*, Gilman contends, provided novelists with a complex structure of irony that was "a way of exploring artistically the dubious relation of modern man to the devaluated society in which he lives." Moreover, Rojas's dramatic presentation of human life as "a mutual affair, a continuing interaction,"[14] helps, I believe, to account for the new perspective of consciousness that sets the modern novel apart from such narratives as *The Odyssey* and *Metamorphoses* (or

*Golden Ass*). In Apuleius, mankind gains the quality of meta-morphosis that Ovid had applied to gods, but no one before Rojas viewed human transformational power as the essential revelation of individual character relentlessly acting in and inter-acting with a world in which all meanings and values were disintegrating—in which the flux of mutual consciousness was that society.

To give an account of self was a dire responsibility of a six-teenth-century Spaniard, and if his background, in the eyes of the Inquisition, were "tainted," he sought to trick others by creating a nonself and by claiming dubious honors. Façades of nobility had become a marketable commodity not simply for the sake of bourgeois vanity![15] In an age of real heroes such as the conquistadores, society was teeming with those for whom heroic grandeur would inevitably and often tragically be denied, yet whose physical and spiritual hunger demanded the acquisition of honor by all means possible. Everyone—from an author's disenchanted or dogmatic perspective at least—was a trickster, deceiver, or confidence man of some sort, and honor, as it is for Falstaff, no more than "a mere 'scutcheon belonging to him who died o' Wednesday."

No wonder that the very name Lazarillo de Tormes parodies its devaluated world: Lazarus the beggar, son of dishonored parents, derives noble pedigree from elemental rootlessness, a river. Unlike the typical hero of legend such as Odysseus, son of Laertes, Lazarillo cannot genuinely relate himself to a mythical time when everything was placed in order and achieved its proper nature; the anonymous author of *Lazarillo* does not grant his protagonist the charter of what anthropologists call a culture-hero. Lazarillo the picaro is a being stripped of social identity; dominated by hunger, he is a wanderer in a world where normal conceptions of good and evil no longer operate, a lost soul who is either playing tricks on people or having them played on him and who, like a god before Prometheus, has no wish to benefit mankind.

There is something so elemental, so primordial, about that solitary, loveless ego called Lazarillo that he impinges on a read-er's consciousness as a mythical being more remote even than

Lear's "bare, forked animal, unaccommodated man," not only detached from human society but, parodistically, the precondition and creator of himself. Shorn of traditionally meaningful spiritual existence, he—through the author's painterlike awareness of reduction to a vanishing point—has come to symbolize the timeless, undifferentiated natural being within every individual. His origins are indeed past finding out! Lacking even physical appearance (unlike Sancho Panza, for example), he seems to exist not only without roots but also without boundaries.

Lazarillo, thus described, is one of the permutations of trickster myth, perhaps the most primitive of all archetypes and one found in most cultures. What trickster stands for is described by Karl Kerényi:

Archaic social hierarchies are exceedingly strict. To be archaic does not mean to be chaotic. Quite the contrary: nothing demonstrates the meaning of the all-controlling social order more impressively than the religious recognition of that which evades this order, in a figure who is the exponent and personification of the life of the body: never wholly subdued, ruled by lust and hunger, forever running into pain and injury, cunning and stupid in action. Disorder belongs to the totality of life, and the spirit of this disorder is the Trickster. His function in an archaic society, or rather the function of his mythology, of the tales told about him, is to add disorder to order and so make a whole, to render possible, within the fixed bounds of what is permitted, an experience of what is not permitted.

Kerényi concludes, "Picaresque literature has consciously taken over this function. . . . In Spain the picaresque novel constituted itself as a literary genus and remained the sole means of revolt against the rigidity of tradition."[16] Claudio Guillén reaches a similar conclusion by a different route: "From *Lazarillo* to our day," he observes, "the picaresque has been an outlet for the expression of human alienation."[17]

Whether consciously transmitted, the trickster myth helps to explain why the picaresque novel has had a continuous life in various cultures over more than four centuries. The timeless schema, always available to consciousness, tends to appear wherever and whenever the modern mind, in flight from decadence, in quest of meaning, declares its freedom from narrow confines of law, custom, and circumstance. Trickster keeps popping up in many guises, often reduced to a harmless entertainer, the merry rogue (who deceives many a critic into thinking him a picaro), sometimes transformed into a devil or divine deceiver or Vice[18] who tells nothing but lies (as in Melville's *Confidence-Man*), but his true nature, as Kerényi maintains, has energy potential as "the spirit of disorder, the enemy of boundaries." Trickster's appearance in picaresque mythology in novels is consistently as a threat to order and meaning—to that totality of significant humanity, that commedia of awareness that would, above all, include love.

A picaresque novel is a seriocomic form that tends to appear at times when the literary imagination is unusually threatened by catastrophe: that is, at times when the very idea of existence commingles with the world of illusion. Broadly speaking, there have been two such times since the waning of the Middle Ages. The first is the period extending from the Reformation through the Counter-Reformation to the middle of the seventeenth century and the so-called scientific revolution. The second is that extending from the loomings of the romantic movement through the intellectual disaster area we call the Darwinian revolution to the present time of intense global conflict. If these periods are not precise, they do at least uncover that interregnum sometimes called the eighteenth-century Enlightenment when catastrophe did not seem to present a problem for creative minds. A sense of the real, a sense that objective experience of the world has validity, tends to distinguish the eighteenth-century mind from the minds of earlier and later periods. And significantly, the eighteenth-century novelists produced a greatly modified version of the picaresque.

At the time when the first picaresque novel, *Lazarillo de Tormes*, appeared—it was published in 1554 but may have been written several decades earlier, almost in the wake of Luther's Reformation—Spanish hegemony spread uneasily over two worlds. The landscape of Europe bristled with men and nations envious of Spanish power. The influx of New World gold, added to earlier price revolutions, overburdened the Spanish economy. And there were other burdens: population explosion, widespread poverty, and the disruptions of long war, of widespread corruption of authority, and of an imperial spirit of self-assertive individualism. [19] Everywhere men quickened with awareness of their worldly environment but consequently felt the precarious reality of their own lives. Yet men continued to be taught that the true reality lay in the supernatural other-world of God. So they, too, would believe in the medieval world—but believe without a living faith. José Ortega y Gasset has described this spiritual state of affairs in fifteenth- and sixteenth-century Spain: "Souls look[ed] simultaneously toward the one world and the other as though walleyed, belonging to neither."[20] According to dogma, the world that begged for every man's conquest was given over to flesh and the devil; men yearned for it all the same and in the process seem to have become darkly conscious of the entanglement of their souls with the accursed externality. Obviously, the drama of life remained the drama of salvation: the individual life was a cultural form analogous to the cathedral-dominated walled city. But how was the individual to accept his part in the drama when the real business of living was being conducted, not in the cathedral, but in the market? How could he accept it if in the struggle for survival he was forced to conform his actions to a world of illusion? This was a question at the heart of *Lazarillo de Tormes*, and the feeling in the question recalls the Gospel query, "If the salt have lost his savor, wherewith shall it be salted?" The feeling expressed might be called anguish or the tragic sense of life.

The feeling of anguish is by no means attenuated in the second picaresque novel, *Guzmán de Alfarache* (1599 and 1604) by Mateo Alemán, and in a third, *La vida del Buscón* (1626) by Francisco de Quevedo. Both these novels are steeped in baroque illusionism: that is, in the feeling that life is a dream and rounded with a sleep. According to one historian, the basis of this sense of the illusory quality of observed reality was "a deeply felt religiosity and more specifically a renewed belief in the transcendence of God as the true reality."[21] At the same time the age was intoxicated with human power and with the life that fled, it seemed, from its own nothingness. Only in death would men find *desengaño*, the disenchantment and spiritual restitution by which they might recognize the proof of divine mercy. The idea may be illustrated from an emblem in *La pícara Justina* of 1605. The emblem represents the Ship of Picaresque Life steered by Time across the River of Oblivion toward a nearby port, where the figure of Death waits and holds out the promised *desengaño*. Aboard ship or beside it, leading it, are Guzmán and Lazarillo, among others then popularly associated with the picaresque, and atop the mast sits Bacchus, symbol of life's intoxicating powers.[22] Of course, as historian Fernand Braudel reminds us, baroque art often smacks of propaganda and may exaggerate, for instructional purposes, the attractions of death, "because this is an art which is preoccupied with convincing."[23] Yet this exaggeration, this self-conscious theatricality, indicates that the need for persuasion was motivated by spiritual desperation.

The classic triad of picaresque novels are likewise emblematic and reveal a paradoxical comic anguish. After the disintegration of existential reality, after the silencing of goodness and trust, something resilient and stoically good-humored still clings to life. "The worst," as Edgar says in *Lear*, "returns to laughter." There is no grandeur in the picaro's life, but it is life of a kind, lived at the diminishing point where life and death, truth and falsehood, good and evil, have arrived as tragically convertible.

Camus has called this feeling "cosmic homelessness."[24] Like the Spanish picaresque novelists, contemporary writers seem to be looking desperately for grounds for living in life itself. Not infrequently, too, they have embodied this spiritual quest in the person of some solitary sinner who, like the picaro, is an outcast of society who wants to enter in. This representative figure, according to R. W. B. Lewis in *The Picaresque Saint*, has appeared in novels by Camus, Faulkner, Graham Greene, Ignazio Silone, and others. Lewis's inclusion of these authors might be considered a distortion of our understanding of the picaresque genre, for indeed, as far as genre is concerned, Thomas Mann, Günter Grass, and Ralph Ellison seem much closer to a central tradition than the authors mentioned. But, again, where picaresque myth is distinguished from genre, the "half-outsider"[25] is a ubiquitous figure in contemporary world literature. In one way or another, then, the original novelistic myth of the picaro continues to live in the mind more than four hundred years since it first achieved form.

The present study grew out of the recognition that there is a continuity of picaresque tradition but that it has not been clearly defined. It was once fashionable to approach a literary kind with a view to its purity. But modern genre theory, according to René Wellek and Austin Warren in *Theory of Literature*, builds on the basis of inclusiveness, seeking to preserve the uniqueness of each work of art while finding the common denominator of a kind, its shared literary devices and literary purpose. "The genre represents," they write, "a sum of aesthetic devices at hand, available to the writer and already intelligible to the reader. The good writer partly conforms to the genre as it exists, partly stretches it."[26] The genre (or subgenre) of the picaresque novel may, I believe, be approached in this way, but only so far. Outside Spain, the generic qualifications of many novels tagged as picaresque—from Alain-René Lesage's *Gil Blas* to Joyce Cary's *The Horse's Mouth*—are virtually negated by an absence or a submergence of the myth of the picaro. When the myth does resurface in the genre, a continuity should be discerned according to a critical approach that includes in its view both technical and cultural characteristics.

The path to critical study of the picaresque has been cleared by Hispanic scholars in comparatively recent times. They have shown that the Spanish novels are works of subtle literary art and that many earlier picaresque studies were superficial. The most typical and influential of these outside of Spain have been Frank W. Chandler's *Romances of Roguery* (1899) and *The Literature of Roguery* (1907). Although now out of fashion, Chandler's views still obtrude when critics emphasize roguery or delinquency. For years there has been much confusion about the nature of the picaresque novel precisely because critics have tried to group works according to their roguish subject matter rather than according to the artistic meaning functioning in the works themselves. Too much emphasis has been placed on social or religious causes, on literary antecedents, or on the etymology of the word *pícaro*. Not infrequently there have been instances of the generic fallacy of assigning to the whole the quality of a part, for example, the psychology of the hero, the formless structure, or the preponderance of special types of subject matter. Among misconceptions of the picaresque novel that have resulted are these: that *pícaro* means "rogue" or "antihero" regardless of the literary context; that episodic structure is primitive and excludes the possibility of symbolic, moral, and psychological coherence in the narrative; or that the only literary interest of the picaresque novels lies in their antiromantic realism. Value judgments, too, have been superficial or colored by emotion. Thus, for instance, Chandler popularized the notion that Lesage's *Gil Blas*, a non-Spanish, nonpicaresque, eighteenth-century novel of manners is the crowning achievement of the genre. The modern emphasis upon the artistic meaning of the three Spanish masterpieces has at last restored critical perspective.

It is now apparent that the significance of the Spanish picaresque novels consists, as Guillén expresses it, "largely in their handling of a theme which was called to play a fundamental part in the modern novel: the dynamic relationship between the inwardness of the individual and his active career in a social and economic environment."[27] The art of the picaresque novels, not their subject matter, establishes them as the first modern novels. Thus from the beginning they are generically distinct from epic, drama, romance, satire, or such rogue anatomies as criminal biographies, conny-catching tales, jestbooks, beggarbooks, pirate adventures, and sketches of low-life manners. While it is reasonably true that the representation of an underdog's precarious life constitutes a substantial parody of the heroic and romantic, it is not true that this is the whole distinction between a picaresque novel and the epic, drama, or romance. The real distinction lies in the manner in which the picaresque novels present the human will in action. Differing from epic, drama, and romance, they do not present isolated human passions checked by external laws or existing in a vacuum but, instead, the unglorified will controlled by the relative contexts of psychological and sociological being actually operating within the story. The picaro is a *persona*, not merely a parodistic antihero. What of satire in the picaresque novels?[28] It is true that the picaresque novels are austerely critical, but it is not true that satire is the sum of their criticism. Unlike, for example, *Gulliver's Travels*, the picaresque novels subordinate satiric perspectives to a novelistic perspective; even allowing for the view that Captain Gulliver is a rounded character, he would have to be regarded, not as a half-outsider but as a misanthropic lunatic. Whereas it might be said that formal satire dissolves reality with reference to the satirist's chosen norms, it might also be said that picaresque satire makes dissolution eventful, a psychological loss of the picaro's sense of reality during his entanglement with his world. And finally, the picaresque novels differ from the rogue anatomies with which Chandler and others associated them. Generally there are two types of rogue anatomy —that which portrays the jests and deeds of a character such as Till Eulenspeigel or that which presents social conditions in a tableau, such as the criminal underworld in Cervantes's sketch, *Rinconete y Cortadillo*. Unlike picaresque novels, however, the rogue anatomies do not combine individual and social planes into a single novelistic point of view.

Therefore, if we are to seek a common denominator of picaresque fiction, we must look for the functional within the novels themselves. Attention must center on the picaro, who is the heart of every true picaresque novel. The term picaro, as used throughout this study, is technical shorthand for "the hero of a picaresque novel." The term, first used in the sense of "scullion" in 1525 and in the sense of "evil living" in 1548,[29] was employed in an early edition of *Guzmán de Alfarache* and by custom has come to apply to the type of hero Alemán had portrayed. Its usual application to the hero of the earlier *Lazarillo de Tormes* suggests that its meaning must be seen not in the much-debated etymological sense but from within the novelistic situation.[30]

And that fundamental situation of the literary picaro is the loneliness of an individual isolated *within* society.

A good way to see what kind of loneliness is represented in the picaro is to distinguish it from other kinds. It is not the individual isolation represented in classical fictions such as the *Metamorphoses* of Apuleius or the *Satyricon* of Petronius. The individual of antiquity may come into conflict with his environment, but, doing so, he is always in the wrong because the world he moves in or out of is a static, timeless continuum, not the active social reality of novelistic literature.[31] The picaro's society acts within him as he within it. Loneliness becomes an evolving state. Neither individual nor society is always in the wrong. Nor is the isolation of the picaro the isolation of the ideal temporarily dislodged from corrupt society: ideal isolation still retains potential identity, stability, and love. The picaro's loneliness is by contrast the outgrowth of the sense of failed identity, of the instability of an inferior social standing, and of the failure to find human solidarity. Unlike Donne's lovers—

> All other things to their destruction draw,
> Only our love hath no decay—
>
> ["The Anniversary"]

the picaro stands in the way of mortality and cannot cross at will the bridge of love. His loneliness is the fear of love. In fact, one of the sure clues to the absence of a picaro in a novel is the representation of a fellowship. *Don Quixote*, *Tom Jones*, and *Roderick Random* do not fully portray picaros because in them the wandering hero is accompanied, the "I" becoming a "we." By a similar token the picaro's isolation is not the romantic rebel's, opposing nature to convention. Byron's Don Juan or Stendhal's Julien Sorel make isolation into an affirmation of natural superiority. But the picaro is a conformist with little antisocial tendencies in the affirmative sense. He yearns to enter into society, implicitly accepting social values no matter how hostile to his dignity they have proved to be.

The extent of the picaro's loneliness may be seen in the compulsive restlessness with which he goes forth in search of life. He is an eternal *buscón*, both seeker and swindler. Yet increasingly those whom the picaro encounters on the road tend to reflect his own lack of significant reality, and his jerky, episodic journey is thus precisely the form this experience takes. The more he seeks, the more disintegrated he becomes. Thus, finally, in order to bring himself into precarious relation to society, the picaro undertakes to form a deceptive identity out of mere appearances. *Creating a self that his will supports but that he knows for an illusion, the picaro evolves into a symbolic being, a confidence man, outwardly one who shares faith in existence, inwardly one reduced to spiritual nothingness.*

The presentation of this functional illusionism in the Spanish picaresque novels is moral in the extreme. Earlier commentators, of whom Chandler is again typical, found the Spanish novels cynical and hypocritical and thought that the picaro's loss of goodness and consequent desire to repent were merely grist for the Inquisition's mill. These critics failed to distinguish between picaros and their creators. Actually, nothing is more characteristic of picaresque writers in Spain and elsewhere than their consistently moral outlook, often conveyed through some ingeniously artistic veil of irony. This essential morality of the picaresque novels is contained in the manner in which individual and society reflect each other; in fact, they *are* each other. If society is morally astray, then the individual may go morally astray, and vice versa.

This moral theme originates in the fact that in the Siglo de Oro "society" had a somewhat different meaning than it has today. It meant not social community in a collective sense but, rather, an aggregate of individuals, each with a supposed function or office that contributed to the common good. But since "society" is an Aristotelian hierarchy, then individual form cannot be transformed into another and still retain a moral sanction. The modern concept that reality consists in pure transformation has not been reached (although it is, indeed, beginning to announce itself in *La Celestina* and the Spanish novels).[32] Suppose, therefore, that a very large number of individuals are abusing their offices, living irresponsibly in some way, and, freed by an unstable historical situation such as a sudden influx of New World gold, are seeking to improve their credit in the world. Two contradictory ideas of reality then appear: one, the absolute reality of the supernatural other-world, the other, the relative reality that the individual experiences in the world. This happens in the Spanish picaresque novels. The perception of an absolute reality is retained by the author, while the perception of relative reality has shifted to a viewpoint inside the narrative. The rhetorical effect is that the reality accepted a priori by the picaro is depicted as a false reality. His will, which supports the painful structure of the confidence game, has elected evil. Social reality stubbornly affirms its unreality: nothing is what it seems. At the same time the picaro sees before him a society that cannot be transformed into another kind of society. By giving himself over to condemned acquisitive instincts, the picaro tries to stabilize himself in a new reality, but these pre-Cartesian evasions of the past do not relieve him of the feeling that he is bitterly entangled in the dark web of dreams. He and the society he sees are fused in the evil of unreality. Consequently, the more unreal the picaro becomes, the more he accedes to social evil and adds to it. Therefore, the critical view that the Spanish picaresque novels are primarily a stage in the development of realism in the novel is more than suspect because, while these novels do indeed represent everyday life and imitate historical actualities (poverty, vagabondage, delinquency, and the like), in the moral scheme of ironic autobiography such realities are conveyed as illusory.[33] This is what Américo Castro means when he refers to the "reality-destroying style" of the picaresque novels.[34]

Since realism triumphs as a rhetoric of fiction from the 1700s onward—recall that Scott Fitzgerald reread *Madame Bovary* every year as an act of aesthetic-religious devotion—it might appear that antirealism or illusionism in picaresque novels must limit their moment to Spanish literature of the Siglo de Oro. But the poetics or myth of picaresque fiction, incorporating techniques not of realism so much as of irony that distorts perceptions of reality, continues in novels from *Lazarillo* to *The Tin Drum* (*Die Blechtrommel*, 1959). The Spanish picaro is characterized as a person with a negative existence, moving along points that may be plotted in a downward direction. This nonlife or *sin vivir*, transformed into the symbolic picaro or confidence man, often as not is nothingness, unreality, or disintegration incarnate.

The common denominator of the picaresque myth may then be summarized by the word *disintegration*. This word implies the undoing of a previously formidable orthodox tradition, the collapse of personality or its submission to an experience of nothingness, and a structural metaphor for what is precipitated from an author's composition. Stuart Miller in *The Picaresque Novel* prefers the word *chaos* and distinguishes between a picaresque novelist's expression of our sense of disorder and other modern writers' expression of philosophical absurdity: "When a modern writer wishes to convey a sense of the absurdity of the universe, he is not trying to shock the reader in the same way that picaresque novelists did. A world which is lamentable because it gives the human being no final philosophic answers is, for whatever it may be worth, a much more relaxed world than the picaresque one. In the picaresque world, the chaos is radical; it extends to the very roots of life."[35] Miller argues, and I think he is right, that when we read an "absurd" novel we react to incidents as symbolic rather than as immediate and literally true. It is the difference of effect between Joseph Heller's *Catch-22* and Ralph Ellison's *Invisible Man*.

In this study I attempt to show that the genre of the picaresque novel includes a variety of particular novels that represent either a personal or a symbolic picaro. Because the method is critical, I have not been concerned to trace all the lines and colors of the picaresque canvas but to describe what I think is the main line of development. I have distinguished what I consider to be a historical achievement of the picaresque novel in three forms: (1) the classic form of the Spanish novels, *Lazarillo de Tormes*, *Guzmán de Alfarache*, and *El Buscón*; (2) the "dialectical" form of the mixed picaresque and nonpicaresque novels of France and England in the eighteenth and early nineteenth centuries; and (3) the symbolic form of certain nineteenth- and twentieth-century novels achieved in Russia and Germany but particularly in the United States, where the picaresque myth seems to have been spontaneously reborn.

When the novel of social realism became prominent in the eighteenth century, the reality-destroying style of the Spanish picaresque novels lost meaning. Rationalism and a new Christian concept of nature and grace, whereby the acquisitive instincts became an acceptable means to salvation, meant that the classic picaro, the acquisitive outsider for whom there was no survival outside and no reality inside, became submerged in a new myth, Hobbes's myth of the natural man. In works by such representative novelists as Lesage, Defoe, Fielding, Smollett, Dickens, and Thackeray, individual loneliness and antisocial behavior were treated simply as one kind of polarity, the antithesis to a thesis of social order. Illusion was no longer functional in the eighteenth-century novel. The individual was not forced to seek his identity within the social framework; it was assumed that every man, no matter what his social status, could, sooner or later, conform to acceptable moral standards. Hence the eighteenth-century novels never truly raise the question of the validity of experience. No manner of self-assertiveness of a Moll Flanders, Gil Blas, or Count Fathom would or could be indicative—as a picaro's is— of a dance of death or a direct devaluation of all cultural content. The eighteenth-century novelists, like their Spanish precursors, were oppressed by the problem of evil. However, they tended to treat private malfeasance not as a reflection of a whole society gone astray, but as the ever-present threat of a loss of meaning should it be permitted to persist. Although the picaresque idea of disintegration continued into the eighteenth century, it did so in the greatly modified form of an antithesis in the dialectics of religious and moral life.

In the nineteenth century the questionable reality of experience suddenly reappeared as a novelistic theme. This revival may particularly be observed in the literature of the United States, where novels express a primacy of passions and ideas over manners. Now the picaresque or part-picaresque novels appeared with a symbolic intention. Like as not, the picaro was called a confidence man, as he was in the title of a novel published by Herman Melville in 1857 and as he was to be again in Mann's *Confessions of Felix Krull, Confidence Man*, in 1954. The picaro who now disguised himself variously as a political demagogue, Russian bourgeois manqué, Wall Street philanthropist, Mississippi tramp, or fake Portuguese aristocrat was symbolically expressive of unreality, nihilism, or the idea of disintegration. Gogol's *Dead Souls*, Melville's *Confidence-Man*, and Mann's *Felix Krull* also express the feeling of comic anguish typical of the Spanish picaresque novels, although the symbolic picaros do not, as a rule, themselves suffer anguish, but rather are vehicles for the communication of the author's own. Thus, for example, Alemán represented in his picaro's frustrated religious quest an old world nearing the apocalypse, whereas Melville makes the apocalyptic extinction of the lamp of faith not a feeling of the picaro, but an allegorical event in which the picaro is instrumentally destructive. The picaresque myth continued, but the form of its achievement changed.

In sum, the hero of a genuine picaresque novel is always to a degree archetypal, and the picaresque genre, when surveyed over four hundred years, makes manifest a literary myth. Pertinent to this argument is the fact that a literary genre may be or become descriptive of the ethos of a civilization. For example, the pastoral is a more or less artificial literary kind that in Europe has long been associated with Sicilian shepherds and English Colin Clouts; but in America pastoralism is the governing belief of people in a simpler, better way of life, the literary expression of which is often tragic disillusionment with the dream's possibility. A similar transformation of the picaresque can be observed. Beginning as a kind of novel depicting the adventures of a trickster or delinquent in a chaotic, decadent world, the picaresque moves through two phases: through a dialectical phase in France and Britain when picarism is antithetical to the bourgeois faith in science and society, and then to a phase transforming the picaresque hero by symbolic modes of perception. And thus, today, the picaresque novel proves to be more than a freak of literary history. Now Western civilization as a whole could be described as "picaresque": the picaro is modern man without a living faith. The critical focus is no longer narrowed to the subject matter or episodic autobiographies of Spanish fiction. Rather, the presence is recognized of something universal, the trickster hero of folklore recreated as the lonely individual cut off from, though yearning for, community and love.

The picaro's lack of love throws into relief the whole myth. Cervantes knew this when he created the double perspective of *Don Quixote* and permitted friendship and community to exist imaginatively together with the picaresque underworld of loneliness. The myth of the picaro emerges as the negative journey of the soul toward order, meaning, and that full humanity implied by the word love.

**2**

# *The Soul's Dark Journey*

The story of a blind master who bashes his servant boy's head against a stone bull was a familiar bit of folklore by 1554 when the incident appears in *Lazarillo de Tormes*. There, however, it passed from the realm of roguery to that of man's inhumanity to man—or to children, to be exact. That cruel blow to the head created, as it were, the modern novel, for the inner psychological dimension of the scene manifests itself immediately, when Lazarillo realizes for the first time how alone he is, how lost his soul is. Indeed, the scene rests upon a foundation in the psychology of learning. How do human beings come to attain the sense of objectivity, the sense of reality, a stable, reliable vision of the world around them, the ability to make clear discriminations between what they know, are taught, or merely believe? How are they able to get straight the orders and kinds of belief and credibility? The capacity for fitting things together into a coherent whole comes from relations with the human world and with the inanimate world. By an insensitive master and a stone bull, Lazarillo is taught to place no confidence in any world, sacred or profane. Thus begins a soul's quest for meaning as the world falls apart.

### *Lazarillo de Tormes*: Death of a Soul

The originality of *La vida de Lazarillo de Tormes y de sus fortunas y adversidades* is worth pondering. *Lazarillo* is in many ways derived from literary tradition. As a narrative comprising a series of tableaux projected in the realistic manner, it is anticipated by such works as the *Metamorphoses* of Apuleius, *Satyricon* of Petronius, and *Decameron* of Boccaccio. But it is somewhat misleading to consider *Lazarillo* merely as a contributor to the rise of realism in Western prose fiction if by the term "realism" we mean the portrayal of the natural and visible: one of the themes of *Lazarillo* is that this kind of reality is unreal. Equally misleading is too ready a classification of *Lazarillo* in that limbo known as "the literature of roguery." Roguery (whatever that means) may be an element in *Lazarillo de Tormes*, but it may also be seen as an element in hundreds of other works, including *The Odyssey*, *Arabian Nights*, and *Canterbury Tales*. Clearly it is absurd to create tradition out of such diversity and impossible to distinguish the originality of *Lazarillo* in terms of such tradition.[1]

Critical priority must be given to understanding a literary work in and for itself, and this, too, has been a four-hundred-year-old problem: the ironies of *Lazarillo* are so deep and deceptive that a majority of critics still regard this novel as essentially optimistic, Renaissance in spirit. Even such a contemporary authority as Marcel Bataillon views *Lazarillo de Tormes* as a "petit livre satirique et plaisant, . . . un tour de force artistique, . . . un livre pour rire, *de burlas*."[2] Without being too solemn about the matter, I think one can say that a novel about a man who becomes his wife's pimp and then complacently assumes each and every one of us to be his *hypocrite lecteur* is scarcely a work to make us slap our sides in merriment and wink at ourselves in mirrors.

The picaro in *Lazarillo de Tormes* acts and reacts within a fictional world or society: that is a technical originality of the work. In antecedent literature the angle of vision had not truly been the trickster's. Rojas's Celestina, that Spanish Wife of Bath, is a complex dramatic character in the delineation of which much was achieved of artistic value to the author of *Lazarillo* several decades later; but in the play that now bears her name Celestina is not the protagonist, whereas Lazarillo is the protagonist and tells his own story. The autobiographical technique of *Lazarillo* leads to comparison of it to the technique of an old "I"-form of story, Apuleius's *Metamorphoses*, a work of certain influence on *La Celestina* (1499) and *La Lozana andaluza* (1528) and popular in Spain following the translation in the early sixteenth century.[3] But *Lazarillo* transforms the technique of autobiographical fiction. What happens to Lucius when he is turned into an ass is implausible; what happens to Lazarillo is something of which psychological analysis might take account.

Another way of distinguishing the originality of *Lazarillo* is to say that the concept of the self is in it inseparable from the concept of time. As Hans Meyerhoff writes in *Time in Literature*, "What we call the self, person, or individual is experienced and known only against the background of the succession of temporal moments and changes constituting his biography."[4] In *Lazarillo de Tormes* episodes are more than stitched together by the continued presence of a single narrator. They are disposed in time; hence their duration is of immense importance in telling us who and what the narrator is.

There are three main grounds for objection to this view of *Lazarillo*'s artistic integrity: (1) the text appears to be corrupt or incomplete, (2) the author is anonymous, and (3) the date of composition is uncertain. These problems are interrelated and affect the criticism of *Lazarillo* as a coherent work of the imagination.

The textual dimensions of the novel are those of the extended short story. Like Flaubert's *Un Coeur Simple* or Joyce's *The Dead* it offsets limited characterization—and the possible numbing spatial effect of banal atmosphere—by means of a scrupulous style expanding the form in depth. The art of a short novel may constrict the sense of life. Yet is constriction a deliberate part of the art of *Lazarillo*? The text appears to be corrupt or incomplete. It is not positively known whether the text we now possess represents a small part or large part or the whole of a possibly lost archetype. Three editions dated 1554 appeared respectively at Burgos, Alcalá de Henares, and Antwerp. While the Antwerp edition seems to be reproduced from the Burgos edition, that of Alcalá is sufficiently different to imply a lost archetype. Yet the evidence of textual analysis and collation is insufficient to describe what this *Ur-Lazarillo* may have been like.[5] A sequel to the 1554 *Lazarillo* was printed in 1555. What sort of relationship, if any, exists between the novel of 1554 and the sequel of 1555? Half again as long as any 1554 edition, *La segunda parte de Lazarillo de Tormes* begins where the original part ends and then takes a titular hero named Lazarillo on a series of fantastic adventures reminiscent of the *Metamorphoses*. It seems highly unlikely that the two parts were composed by the same hand, but perhaps two authors drew upon a common source. Again, why does *Lazarillo* exhibit such a chopped-up appearance? Of the eight printed divisions, a Prologue and seven *tratados* (literally, "treatises"), only the first three seem substantially worked out; Tratado IV consists of a paragraph and Tratados V–VII combined do not equal the length of one of Tratados I–III. Is the answer censorship, precensorship, or a manuscript damaged in circulation? We do not know, but the printed divisions may be misleading, may, in fact, as the rubrics seem to suggest, be the work of an editor. Thus the student of *Lazarillo de Tormes* meets at the outset an almost insurmountable textual problem. But his most reassuring piece of evidence is the novel itself, which, in spite of its superficial appearance, is magnificently unified in style, tone, and characterization. Indeed, from the point of view of style, most of the novel, with the exception of Tratados IV–VI, is highly finished, which leads to the theory that the artist left part of his work incomplete.[6] From the point of view of characterization, however, even these "unfinished" parts can be seen as artistically necessary. Common to both views is a feeling that the extant novel is essentially complete in its dimensions and may, therefore, bear close critical scrutiny. Such scrutiny reveals that what seems unfinished is in fact a superbly artistic rendering of an irretrievably dead soul. If the author had expanded Tratados IV–VI—if he had added anything at all to the drama of spiritual death—he would, conceivably, have botched a literary masterpiece.[7]

Two other problems confronting the student of *Lazarillo* are the related ones of authorship and composition date. If the problem of authorship so far fails of solution, it has not been for lack of candidates. The most frequent suggestions are the diplomat Diego Hurtado de Mendoza, Father Juan de Ortega, the Toledan poet Sebastián de Horozco, and the prominent follower of Erasmus, Juan de Valdés. If Mendoza were the author, it is conjectured, the earliest date of composition would be in the late 1540s, if Ortega or Horozco, in the late 1530s, or if Valdés, in 1525. Whoever the author may have been, it is certain from *Lazarillo* itself that he was greatly concerned with the religious problems of the age. His anonymity may have been essential, allowing him to express heterodox—possibly *converso*—views. A more likely explanation is that the book was left unsigned and was posthumously published. And it is not sophistry to argue that the author chose anonymity in order to dissociate himself from a society athirst for fame and self-display and diseased by each man's concern for honor. *Lazarillo* may be a rejection of Spain so complete that the author—with what mixture of pride, revulsion, and self-abasement we can only guess—finally rejected himself.[8]

The authorial problem leads to the problem of composition date. Internal evidence shows 1525 to be the earliest possible date; 1553 would be the latest possible date. Therefore *Lazarillo* was composed at some time during a twenty-eight-year period crucial in the Siglo de Oro. In 1525, for example, the melioristic ideas of Erasmus flourished in influential places, but by 1537 the *erasmistas* were in disgrace, their leaders either in exile or imprisoned by the Inquisition.[9] In 1540, Loyola founded the Society of Jesus, in 1545 the Council of Trent was assembled, in 1554—the very year *Lazarillo* was published—the first *Index Expurgatorius* appeared, and, nine years later, with the conclusion of the Council of Trent, the Counter-Reformation was in full swing, hardened against the relative freedom of the earlier generation. It is not without significance that an expurgated *Lazarillo* appeared in 1573. During this same twenty-eight-year period the star of Charles V, one of the last chivalric kings, ascended, and Spanish hegemony spread over two worlds. Ruler of Spain in 1516, Holy Roman emperor in 1519, successful against the rebel Commoners in 1521, Charles had in 1525 won the greatest victory of the age when he defeated François Ier at Pavia and forced the French king to spend a year in Madrid as prisoner of war. Charles, who was to abdicate in 1556, outlasted this stubborn enemy, who died in 1547, leaving the emperor free to defeat the Protestant League at Muhlberg. But the great years of glory and conquest had been earlier, between 1521 when Elcano circumnavigated the world and 1534 when Pizarro conquered Peru, the Mexican conquest by Cortés having occurred in 1526. The spirit of romance and chivalry permeated the age and seemed in Charles to be incarnate. Yet there were already signs of impending economic disaster as increasing numbers of the Spanish population were forced from sheer want into vagabondage. While the power and glory of imperial Spain rose, the seeds of decadence had already been sown.[10]

It is tempting to regard the author of *Lazarillo* as a reformer in mild dissent, as one more inclined to treat social evils as the result of official abuse than as a symptom of man's willful surrender of interior light and personal authenticity. If we are thus tempted, the intellectual context of the novel might seem to shift in the direction of 1525, a time of comparative license in doctrinal matters, of proud assent to the imperial success, and of a certain simplicity in social and economic thought, whereby the problems of an impoverished populace were charged, in the traditional form of satire, to ecclesiastical corruption and to faulty distribution of wealth. However, the death of a soul is a subject cutting far beneath the level of satire.[11] The character of Lázaro (the mature Lazarillo) freely accepts evil when he does not even have the excuse of hunger.[12] In other words, the moral lesson of *Lazarillo de Tormes* is so bitter and so profoundly pessimistic that it is misleading to read the book as inspirited with Renaissance optimism and early post-Reformation meliorism.

As for dates of possible composition, 1525–26 and 1538–39 have usually been the ones proposed. Concluding his memoirs, Lázaro states: "Esto fué el mesmo año, que nuestro victorioso emperador de esta insigne ciudad de Toledo entró y tuuo en ella cortes y se hizieron grandes regozijos." (This all occurred the same year our victorious emperor entered this great city of Toledo and here held court, when so many wonderful celebrations and fiestas took place.) (*Lazarillo*, pp. 241–42).[13] Twice before 1554, the imperial court met in Toledo, in 1525 and 1538. Both years were festive occasions, but the term "victorioso" would seem to point to 1525 and the victory of Pavia.[14] Elsewhere reference is made to the captivity of François I^er: "En aquel tiempo no me deuian de quitar el sueño los cuydados de el rey de Francia." (At that time not all the cares of the king of France should really have kept me awake.) (*Lazarillo*, p. 133). Here again the event alluded to occurred shortly after Pavia. Finally, internal chronology seems to indicate 1525 as the earliest date of composition.[15] Lázaro says that his father died at the battle of Gelves. At the time he was eight years old, and if the reference is to an important battle of 1510 and not to a minor expedition of 1520, then Lázaro would have been born in 1502 and twenty-three the year of his marriage, following an apprenticeship of about ten years. To put the marriage in 1538 would seem to make the hero too old for a novel about the disintegration of a youth's character. Nevertheless, the nature of internal references remains in dispute; for example, the reference to "the cares of the king of France" need not be to François Ier.[16] The latest investigations, in fact, favor a late date of composition, just before *Lazarillo* was published in 1554.

What, if anything, may we infer from these related matters of text, authorship, and composition date? First, *Lazarillo de Tormes* is a masterpiece as it stands. Second, the author's anonymity or concealed identity is probably in some measure a result of deliberate deception and a kind of enticement to the hypocrite lecteur to find in the work itself keys to its interpretation. Third, whatever composition date between 1525 and 1554 is finally favored, *Lazarillo* is unlikely to be pegged as either a roman à clef or a historical portrait of decadence. There are good reasons for proceeding with examination of *Lazarillo de Tormes* as the progenitor of the myth of the picaro.

It is useful to see the structure of *Lazarillo* as a "temporal disposition" of stages in the picaro's life.[17] To simplify analysis, these stages will be discussed separately as structural units, some account of the picaro's temporal development will be given in each, and some technical aspects of the story, such as parody, may be considered.

The autobiographical form of the novel signifies an interplay of past and present that gives a confessional design: the uncovering of the past is a revelation of the present.[18] Bearing this form in mind, we may divide *Lazarillo* into four narrative units: (1) Family (Tratado I until Lazarillo serves the blind man); (2) Education (Tratado I from the episode of the blind man to the end of Tratado III); (3) Maturity (Tratado IV until the appointment of Lázaro as town crier in Tratado VII); and (4) Frame (Tratado VII after the appointment, and the Prologue). This re-orientation of the Prologue is particularly needed because it makes the Prologue an expression of the mind of Lázaro in the present time at furthest remove from the childish mind of Laza-rillo represented in the first tratado. This Prologue actually forms part of the conclusion of the narrative and helps to explain what became of Lazarillo after his adventures.

### Family

Lazarillo, son of Thomas Gonzalez and Antonia Perez, was born, we are told, in the middle of the river Tormes. When he was eight, his father's thefts led to arrest, exile, and death in a military expedition against the Moors. Antonia rented a cottage in Sala-manca and worked as a cook and laundress to support the family. Soon she formed an alliance with a colored slave, Zaide, whose bribes of stolen food and firewood made him welcome to the boy, who, indeed, found no objection to the arrival of a colored half-brother. However, Zaide was seized, convicted on the evi-dence of the unsuspecting Lazarillo, and, after a cruel whipping, forbidden to consort further with Antonia. She, now victim of slander as well as poverty, removed her family to a nearby inn where Lazarillo was put to work running errands. When a blind man stopped at the inn and requested that Lazarillo be entrusted to him as servant and son, Antonia gave Lazarillo her blessing, and they parted.

If Lazarillo suffers from shame over family dishonor, his later actions may be seen as overcompensatory; but, it seems to me, this psychological possibility is not as evident in *Lazarillo* as it is in the later Spanish picaresque novels.[19] True, he colors his child-hood memories with the wash of ridicule, but the tone is not so much resentful as playful and complacent. His sympathy for Antonia and Zaide seems genuine:

Ella y vn hombre moreno, de aquellos que las bestias curauan, vinieron en conoscimiento. Este algunas vezes se venia a nuestra casa y se yua a la mañana. Otras vezes de día llegaua a la puerta en achaque de comprar hueuos y entrauase en casa. Yo, al principio de su entrada, pesáuame con él e auiale miedo, viendo el color y mal gesto que tenía; mas, de que vi que con su venida mejoraua el comer, fuyle queriendo bien, porque siempre traya pan, pedaços de carne y en el inuierno leños, a que nos calentauamos.

She became acquainted with a dark man who helped take care of the horses. He sometimes came to our house in the evening and would leave on the following morning. On other occasions, he would come to the door on the pretext that he wished to buy eggs, and then he would enter the house. When he first began to visit us, I did not take to him at all. I was really afraid of his black color and unprepossessing appearance. But when I saw that the quality of our food greatly improved with his visits, I began to grow fond of him, for he always brought bread and pieces of meat with him, and when winter came he would bring firewood, which kept us warm. [pp. 69–70]

The emphasis of this passage, with its fidelity to the child's point of view, is not on a flickering resentment of an adulterous mother but on the humorous incredulity and irrationality of the boy himself. Zaide's color, not his bribery, alarms Lazarillo. When he knows Zaide's motives are amorous and his mother's are ruled by necessity, he adjusts to the new situation. Later, when Zaide's "charity" leads to punishment, Lazarillo is stung by remorse for having inadvertently betrayed him. When innocence so evidently produces evil, it is better to abandon innocence: the blind man's teaching is carefully foreshadowed.

I find it difficult to agree with Francisco Maldonado de Guevara that Lazarillo is perverted in his birth; in his early years he seems uncorrupted by the venial family sins.[20] What evil exists is initially associated with the social order. The punishment meted out to Gonzalez and Zaide is out of proportion to their crimes and inflicts much suffering on the innocent. Antonia at least does her duty, but she stands alone against the tide of social evil that sweeps in upon her son.

This family unit of *Lazarillo* gains artistic energy from its parody of heroic myth. Anticipating Cervantes, the author probably reacted against the *libros de caballería* popular with his contemporaries. Certainly many of those books of chivalry that were later to unhinge the reason of Don Quixote reached the heights of popularity during the first half of the sixteenth century.[21] *Amadís de Gaula*, the first known edition of which appeared in 1508, achieved more than two dozen editions before 1587, and its continuations in 1510 and 1514 were almost equally popular. Of *Palmerín de Oliva* there were ten editions between 1511 and 1580. There were ten editions of *Primaleón* between 1512 and 1588, and the same number of editions of *Lepolemo* between 1521 and 1600. *Clarián de Landanis* appeared in 1518–24. At least eight other romances appeared before 1525. In sum, between 1508 and 1550 romances appeared at an average rate of almost one a year; nine were added between 1550 and the time of the Armada; and there were three more before the appearance of *Don Quixote* in 1605. Lazarillo's blurring the details of his birth and assigning to himself a mythical origin in the river strike a more or less conventional motif of heroic literature. Amadís de Gaula, called the Child of the Sea, was launched, like Moses, on the water. Palmerín de Oliva was abandoned on a mountain covered with palms and olives. In Greek literature and myth the early forsaking of the hero—Oedipus, for instance—was a sign of destiny. Thus Lázaro sees himself as abandoned to destiny, vaingloriously honorable to him though, to the reader, futile and drifting. As Maldonado says, *Lazarillo* is "una parodia del mito del héroe-niño abandonado."[22]

Biblical passages, too, are parodied. Lazarillo says of his father that he was "preso y confessó e no negó y padesció persecución per justicia" (p. 66), an echo of *confessus est et non negavit*, John 1:20. This is followed by, "Espero en Dios que está en la gloria, pues el Euangelio los llama bienauenturados" (pp. 66–67), which parodies *beati qui persecutionem patiuntur propter justitiam* of the Sermon on the Mount. As both passages refer in the context of the novel to Lazarillo's father, it is significant that Antonia later recommends Lazarillo to the blind man as the son of a man who died "por ensalçar la fe" (to exalt the Holy Faith) (p. 75).[23] Since in the sixteenth century the imitation of Christ was an act of honor and reverence, it appears that Lázaro wishes to transform his father's ignoble death into a martyrdom, a desire that links with his general propensity for placing his own life in heroic contexts.

Such parodies, implied or specific, help to reveal a fusion of layered ironies. Lazarillo, the witty, vulnerable, initially truthful boy, appeals to the reader's sympathy and trust as might a virtuous hero; at this level of response, we may indulge his pretensions to nobility as, at worst, adolescent fantasies. But the boy's story is being narrated by a mature Lázaro, who is not only complacent, odious, and spiritually dead, but who has also suppressed, if he has not altogether extinguished, that earlier possibility of internal truthfulness. The adult who can lie to himself is quite capable of believing in some image of himself as a godlike hero, immortal and infallible. In childhood, Lazarillo could distinguish appearance from reality: "Quantos deue de auer en el mundo, que huyen de otros, porque no se veen a si mesmos!" (How many there must be in the world who flee from others—simply because they cannot see themselves!) (p. 72). In maturity Lázaro can no longer be relied upon to see himself. It is as if a spiritually dead man were peering back, over an impassable frontier, at the earlier authentic life, the soul of which can no longer be identified by himself—though it may be by the reader. Like the self-destroyed Macbeth, Lázaro might, but for blindness, conceive of his life as "signifying nothing."

### Education

Having left his mother, Lazarillo was cruelly deceived by the blind man. When they came to a bridge near which stood a stone bull, the blind man enticed Lazarillo to place his head close to the stone in order to hear a great sound. As he did so, the blind man struck him brutally and, laughing, warned that a blind man's servant must learn to distrust everyone. Lazarillo thereafter learned to look out for himself, even stealing food from his master-teacher. But after some failures, which led to further persecution, he took his revenge and ran away, and in the village of Maqueda he became altar boy to a priest. The priest proved more niggardly and avaricious than the blind man. At the end of three weeks Lazarillo was weak from starvation. Only when he attended his master at funerals did he eat well (so well, in fact, that he prayed for people to die), but between times he maintained life by stealing from the priest's breadbox. Eventually his stratagems failed, and he was dismissed. Then with little strength remaining he came to Toledo and served a prosperous-looking squire. This new master proved as poverty-stricken as he. At first Lazarillo begged in the streets to support himself and the squire. After a sudden crop failure in the region, poor strangers in the city were restricted, so the boy withdrew to his master's empty house to wait for what seemed inevitable death from starvation. At last the squire, hearing that bailiffs would seize his property, deserted Lazarillo, who was cleared of responsibility for the squire's debts and came under the protection of some spinning women.

This unit, the core of the novel, is an embryonic *Bildungsroman*. It exemplifies (in spite of a certain farcical crudity in the three episodes) a process of learning and development. The key incident of the stone bull sets the pattern:

Salimos de Salamanca y, llegando a la puente, está a la entrada della vn animal de piedra, que casi tiene forma de toro, y el ciego mandome que llegasse cerca del animal e, alli puesto, me dixo:

"Lázaro, llega el oydo a este toro e oyrás gran ruydo dentro dél."

Yo simplemente llegué, creyendo ser ansi. Y, como sintió que tenía la cabeça par de la piedra, afirmó rezio la mano y diome vna gran calabaçada en el diablo del toro, que mas de tres dias me duró el dolor de la cornada y dixome:

"Necio, aprende: que el moço del ciego vn punto ha de saber mas que el diablo."

Y rió mucho la burla.

Paresciome que en aquel instante desperté de la simpleza en que como niño dormido estaua.

Dixe entre mi:

"Verdad dize éste, que me cumple abiuar el ojo y auisar, pues solo soy, y pensar cómo me sepa valer."

Commençamos nuestro camino y en muy pocos dias me mostró jerigonça. Y, como me viesse de buen ingenio, holgauase mucho y dezia:

"Yo oro ni plata no te lo puedo dar; mas auisos, para viuir, muchos te mostraré."

Y fué ansi, que, despues de Dios, este me dió la vida y, siendo ciego, me alumbró y adestró en la carrera de viuir.

We left Salamanca, and when we reached the bridge we observed there a stone animal which had almost the form of a bull, and the blind man requested me to approach the animal. When I had come near, he said to me:

"Lazarus, place your ear up close to the beast, and you will perceive a great sound within him."

I, in my simplicity thinking it to be so, obeyed. When my master felt that I had my head alongside the stone, he knocked it with a terrific blow of his hand against the beast, so that I had a headache for three days afterward from my butting of the bull. And he said to me:

"Idiot! Be now aware that a blind man's boy has to know somewhat more than even the devil himself."

And he laughed heartily at his little trick.

I seemed at that instant to awaken from the simplicity in which like a little boy I had slept, and I said to myself:

"He is very right, and I must indeed have an alert eye and I must be ever watchful, since I am alone, and I must learn to take care of myself."

We began our journey, and in a few days the blind man taught me some thieves' slang, and when he saw I was an intelligent lad, he was quite pleased and said to me:

"Gold and silver, I can give you none, but wise counsels for living, I can give you many."

And so it was indeed: for, after the Lord God, my old master took best care of me, and, although he was blind, he illuminated me, and in his own way gave me the only education I ever had. [pp. 76–78][24]

The scene is striking for two reasons: it is an *exemplum* of false teaching, and the reaction of the protagonist is internalized. There is clearly an ironic counterpoint in the "illumination" of a boy by one denied the light. There is a darker meaning, revealed in the blind man's "gold-and-silver" speech. For this speech is another biblical parody and refers to the miraculous healing of a paralytic by Saint Peter.[25] The blind man, in truth, does the opposite: he cripples the mind of his pupil. He figures in the novel, then, as a false apostle, a deformer of Christian truth. At the same time that Lazarillo's teacher is unmasked, the boy himself draws back into his loneliness and accepts his bitter lesson. Once before he had felt guilty over his innocent betrayal of Zaide, and now his confidence in the value of innocence and trust has been thoroughly shaken. What trust remains to him he places in the blind man, who, under the existing social code, is in charge of his religious and social training. But for the budding confidence man, this poses a dilemma: he must depend upon the trust of others while in himself he must meet the world with deception. In this new scheme of things nothing seems to retain its former objectivity. Even the stone bull seems strangely animated, and Lazarillo speaks of it as if it had gored him.[26]

What follows this incident of the stone bull intensifies Lazarillo's distrust and, consequently, his sardonic faith in the blind man. Like a Pavlovian experiment in conditioned response, the remainder of the education unit shows a mind trapped in a vicious circle. Starved, Lazarillo resorts to stratagem; discovered, he is punished; yet he sees no alternative but to try again, each trick more slippery than the one before. As his anxiety increases, he no longer seems to act with a will of his own. He feels transparent, overexposed; and this identity as externally visible man leads to the passive "invisible man" condition of Lázaro in the final tratados.

Lazarillo's revenge is also, I think, psychologically plausible, and it certainly is no proof, as Chandler thought, that the picaro is almost by definition a "heartless" person who "lack[s] pity for the crippled."[27] Lazarillo, who betrays his master into hurling himself head-foremost against a stone pillar, repays in kind, meeting violence with violence according to the blind man's own precepts. If he seems malicious here, the instance is temporary, for his charitable good nature is to manifest itself in the episode of the squire. Moreover, inspection of his motives for this violent revenge shows that Lazarillo feels humiliated by the man he has accepted as his teacher: not only does the blind man punish him unmercifully, once even breaking a jug of wine over his head, but he also entertains outsiders with the story of Lazarillo's tricks, thus making his pupil appear foolish. What Lazarillo fears most, next to starvation, is public ridicule. It happens, then, that the picaro, who wants to conform, is unjustly and unnecessarily cut off from the community. Violently disillusioned, he takes violent revenge, but he is still a child, whose basic goodness of heart has been outraged. It is a commonplace of psychology, of course, that violence is a concomitant of repressed emotion, a kind of "innocence," and that a degree of self-assertion or benign aggression is indicative of mental health. Although Lazarillo endangers the blind man's life, his revolt against false authority, as compared to Billy Budd's in Melville's novel, does not carry to homicide and tragedy. The scene exemplifies Lazarillo's interior self as still, at this stage, instinctively well, emotional turbulence still finding release, albeit in a form of aggression bordering upon the malignant.[28]

The priest of Maqueda ratifies the blind man's hypocrisy but is more diabolic in that he is hypocritical to Lazarillo, whereas the blind man is not. In Tratado II the hunger motif emerges as a metaphor of the spiritual life. The priest's battered chest contains loaves of bread donated by members of his flock in remembrance of their dead. Although this bread is not literally the Communion substance, the *bodigos*, according to Anson Piper, are "prepared for a distinctly religious purpose," and the chest is "a religious symbol, an altar erected to a beneficent god whose earthly minister is a cruel and niggardly hypocrite."[29] To the boy, the chest so zealously guarded by the priest is "paraíso panal" (breadly Paradise) (p. 125), and twice its contents become for him "cara de Dios" (the face of God) (pp. 124, 128). To the priest, the thief of bread is identified as a serpent. But the priest— the church militant against heresy—is the true satanic serpent because he denies compassion, literally the sharing of bread, and his final dismissal of the boy, which is the gesture of excommunication, represents an abuse of his office.

The climax of Lazarillo's education occurs in the episode of the squire. The tempo picks up. Early one morning the boy meets the squire; by eleven o'clock he is anxious about food; by one o'clock, unfed, he suspects the truth when he sees his master's dark, empty house; by two o'clock he is completely undeceived and melancholy. That evening he identifies his master's helplessness before evil as "la negra que llaman honrra" (the dark disease of honor) (p. 163). Such intensified awareness of time shows both how far along Lazarillo has traveled in distrust and how his anxiety is working to a climax.

Why does he cling to the squire? Why does he reverse the social order by charitably supporting his master? This is a masterstroke of the novel, one which by placing in relief all that has gone before gives Lazarillo the roundness of an autonomous literary character. Gifts intended as bribes, demonstrated by Zaide, have been the boy's nearest approach to charity, although the blind man never explicitly taught that the proceeds of begging could not be shared. Like Huckleberry Finn, Lazarillo has never been taught to love, but he *naturally* loves, that is, in the novel's past tense, loved when his soul was alive. Does he love the squire as social superior, prototype of the true aristocrat? If he does, there is textual evidence that the author of *Lazarillo de Tormes* presents the squire ironically, not as prototype of the true aristocrat but, Donald McGrady argues, as "an impostor, a New Christian upstart who is attempting to worm his way into privileged rank without possessing the prerequisite virtue." The squire's preoccupation with cleanliness, according to this hypothesis, echoes the aristocracy's (and a *converso*'s) concern with purity of blood. It follows that Lazarillo indeed loves the squire but loves (and later, as Lázaro, adopts) "only the outer shell of honorableness, caring nothing for the virtue on which honor is based."[30] Surely the most important motive for Lazarillo's charity is his wistful yearning after honor, even after the hollow semblance of honor. For once he may put his education to good use, make dishonor serve the cause of seeming honor and at the same time rationalize his sense of guilt. Lazarillo may lack a moral vision to discern true virtue, but *caritas*, the self-sacrificing agape or mind of love, temporarily balances with Eros, the principle of self-love. Lazarillo's thwarted compassion lends tragic dimension to the picaro who, outcast at an early age, nursed in disillusion, physically tormented and spiritually deformed, desperately anxious and with no balm of quixotic madness to soothe his torment, nevertheless desires to enter into some form of community with his fellow man. In the episode of the squire we see community happening, though only for a brief while—then all collapses.

The breakdown comes after Lazarillo, no longer able to beg, has withdrawn to the squire's house to wait for death. Suddenly one day the squire obtains a *real*. Overjoyed, Lazarillo goes out to buy food and drink but on the way is arrested by sight of a funeral procession and by the figure of a keening widow: " 'Marido y señor mio, adonde os me lleuan? A la casa triste y desdichada, a la case lobrega y obscura, a la casa donde nunca comen ni beuen!' " ('O my dear husband and my lord! Where do they bear you now? Alas, to that sad and cheerless dwelling where there is never eating or drinking!') (p. 184).[31] Lazarillo is seized by panic: the dead man is being carried to the squire's very house! He races back through the streets, bars the doors, and waits nervously for the procession to arrive. Long after it has passed on and he has realized the truth, he remains deeply disturbed and, though starving, takes no joy in his food.

This scene comes at a critical moment. Not only does it dramatize the picaro's naked anxiety before the fact of death, it also indicates how inseparable in his mind now are illusion and reality. Ever since the stone bull affair his sense of objectivity has been crumbling. Now he speaks of the squire's empty house as "encantada" (p. 152). Recalling, moreover, that he has earlier witnessed funeral processions without a morbid reaction, we have a measure of how great his anxiety has become. The scene of the funeral procession, then, may with some justification be regarded as the psychological climax of the novel. Gilman's treatment of the scene as emblematic of Lazarillo's spiritual death is neat and irresistible: the squire's bed, black with dirt (despite his obsession with cleanliness) and almost without wool, can be visualized as an emblem of a tomb, with Lazarillo stretched like the traditional dog at his master's feet. From this moment, we will see an archetypal Lázaro returned from the dead yet spiritually no longer alive.[32]

In summary, the pattern of the education unit shows increasing anxiety and loneliness culminating in a partial breakdown of objective reality. Common to this world where little is what it seems is the lack of solidarity. For a brief moment the light of compassion bursts forth, showing the world what once it seemed to be and might be again. Then the light goes out: things fall apart, the center cannot hold.

The satiric savagery of this narrative sequence varies. Avarice and fraud rule the blind man, avarice and hypocrisy the priest; but the squire's vice is affectation. Except for the priest, the reader can sympathize, with the blind man because of his embittering handicap and with the squire because he is gentle and stoical in adversity.

What, then, is the function of satire in *Lazarillo de Tormes*? Is it the exclusive purpose of the picaresque novel? Until recently criticism of the picaresque novel followed Chandler's dictum that the picaro is "nothing in character,"[33] little more than a technical device for the satire of manners. And, of course, Lazarillo's peregrination provides an opportunity for diverse satiric portraits. But on the other hand it should be by now plain that he is a *persona* and not a device. He is an object of satire himself. Lazarillo does not represent any normative point of view; he forfeits this role because he is self-deceived. By the end of the novel Lázaro no longer effectively criticizes anyone because he himself has disparities in his present life.[34] He has come to accept in full the blind man's debilitating view of a glacial world animated by egotism and ruled by necessity. In short, the picaro and *picardía*, his world of persons living marginal lives, are not opposed but are reflections of each other. Nor is the norm located outside the picaro but still inside the novelistic milieu. We might expect the squire to represent the social norm in a Renaissance work, but the squire is satirized for affecting the appearance but lacking the substance of honor. Like the blind man and the priest, he abuses the office society has entrusted to him; unlike them, his title to office is already suspect. Now, curiously, there is a hint of normative good inside the novel—*los buenos*, the good people, who hover on the periphery of the action and who in the education unit are represented by the kindly spinning women. This shadow chorus of good people might represent a norm from which the picaro himself may be seen to deviate and to which in the ironic anagnorisis he later yearns to return. But even *los buenos*, if Gilman surmises correctly, are not authentic but a sort of societal commonplace like the terms for God and just as remote to the spiritually starved.[35] More evident of a norm than the chorus, finally, is the author himself, who, like a sixteenth-century Flaubert, practices irony-to-all-sides. In this sense normative good is outside the novel.[36]

What *is* satirized? First, the blind man. In keeping with the mock-heroics of the novel, he is a kind of anti-Tiresias, a cynical prophet of his servant's destiny. But as an object of satire he may best be seen as charity gone bad. His begging is supposed to relieve social guilt, to create an agency whereby others may store up credit in heaven. When he perverts this "divine" confidence trick into an earthly game of acquisitiveness, he abuses his function. The squire is a parody incarnate of the ideal courtier and gentleman; through idleness and a superficial code of honor, he demonstrates a lack of grasp of moral foundations. Finally, the priest's contribution to social chaos is unmistakable: hypocritical advocate of temperance, he gormandizes at funerals and makes a farce of the sacraments. This monstrous Goya-like figure is, moreover, no static caricature of the medieval type, partly because we are not simply told of his viciousness; it is rendered through symbolic action. Earlier we noted that his chest, to Lazarillo, is a symbol of paradise, its contents the face of God. If we examine these symbols carefully, a pattern emerges suggestive of a hidden fable.[37] For instance, when Lazarillo has been starved for three weeks and is unable to steal from the breadbox, he meets a tinker whom he persuades to duplicate the breadbox key. To him the tinker is an angel of divine intervention: "Yo creo que fué angel embiado a mi por la mano de Dios" (p. 123). Lazarillo claims that the key trick occurred to him because he was "alumbrado por el Spiritu Sancto" (illuminated by the Holy Spirit) (p. 123)—heretically, he has achieved a state of grace in spite of the church. There is now, as it were, a duplicate key to the Kingdom, and the individual desecrates the altar chest and advances to Communion without the intercession of ecclesiastical authority or, for that matter, the authentic Communion wafer. There then follows a curious beast symbolism. Lazarillo has poked holes in the box so that the priest may blame mice for the thefts. The priest plugs up the holes, and when this device fails to stop them, he plants a mousetrap—and Lazarillo eats the cheese! In desperation, the priest, at last convinced that only a serpent could be to blame, waits in ambush. The culprit is found, and Lazarillo is driven from the house with these words: " '[D]e oy mas eres tuyo.' " ('From now on you belong to yourself.') (p. 145). Is there a possibility here of a twice-told tale? While specific allegorical interpretations are hazardous, the logic of the action is that the priest makes no essential distinction between mice, serpent, and Christian individual: all, somehow, are enemies of the church.[38] One who seeks his own salvation, his own self-creation, might well be a heretic (= mouse) or Satan (= serpent), the former of which is supposed to be prevented by the Inquisition (= mousetrap). But the real thief is neither heretical nor possessed, but a boy excommunicated from the only thing in which he can believe, bread. Lazarillo wants to "enter in," and he is denied because those responsible for his welfare are abusing their offices. Society as a whole is hypocritical; the mature Lázaro will soon reflect its face.

### Maturity

After brief service with a friar, Lazarillo enters the service of a pardoner, a confidence trickster of the classic variety, who persuades people of the miraculous value of indulgences by means of a sham drama of divine justice. After serving this master and others, Lazarillo (now Lázaro) attains his manhood and begins to prosper.

In elliptical fashion the maturity unit presents the complacent life of the mature picaro. Here for once Lázaro seems little more than a titular link between episodes; yet it is plausible to see this unit as a swift dénouement. The character of Lázaro is now formed. He reacts negatively to events, drifts on the surface of life, and uses his fading energies to keep up respectable appearances. He buys a suit, saves money, conforms. To him the task of water bearer to a chaplain is "el officio" (p. 230) and "el primer escalon" (the first step) on the ladder to "buena vida" (success) (p. 229). His great aim is to be an "hombre de bien" (a respectable man) (p. 230), a goal achieved, he claims, when he serves a bailiff; but he finds the compensations of being on the right side of the law are outweighed by the danger involved. Here Lázaro consistently rationalizes his failure as success because illusion has become his reality. His reactions are weightless, without force. Thus, for example, after watching the pardoner pretend that he is in a state of divine ecstasy, Lázaro comments tamely, "Y, aunque mochacho, cayome mucho en gracia." (And, despite my being so young, I was amused.) (p. 228).

Textually problematic as the short maturity unit is, and psychologically deflated as is the character of the picaro, there is a case for artistic necessity.[39] It rests on the assumption that in the autobiographical novel the time duration of events is controlled not by calendar but by memory. A decade more or less must in the maturity unit pass rapidly in order to bridge the education unit, in which Lazarillo's character became definitive, and the frame unit, Lázaro's cynical adulthood. The tempo of the maturity unit is slowed to contrast with the education unit in which time was a matter of hours and days. He no longer laughs, even to himself, and is immune to laughter at his own expense. His intimate thoughts, earlier expressed as asides, have disappeared. "The result of these three brief chapters," Howard Mancing observes, "is to disengage Lazarillo both from his previous existence and from the reader's sympathy, as well as to foreshadow carefully the protagonist's status at the end of the book."[40] Lázaro is beginning the "rise" to prosperity that is the "fall" from grace.

He is spiritually dead.

### Frame

Lázaro at last found the "respectable" post he wanted, town crier of Toledo. About the same time he met the archpriest of San Salvador who arranged the marriage with his servant—in reality, his mistress and mother of his children. Lázaro accepted the arrangement and secured material comforts in return for pimping. Toledans who mentioned the scandal were cowed into silence. Then after a short period Lázaro obeyed the request of the archpriest's noble friend and protector to give a complete account of his life.

The mature Lázaro is in full flight from reality, a deliberate strategy for maintaining his precarious hold on life. Pressing back his fear and anxiety, he now overcompensates for his acceptance of dishonor by insolent self-assertiveness: "Hame succedido tan bien, yo le he vsado tan facilmente, que casi todas las cosas al officio tocantes passan por mi mano. Tanto, que en toda la ciudad el que ha de echar vino a vender o algo, si Lázaro de Tormes no entiende en ello, hazen cuenta de no sacer prouecho." (Things have gone so well with me, and I have occupied myself so diligently, that all the matters I have mentioned above now pass through my hands. I am now so influential that if in all the city any man wishes to sell his wine or anything else, Lazarus of

Tormes had better be informed of it, or the business will not go well.) (pp. 233–34).

Toward the noble protector he gives himself the lofty airs of the parvenu: "Y tambien porque consideren los que heredaron nobles estados quán poco se les deue, pues fortuna fue con ellos parcial, y quánto mas hizieron los que, siendoles contraria, con fuerça y maña remando salieron a buen puerto." (It will be clearly seen from this narrative that those who have inherited noble houses ought not to be presumptuous, since they have been favored by Fortune. And it will likewise be seen that those to whom she has not been partial have often done much more than those who have inherited their wealth, for many times, through their own energy and pluck, the less favored have, despite ill fortune, eventually reached port.) (p. 64). The words scarcely veil the demand that nonexistent merit should be rewarded equally with real merit. Lázaro even credits himself with Machiavellian energy and cunning that he has never possessed. He has arrived at his mature state of moral complacence, examples of which abound. Thus, following the incident of the stone bull there is a "time shift" to the present time of the frame, and Lázaro moralizes: "Huelgo de contar a V.M. estas niñerías, para mostrar quánta virtud sea saber los hombres subir siendo baxos y dexarse baxar siendo altos quánto vicio." (I am happy, sir, to recount to you these childhood memories to demonstrate how virtuous it is for men to rise from low estate, and, contrariwise, how vile it is to fall low from high position.) (pp. 78–79). This parodistic *Poetics* is a smug reversal of the wheel of fortune. Since structurally the idea of fortune as the servant of the Christian God results in an equation of good fortune with virtue, it would appear that the rise of the picaro has been based on personal merit —which is manifestly untrue.[41] Even the post of town crier—he accompanied criminals to their punishment or execution—is thoroughly disreputable.

It would seem logical for the self-deceiving picaro to avoid exposure in his "confessions," but, now, fame is the spur. Lázaro has convinced himself that writing his success story, even writing it badly, gives him a claim to esteem. He quotes Cicero to the purpose: "La honra cría las artes" (Honor promotes the arts) (p. 62). But, as far as he is concerned, the exterior appearance of honor is good without the content of a noble action: "Suplico a vuestra M. reciba el pobre seruicio de mano de quien lo hiziera mas rico, si su poder y desseo se conformaran." (I beg Your Worship to receive this poor offering of one who would have made it richer had his gifts and his desires been of equal magnitude.) (p. 64). Lázaro's act of artistic creation helps him to extend that masquerade of honorable appearances for which the squire had set the supreme example. The *author's* purpose, on the other hand, is signaled when Lázaro says he is writing in obedience to an inquiry into "el caso" (the matter) (p. 64)—which turns out to be the *ménage à trois* at the end! Among the most recent critics, Francisco Rico regards "el caso" as both the pretext and the heart of the novel; Fernando Lázaro Carreter also considers it the illuminating focus of the whole novel; and Howard Mancing sees it as the moment, for the reader, of moral truth.[42] There can be no doubt that Lázaro is a base and repulsive creature, even though generations of readers have been beguiled into thinking *Lazarillo de Tormes* the story of a charming little chap.

As Albert Sicroff has observed, one purpose of the Prologue lies in Lázaro's pretense of honor.[43] Thus the frame of the novel may be seen as part of the parodistic pattern of the other units. Lázaro deliberately rejects the epic convention of in medias res as unfit for his story: "[P]aresciome no tomalle por el medio, sino del principio" (I have thought it best to start not in the middle but at the beginning) (p. 62). This rejection of epic is a significant clue to the whole genre of the picaresque novel. Lázaro does not mean that he is unaware that great events, sufficient to fire the imagination of an energetic poet, are taking place. Indeed, the most extreme parody of all is revealed when Lázaro marries another's mistress the same year that the triumphant emperor enters Toledo: side by side we have the triumph of chivalry and honor and the fake triumph of materialism and dishonor. The point is that although autobiographical form lends itself to such a conversion of values, it also supports the author's vision of time as being out of joint. In autobiography the vantage point is not in the middle, cohesively centered in a point of lost time. The point of departure lies inevitably in present time, and out of this situation emerges the interplay of past and present. Fittingly, then, we have the "I" of Lázaro as a defining limit. Only once—in the episode of the squire—does the "I" seem to expand spatially into the "we," and this is a short-lived flowering. The rest of the time the world outside the "I" is dead time, a fantastic memory of a journey to the end of night. To project his life in terms of an ulterior order, in terms of time itself, would be for the picaro, whose world is disintegrating, a contradiction. Comparison with Augustine's *Confessions* is instructive on this point. Augustine, too, recollects scattered fragments of time, but he does so in order to represent plastically the coherence of human existence apparent to him after his religious conversion. The *Confessions* exhibit an ethical energy in that particular circumstances and particular personal relationships precipitate an inward religious experience. But the world of *Lazarillo de Tormes* is a world without a living faith: the picaro, whose identity is bound up with the concept of time, has been socially and religiously deformed. His search for inner standing is a disaster in which material success, not faith, appears as a unifying thread; and, because success is here inseparable from amorality and spiritual death, the picaro's life remains little more than random self-assertiveness.

*Lazarillo de Tormes*, it may now be claimed, is a novel of character, and what happens to the picaro is therefore of consequence for a statement of the theme. That theme, it seems to me, may be called disintegration.[44] To demonstrate the comprehensiveness of the theme in its various philosophical, socioeconomic, and religious aspects, I have subdivided its discussion in three parts: (1) the disintegration of reality, which is the problem of knowledge, (2) the disintegration of goodness, which is the problem of morality, and (3) the disintegration of trust, which is the problem of faith.

## The Disintegration of Reality

*Lazarillo de Tormes* sets for the novel generally the conflict between illusion and reality. It turns attention to an epistemological problem that has intensified since the breakup of the medieval synthesis—the problem of how we know and of how reliable our knowledge is. The first picaresque novel thus gives evidence of a shift from the view of reality as absolute to the view of reality as relative.

In *Lazarillo* the disintegration of reality as absolute is caused by a breakdown in the individual psyche. The narrator is a *persona* whose experiences, instead of being anomalous facts, acquire symbolic value. The real connection of events entirely relative to the *persona* comes from what Rousseau calls the "chain of feeling."[45] Truth is subjective; we must rely on Lázaro; but Lázaro is unreliable, the student of a false teaching. He has elected a dishonorable course of life because he sees no alternative to compromise: there is no escaping reality—except, as happens, through the will to illusion.

From the beginning Lázaro expounds his relativistic philosophy with scholarly sophistry. The soldier, he declares, acts dangerously not because he is brave but because he desires to win esteem. The friar preaches well not because he desires the salvation of his hearers but because his eloquence may win praise. The author writes not for intrinsic merit in the act but to make his reputation. This situation being true—Lázaro argues—one may see the difference between a peasant and a nobleman as a matter of luck, not merit: "Y tambien porque consideren los que heredaron nobles estados quán poco se les deue, pues fortuna fue con ellos parcial." (It will be clearly seen from this narrative that those who have inherited noble houses ought not to be presumptuous, since they have been favored by Fortune.) (p. 64). And so forth. Father Gonzalez was a martyr, the blind man an apostle of light, the squire an honorable man, the pardoner a contributor to the good life, and the archpriest a model of respectability. This topsy-turvy world does not mean that standards have disappeared but that they have lost their reliability and no longer describe a fixed order of reality. Standards become creations of the individual; indeed, the relativism of Lázaro leads to an apotheosis when distinctions are blurred between the emperor and the picaro.

In this world of uncertain knowledge even material objects tend to lose reliability. The stone bull, strangely animated, has "gored" Lazarillo. The wine jar the blind man smashes against his mouth contains an element "dulce y amargo" (bittersweet) (p. 87) because it both hurts and heals. Lázaro converts *maravedís* into half their value, bread into God, a chest into paradise, and an empty house into a place of enchantment. Yet all objects do not share a similar fate. There is the unstuffed mattress on which Lazarillo and the squire sleep: untransformed, it remains tangible enough to be seized by the bailiff, evidence that Lázaro is not quixotic but a willing agent in the metamorphosis of reality.

The word "metamorphosis" reminds us of a possible source of *Lazarillo de Tormes*. Apuleius, with his frivolity and his liking for what Erich Auerbach calls the "spectrally sadistic,"[46] distorts reality, because reality in the modern sense does not interest him. He delights in the fancifully erotic, in, for example, the sexual encounter of an ass and a vulgarized Pasaphaë, because he lacks human feeling toward his own characters. The accent in *Metamorphoses* falls on spontaneity and inventiveness, although, of course, a lazy dichotomy of man and beast, soul and body, lust and asceticism, glosses the playful obscenities with a film of morbid puritanism. *Lazarillo de Tormes* is quite different. The author's talent is systematic rather than spontaneous, synthesizing rather than inventive. He still has a taste for old jokes, but it fades before the essential dignity with which he imbues the youthful protagonist in the first three tratados. Seriously represented, the mature Lázaro, unlike Lucius, cannot be altered in appearance without an accompanying change in spirit, which is another way of saying that, once transformed from one state of being to another, he cannot change back. Time, with which he maintains a state of tension, is not frivolous.

But if this is simply to say that *Lazarillo* is humanly impressive, it is also to suggest again how great is the distance that separates author from protagonist, because it is as if Lázaro thinks of himself as another Lucius, as victim of a fate that strikes from outside and that animates perpetually the dead fixedness of life. The sort of pattern that life offers may, he thinks, be summarized as *fortunas y adversidades*. Moreover, a change of fortune is preceded by a supernatural signal device that he calls "illumination."[47] The blind man "illuminates" Lazarillo by teaching him to prosper materially. The goddess Fortuna herself seems to illuminate him just before his success as town crier. Yet Lázaro, as the author's uncompromising irony tells us, is not finally a victim of fate at all nor has he ever intuitively perceived or been illuminated by some supernatural reality. Just as his illuminations were deceptive, so the fortuitous pattern of his life denotes his complacent attempt to give form to futility. His best efforts at transforming himself have failed, but, since this idea is intolerable, he prefers to see himself as a necessary part of cosmic drama. Yet all the time he *has* changed. The outward signs of prosperity serve finally as a critique of an inner catastrophe for which Lázaro must be responsible.

So in the end the disintegration of the picaro's sense of the natural order is not just a matter of his subjective, relativistic concept of knowledge or of his desperate playfulness with material reality, but, superintending these, of the dissolving structure of his thought.

## The Disintegration of Goodness

Of the picaro in *El Buscón*, T. E. May writes: "[He is] the embodiment, in the novel, of that experience in which the good seems actually to be weakened into evil; or in which the evil will, since evil has no existence of its own, has to wear the mask of the good, which however it deforms inevitably in the wearing."[48] To the extent that the hunger motif is not deterministic this also describes *Lazarillo de Tormes*. Benedetto Croce saw the novel as an epic of hunger and not at all as a drama of moral choice.[49] Superficially, at least, Lázaro seems to lack a will of his own, but, it seems to me, this apparent lack of will is not a condition of his literary being but a symptom of his final disintegrated state.

Hunger loses its force as a determining factor when Lazarillo leaves the house of the squire. What occurs at the end of the novel is not a struggle between good and evil but a situation in which goodness has lost its savor and left the world to the murky combat of picaro and *picardía*. To see this development, we have to recall that the forces of love and goodness have shown themselves to and in Lazarillo from the beginning. Not corrupted in his birth by the venial sins of his family, the mature Lázaro has reason to regard childhood as a period of goodness and innocence. His mother may have erred because of poverty but she never shirked her duty to teach her child the rudiments of piety and charity. In fact, until his ninth or tenth year he was naturally trustful, living in a state of innocence without which the betrayal of Zaide and the anguish of the stone bull incident would have been pointless. Satanism, or the determination to oppose the good, begins only when the blind man warns Lazarillo that he must know "somewhat more than the devil himself." Yet even the periods of service to blind man, priest, and squire do not utterly efface the boy's belief in goodness: there are *los buenos*, the good people who seem to him to rim and contain the eruption of evil. Even if the idea of their goodness may finally be converted in his consciousness into a dubious respectability, they are remembered for their kindness. Lázaro, after all, is able to distinguish good and evil, as the episode of the squire shows in large measure. Toward this master, Lazarillo is compassionate because the squire is potentially virtuous. At the same time, the squire's evil condition is related to the spiritual unreality of his code of honor. The picaro sees that innocence, love, and virtue are punished, while evil that wears the mask of goodness is rewarded.

Capable of moral choice, Lázaro chooses evil when he agrees to pimp for the archpriest. His choice results in something more than complacent hypocrisy and comes closer to a condition of total amorality. To an extent his choice has been determined by necessity, but, unless he is made responsible for his self-destruction, the exhibit of his impudent and odious hypocrisy in the Prologue and Tratado VII is meaningless. He has learned from each master, but he knows that he has been falsely taught and that illusionism does not really solve his problem.

It would be interesting to know whether *Lazarillo de Tormes* was originally conceived as a parody, not only of heroic literature, but also of the sentimentalized picaresque tradition, for Lazarillo is not the lovable rogue or simple trickster of legend, another Robin Hood, Till Eulenspiegel, or Reynard the Fox. He cannot be sentimentalized at all, certainly not as a romantic rebel opposing nature to convention and symbolizing human freedom. His critical position involves a paradox: he is an outsider who wishes to enter in, an unwilling, unromantic outcast without moral grandeur. He cannot oppose society without opposing himself because society (in the Renaissance generally) held just this sense of a composition of individuals, of an ordered world in which the individual was integrated, theoretically, into the whole.[50] Turmoil in society was to be attributed to an alteration in individual conduct. The Renaissance writer was not apt to see a qualitative difference between individual morality and social morality—witness the trail of evil that follows upon the murder of Hamlet or the abdication of Lear—and, consequently, the notion of rebelliousness for its own sake would probably have seemed dangerous nonsense. Rebellion, too, often meant usurpation, and both were rooted in the sin of pride that individuals might improve their lot through their own efforts.[51] The picaro is a potential usurper. Set adrift on the perimeter of a world breaking up, he is nevertheless as much to blame for decadence as any other individual. He, too, contributes to the sum of social malaise, and society will increasingly reflect back to him his own distorted image. As an individual he is not free from the burden of social guilt. He is a fallen man in a fallen world, an Adam who belongs to himself. It is typical of the moral austerity to be found in the Spanish picaresque novels that Lázaro is left in his disintegrated moral state unredeemed, even by the sense of life itself. While there is, to be sure, a strategy of redemption in *Guzmán de Alfarache*, an atmosphere of damnation is not screened out by comic effects in the classic triad of Spanish picaresque novels.[52]

## The Disintegration of Trust

The problem of religious faith in *Lazarillo de Tormes* involves not a question of the sincerity or hypocrisy of the picaro's piety but of the picaro's conception of his worldly environment. According to Ortega y Gasset, secular man of the Spanish fifteenth and sixteenth centuries until the Council of Trent was "lost in himself, torn away from one system of conviction and not yet installed in another, without solid ground on which to stand."[53] He still believed in the medieval world, that is, in the supernatural other-world of God, but he believed without a living faith because, for men nauseated by ecclesiastical corruption, the source of dogmatic theology had dried up. But, above all, the new anthropocentric life appealed to him. Having segregated Christ from the Trinity, he sought a new version of saintliness in the imitation of Christ's conduct. The individual thus might evolve a new relationship to God without the ritual intervention of the church. Because such "heresy" was supplanting the traditional role of ritual and God became inscrutable (raised to dogma by the Protestants), the individual of this age soon preoccupied himself with his worldly environment. Before long, good works would become central to salvation, and this evolution was to lead, as R. H. Tawney and others have shown, to the development of a middle-class formula of salvation by material success.[54]

Does Lázaro think to redeem himself, then, by the exercise of his acquisitive instinct? We have seen how the rise to prosperity that Lázaro projects as the triumph of materialism issues in fact out of defeat, despair, and a spiritual death. However much we may sympathize with him, he is damned, and the distinction helps to focus the author's attitude more sharply: it is not man who is condemned but acquisitive man, he who uses his worldly environment for selfish purposes. In this sense *Lazarillo de Tormes* represents the negative impression of God, the protagonist, whose acquisitiveness makes him man without grace, helping us to understand what grace is, or once was believed to be.

If the movement of the novel is interpreted as the fall from hope of grace, confirmation appears in the disputed fifth tratado.

The pardoner, unlike any other character in the novel, is a "divine" confidence man, perhaps Satan personified. Blasphemously he pretends to live in a state of grace, to be a minister of divine justice. So cleverly does he act his part that even Lázaro is at first deceived; yet when Lázaro is undeceived, he reacts so calmly that it would seem that he is now too disillusioned to care: "Y, aunque mochacho, cayome mucho en gracia." (And, despite my being so young, I was amused.) (p. 228). The half-theological idiom *caer en gracia* implies that amusement hides Lázaro's fall from grace.

Johan Huizinga writes that among the many spectral fancies of the waning Middle Ages there was one according to which the biblical Lazarus, after his resurrection, lived in continual horror at the thought that he should again have to pass through the gate of death.[55] What interests me here is the new emphasis in feeling about the Christian miracle, whereby joy and awe have been replaced by anguish. Now Christ has become inscrutable, but Lazarus of Bethany (as distinguished from the beggar in the parable of Dives) has become too intensely human an image of our destiny. So, too, with Lázaro of Tormes, that strange, inaccessible self held over from the loss of the world, who lives at the contingent edge of life and will soon plunge back into darkness. He, too, has found death-in-life because he distrusts his own idea of significance: the sound of life, like the sound of the stone bull, is treacherously hollow. His journey into self is a confrontation with death and emblematically an experience of it.

The idea of death is linked in the novel with the idea of freedom. The systematic procedure, the ironic *Bildungsroman* of character deformation, betrays in some of its largest configurations a story of the prying loose and casting out of a free individual and of the spiritual death that results. Responsibility for this state of affairs is made to rest on the individual, first because he is an inseparable integer of society, second because he makes a choice of the freedom that destroys him. In other words, Lázaro's final isolation grows out of, but is not dependent upon, his victimization by selfish masters. For Lázaro desires his freedom. He took destiny into his own hands when he deserted the blind man. He was not required to steal from the priest, although the alternative was a saintly renunciation of the means to life, and Lázaro knows well he is not a saint; as he says in the Prologue: "[C]onfessando yo no ser mas sancto que mis vezinos" (I will confess I am no more saintly than my neighbors) (p. 63). Harsh as the judgment is, Lázaro is a sinner, his sin is, above all, pride, and what tempts him is the desire to belong to himself. We are thus prepared for Lázaro to accept, freely, the role of cuckold and pimp in return for freedom from want. But it is clear that the freedom Lázaro gains is completely intolerable. In exchange for comfort and the appearance of respectability, he must consent to observe the dissolution of his spirit because he has no values, symbols, and patterns: he accepts a condition aptly termed by Erich Fromm "moral aloneness," a condition in which freedom is destroyed. Fromm says: "[M]an, the more he gains freedom in the sense of emerging from the original oneness with man and nature and the more he becomes an 'individual,' has no choice but to unite himself with the world in the spontaneity of love and productive work or else to seek a kind of security by such ties with the world as destroy his freedom and the integrity of his individual self."[56] If we agree with Fromm that love and productive work are major freedom-preserving actions, we can see how Lázaro once possessed the dignity of freedom when he served the helpless squire, for then only could his confidence game become holy. Once the squire departed, Lázaro escaped permanently behind his mask of fear.

The somber link between freedom and death expresses an introvertive individual myth that symbolically portrays an important intrapsychic happening. It is difficult to conceive of the first picaresque novel as mythless. We should observe the mythoclastic role of *Lazarillo de Tormes*: Is it entirely possible to destroy one myth of the hero without replacing it with another? Cervantes, for example, shared Quixote's fondness for chivalric romances, and his parody of them is a rear-guard action fought for the preservation of a dying myth. Similarly, Lazarillo is a picaro who falls far short of heroic measure, who reinternalizes the old myth, and who is "born again" (the Lazarus archetype) as nonheroic economic man. But in the context of *Lazarillo* this is a very bad state of affairs. The emergent myth is undesirable, and the misadventures of the new hero are presented as a cautionary tale.

The matter may not be so puzzling when we remember that the picaro is in some of his aspects a reincarnation of the epic hero. Odysseus was wily, cunning, and adaptable, a grandson of the archrogue Autolycus and favored by Athena for his intelligence. According to W. B. Stanford, "Odysseus's famous deception of the Cyclops and the Suitors, his ingenious stories and his skilful maneuvers when still disguised as a beggar in Ithaca, his masterly stratagem of the Trojan Horse . . . marked him out for posterity as the supreme man of wile in classical mythology." Intelligence, however, is a neutral quality and "may take the form of low and selfish cunning or of exalted, altruistic wisdom."[57] There results from the ambiguity a gradual transformation of Odysseus as a heroic myth develops through the ages: Odysseus appears as an opportunist in the sixth century, a wanderer, bold baron, or learned clerk in the Middle Ages, a prince and politician in the seventeenth century, and a salesman of the metropolis by the twentieth century. If Lázaro is placed into this cycle, we see that he shares certain Odyssean characteristics, chiefly wiliness, inventiveness, and adaptability. He does, then, have some claim to superiority. But he forfeits his claim through a lack of other heroic qualities such as prudence, magnanimity, and courage.[58] As Guillén observes, the picaro is "the coward with a cause."[59]

The critical irony with which the story of Lazarus was treated was overlooked outside of Spain. Englishmen read *Lazarillo* because they thought it was funny and realistic. David Rowland, whose translation entitled *The Pleasaunt Historie of Lazarillo de Tormes* appeared in 1576, writes that he was attracted to the novel, "finding it for the number of strange and merry reports, very recreative and pleasant."[60] The near-starvation of a child struck Rowland as a good subject for mirth, though he adds that "besides much mirth, here is also a true description of the nature and disposition of sundrie Spaniards."[61] Apparently, many later readers have seen in the novel no antagonism to contemporary myth, despite the gulf separating the treatment of acquisitive man in *Lazarillo* and in, say, *Robinson Crusoe*; as late as 1895, William Dean Howells, American apostle of the dream of success, praised *Lazarillo*, a lifelong favorite, because it showed, he said, "the life of a man who has risen, as we nearly all have, with many ups and downs."[62] In the Gilded Age, the disintegrated picaro finally became a respectable citizen!

The anguish of Lazarillo de Tormes differs somewhat from the *Angst* of the so-called existentialist hero such as Dostoevsky's underground man. There are, of course, resemblances. The picaro and the existentialist hero create themselves out of a world of appearances. But the existentialist hero is a nonconformist. The picaro conforms and will sacrifice moral principle in order to conform. But if we are now beginning to understand the feeling behind creation of the first literary picaro, it may well be because the typical literary hero of our times suffers, too, a dreadful freedom.[63]

## *Guzmán de Alfarache*: The Structure of Despair

The second Spanish picaresque masterpiece is *Guzmán de Alfarache: Atalaya de la vida humana* or, as it came to be known, *La vida del pícaro*, by Mateo Alemán.[64] The appearance of the first part of the work in 1599 created a sensation, and the addition of a second part in 1604 gave it a sudden popularity apparently unmatched by any other work in the history of Spanish literature; not even *Don Quixote* (1605, 1615) matched *Guzmán*'s record thirty editions during its first six years.[65] Nor was its popularity limited to Spain and Spanish America.[66] French, German, and English translations helped the rise of the novel in those countries.[67] Gabriel Chappuys (1600), Jean Chappelain (1619–20: ten editions by 1689), Gabriel Brémond (1695), and Lesage (1732: twenty-six editions by 1883) offered French translations. Of these, that by Chappelain, the classical critic, followed Alemán's original; that by Lesage was a "traduction purgée des moralités superflues."[68] In England a brisk and exuberant translation by James Mabbe in 1622 achieved four editions by 1656. The fact that the Shakespeare Third Folio was not issued until 1663 gives some idea of the popularity of Mabbe's *Rogue*. In Germany,

Aegidius Albertinus's translation in 1615 prepared the way for Hans Jacob Christoffel von Grimmelshausen's *Simplicius Simplicissimus* (1669). Nowadays, whereas *Celestina*, *Lazarillo*, and *Don Quixote* constantly find new readers, outside Spain *Guzmán* is all but forgotten. Nor is the reason for this bibliographic curve hard to find: *Guzmán* is composed of two apparently conflicting elements, the narrative and the moral commentary, thus creating a story described by one critic as "Charlie Chaplin viewed by a sixteenth-century Calvinist minister."[69] Such a dualism was bound to lose aesthetic force as later novelists learned to make morality implicit in the action.

Lesage signaled this decline of *Guzmán's* popularity when he rejected its "moralités superflues" in favor of "des tableaux de la vie civile." According to Lesage, Alemán, a student of Horace, lacked Horatian restraint: Alemán had gone beyond his material and indulged an appetite for the *utile*, thus denying his readers "le secret plaisir"[70] of reflecting for themselves. Nineteenth-century commentators followed suit. Typical was George Ticknor, who decided that the moralism was superfluous because it was hypocritical: "The long moralizing discourses with which [*Guzmán*] abounds, written in a pure Castilian style, with much quaintness and skill, though in fact to us dull, were then admired, and saved it from censures which it could otherwise hardly have failed to encounter." Alemán's novel was, Ticknor continued, "Chiefly curious and interesting because it shows us, in the costumes of the times, the life of an ingenious, Machiavellian rogue, who is never at a loss for an expedient, who always treats himself and speaks of himself as an honest and respectable man, and who sometimes goes to mass and says his prayers just before he enters on an extraordinary scheme of roguery, as if on purpose to bring it out in more striking and brilliant relief. So far from being a moral book, therefore, it is a very immoral one, and Lesage spoke in the spirit of its author, when . . . he boasted that he 'had purged it of its superfluous moral reflections.'"[71] Chandler offered a similar explanation. "The Spanish picaresque author," he wrote, "was fearful of being identified with his anti-hero, and often found himself forced to maintain his own integrity by declaring a moral purpose scarcely shown in his work."[72] By

1925 the image of Alemán as a hypocrite had assumed the status of a critical cliché. That year George Tyler Northup declared in his *Introduction to Spanish Literature*: "To satisfy clerical censors and to lend an air of serious purpose Alemán indulged in excessive moralizing. The story advances so slowly in consequence that the modern reader is bored; yet there can be no doubt that formerly this pietism contributed to the book's success. Alemán's style was highly individualistic, his experiences of life rich. In view of his own picaresque career his moral sincerity is sometimes open to question."[73]

What relationship did the man, Alemán, have to his work?[74] Baptized in Seville in 1547, where his father became physician to the royal prison in 1557, Mateo was a medical student at three different universities from 1564 to 1568 but left the University of Alcalá de Henares without graduating and launched himself into business ventures. To avoid imprisonment for debt, he married in 1571. A decade later, his life was still marked by education, business, and domestic upheaval; he received a judgeship by 1583 but was subsequently imprisoned for overstepping his powers. In 1593 he was again named a judge to investigate working conditions of slaves at the royal quicksilver mines in Almadén. In spite of *Guzmán*'s becoming a best seller in 1599, Mateo's life continued to be punctuated by quarrels, imprisonment, and unsuccessful business transactions, but in 1608 he was permitted to emigrate to Mexico where he was protected by the Archbishop García Guerra, published several nonfiction works, and vanished from record, a resident of the village of Chalco, Mexico, in 1615. A life of such turbulence could well invigorate the pages of a novel such as *Guzmán*, with its scenes of student life, prisons, corrupt officialdom, unhappy marriage, and the like. Moreover, a fact of significance for determining the tone of *Guzmán de Alfarache* is that the Alemán family was known to be of Jewish origin; like all those descended from New Christians, Mateo had to be scrupulously pious and doctrinally pure and sincere, upon pain of death for infringement upon orthodoxy. Alemán's Christian faith is not surprising, but, as a recent biographer writes, "it is perhaps surprising that his profound religiousness did not interfere with his immoral business tactics."

The duality is found in Alemán's creature, Guzmán, "not due to a split personality, but to the fact that he is really two persons: the young rogue who commits sins and the mature man who relates them both as entertainment and as an example of bad conduct."[75] Was Alemán having his cake and eating it too? Was the ardent Christian cynically relishing his "other" life of apparent immorality? Or does the author of *Guzmán de Alfarache* make avowals that are not in accord with what he feels or believes? Since Alemán's secret report on his 1593 visit to the Almadén mines has recently surfaced, a picture of a man of sincerity, rectitude, and compassion is at last coming into focus. We see a trusted administrator especially commissioned by the crown to investigate conditions of prison workers assigned to the mines from the galleys. We see an incorruptible judge performing his office in spite of the opposition of the mine owners, who were none other than the Fugger family, powerful international bankers. We see him face to face with the prisoners, taking down details—in first-person narrations—of their wanderings and sufferings and finding their working conditions cruel and intolerable, their lives a testimony so painful that the life of Guzmán must certainly, a few years later, have been invested with the author's sympathetic understanding. In short, the Alemán we now see is akin to the Hugo of *Les miserables* and to the Dickens of *Hard Times*—authors stirred deeply by the plight of social outcasts. We may even infer that Alemán emigrated to the solitude of Mexico because of feelings and opinions amounting to helpless disgust with society, a real life resembling a literary one, that of Molière's obsessively sincere misanthrope, Alceste, of a generation later.

The nineteenth-century attack on Alemán's moralism has been countered in the twentieth. Fonger De Haan claimed in 1903 that "the interest of the story is secondary to those very digressions."[76] In 1937, Miguel Herrero García interpreted *Guzmán* as a novel form unique to the Counter-Reformation, whereby a sinner's autobiography was presented in the light of Catholic doctrine.[77] The idea was systematically studied by Enrique Moreno Báez in 1948 in a book that added greatly to a critical awareness of *Guzmán*'s complexity.[78] Enrique Moreno Báez contends that

Alemán had a thesis intention that converted the moralism into a necessary part of a novel of character. The picaro typified the vicious man, whose wretchedness would serve to warn others, but whose ultimate repentance and conversion to orthodoxy would provide an inside narrative of grace abounding. The theme of the work had been a Catholic thesis, "la salvación del más miserable de los hombres."[79] This view of the novel has been accepted without modification in some quarters; Gerald Brenan, for example, finds that *Guzmán*'s merit lies "in the running commentary" for which "the story is there merely to give the cues," concluding, "Alemán's book then can be described as a dissertation upon original sin."[80] Moreno Báez's thesis, however, has been rejected by many critics; Donald McGrady summarizes their view as being that *"Guzmán* is first and foremost a *novel*, not an ascetic treatise."[81]

Recently the feeling has grown that, while we may not understand the picaresque narrative of *Guzmán* without the moral discourses, neither may we convert the hero's career into a simple illustration of the doctrines expressed by Alemán. In 1926 an editor noted "una falta de armonía artística" resulting from the conflict, not between moralism and picarism as such, but between "el concepto superior del hombre" and "la visión fragmentaria de la vida, esencial en el pícaro."[82] Américo Castro then suggested that *Guzmán* be viewed in a double context, as baroque asceticism and as Judaic desperation.[83] This suggestion has given rise to a new stress upon heterodoxy, as opposed to militant Catholicism, in the novel.[84] The current general view is that Alemán, outwardly and sincerely orthodox, was conditioned by his *converso* background, felt spiritually estranged from the society whose highest ideals he upheld, and was driven into a solitary, personal asceticism. This view takes into account a startling fact: the novel received no adverse comment from Protestant zealots.[85] To the contrary, William Chillingworth, for example, refers approvingly to *Guzmán* in his *The Religion of Protestants a Safe Way to Salvation* (1638).[86]

A critical approach to *Guzmán de Alfarache* may be summarized as follows: there is a conflict of form in the novel originating from a disparity between the novel Alemán intended to write and the one he actually wrote. Hence the moralizing element was due to authorial intrusion on the narrative, but the intrusion did not make moralism superfluous because many of the moral and satiric comments have a bearing upon the protagonist's fictive being. The plot is unified precisely because it is subordinated to a moral and thematic unity—a characteristic feature of the baroque.[87]

During the sixteenth century, Aristotelian and Horatian literary concepts were fused.[88] In their commentaries on the *Poetics*—translated by A. Paccius in 1536—the Italian scholiasts Franciscus Robortellus (1548) and Madius (1550) interpreted Aristotelian ideas in terms of the didactic function of art set forth in the *Ars Poetica*. Madius "accepted the *Ars Poetica* as a Horatian adaptation of the *Poetics*."[89] This fusion would mean that a Spanish writer during the Counter-Reformation would feel himself bound by traditional authority to incorporate entertainment in a moral purpose.

Only two Aristotelian loci need be stressed here: the theory of catharsis and the distinction between history and poetry.

The reference to the tragic catharsis concludes Aristotle's definition of tragedy: "With incidents arousing pity and fear, wherewith to accomplish its catharsis of such emotions" (*Poetics*, p. 11). The modern pathological interpretation (for example, the excitement of music) did not attract the scholiasts. Robortellus, holding fast to the notion of utilitarian tragedy, argued that exposure to the emotions of pity and fear would prepare spectators for misfortune and thus prove a source of comfort. Madius went further: pity and fear were active agents in purging the mind of evil passions. To the point, he believed, was *Poetics*, 13: "Good men must not be shown passing from good into evil fortune; for that arouses neither pity nor fear, but aversion. Nor must evil men be shown passing from misfortune into good fortune. . . . Nor again must a very wicked person be portrayed as passing from good to bad fortune; for even though such a plot would satisfy man's general sympathetic feeling for man it would not arouse pity and fear" (*Poetics*, pp. 23–24). Madius took this dictum to mean that examples of evil men falling from happiness to misery would teach mankind to abstain from villainy. Art, he implied, was auxiliary to the social, political, and religious orientation of culture.

This neo-Aristotelian interpretation of catharsis had general acceptance among the writers of Counter-Reformation Spain. Cervantes, for example, has the Canon describe a good play thus: "The audience would come out from a well-written and well-constructed play entertained by the comic part, instructed by the serious, surprised by the action, enlivened by the speeches, warned by the tricks, wiser for the moral, incensed against vice, and enamored of virtue" (*Don Quixote*, pp. 429–30). Mateo Alemán, although not, like Cervantes, a playwright, seems to have applied similar criteria in the construction of his novel. In his "Declaration for the understanding of this book" he writes:

Escribe su vida desde las galeras, donde queda forzado al remo, por delitos que cometió, habiendo sido ladrón famosísimo, como largamente lo verás en la segunda parte. Y no es impropiedad ni fuera de propósito, si en esta primera escribiere alguna dotrina; que antes parece muy llegado a razón darla un hombre de claro entendimiento, ayudado de letras y castigado del tiempo, aprovechándose del ocioso de la galera.

He writes his life from aboard the galleys where he was put to the oar for his crimes, he having been a celebrated thief as you will see at length in the Second Part. Nor is it inappropriate and beyond my intention for me to set out in this First Part some doctrine, it seeming reasonable to represent by this a man of clear understanding, helped by learning and scourged by time, and turning to good account that idle time he had in the galleys. [*Guzmán*, 1:36][90]

From this declaration it is difficult to judge Alemán's awareness of disharmony in his plan; rather, it would seem he was at pains to have his moral purpose taken seriously as an integral part of the whole. In the eighteenth century a similar anxiety is often expressed by the English novelists, although our contemporary feeling tends to be that Defoe, Fielding, and Smollett protest too much. Nevertheless, Alemán, provoked by his work's commercial exploitation in a spurious sequel of 1602, prefaced his authentic continuation with a reminder of his moral purpose. By the account of Guzmán's life he intended: "sólo . . . descubrir como atalaya toda suerte de vicios y hacer atriaca de venenos varios, un hombre perfeto, castigado de trabajos y miserias, después de haber bajado a la más ínfima de todas, puesto en galera por curullero della." (only to discover as from a watchtower all sorts of vices and to draw remedy out of divers poisons, showing finally a perfect man, punished by troubles and griefs, having fallen into infamy and been condemned to the galleys where he could not escape.) (*Guzmán*, 3:52–53).

Early commentators and translators accepted Alemán's intention at face value. His eulogist, Alonso de Barros, proclaimed that the author mixed "lo deleitoso y lo útil que desea Horacio" (delightfulness and utility as Horace required) (*Guzmán*, 1:41) because punishment of the picaro was an "aumento [*sic*] de contrario" (argument *ex contrario*) (*Guzmán*, 1:39).[91] Jean Chappelain declared that all over Europe the book was considered "le meilleur de tous ceux qui iamais ayent esté faits en ce genre," surpassing *The Golden Ass* and *Lazarillo de Tormes* in invention, abundance, diversity, and "traicts d'erudition," and, though the moralizing was "de trop longue haleine," it was prudent and profitable.[92] James Mabbe, too, must have subscribed to an English eulogist's recommendation of the novel:

> His whole Theame is Man
> . . . for his life alone,
> Is Precept with Example; so that none
> Can better teach by worse meanes;
> Who by strange bifronted posture,
> Ill, to good, doth change.[93]

This "strange bifronted posture" of the picaro delighted an age fond of baroque illusionism, of the finite illuminated by the infinite.

Aristotle's distinction between history and poetry occurs in *Poetics*, 9: "The difference between a poet and an historian is this: the historian relates what has happened, the poet what could happen. Therefore, poetry is something more philosophic and of more serious import than history; for poetry tends to deal with the general, while history is concerned with delimited particular facts" (p. 18). The historian follows the order of events as they occur, a disjointed order in which events are not necessarily interrelated nor their temporal origins adequately clear. The poet, on the other hand, seeks for the inner coherence of possible events "according to the law of probability or necessity" (*Poetics*, p. 18).

Aristotle's distinction challenged the originators of the novel form: was the novel an amalgam of history and poetry, setting out particularity in its background and universality in its characterization? And what of "history" itself, which might denote either "fiction" or "chronicle"? Here was one of the most difficult of all problems facing the novelist, the problem of structure arising from the conflicting demands of "life by time" and "life by values."[94] Spanish novelists adopted two solutions: the first, used by the picaresque novelists, was the narrative of self-revelation, the second, employed by Cervantes, was a narrative in the epic manner.

Autobiographical narration had the virtue of seeming to particularize and universalize at once the individual consciousness: it asserted the self in a pre-Cartesian *cogito ergo sum*. The individual could be represented as in touch with his own continuing identity through the duration mechanics of memory. To the extent that the Spanish picaresque novelists accomplished this aim they anticipated Defoe, whom Ian Watt credits as the first to present "individual life in its larger perspective as a historical process."[95] But the claim should be modified for *Guzmán de Alfarache*. The structure of *Guzmán* unfolds the historical process too unevenly: perspectives evolved from delimited facts do not consistently create an aesthetic distance between author and protagonist. Was Alemán foundering on the Aristotelian rock? What could constitute the raw historical material of the picaro's memory? If I judge from the content of *Guzmán*, the historical aspect included the author's experiences, inventions, borrowing, *cuentos*, interpolated stories, and received theological doctrine—all subordinated under the narrative "I."[96] It is some tribute to Alemán's art that he gave coherence to so many types of "history," but the fact remains that he did not renounce a claim to a place in his narrative. Although he refers to *Guzmán* as "esta poética historia" (*Guzmán*, 1:35) and as "historias fabulosas" (3:53), he fails to absorb himself, as author belonging to history, into Guzmán, the protagonist belonging to poetry. When at the end of the novel Guzmán conforms to orthodoxy, the historical reality at work is Alemán's own—yet the reader must choose between creator and creature here. If we accept the plot mechanism of repentance as Alemán certainly intended, then the illusion of Guzmán's particularity suffers, yet if we accept it as a consequent effulgence of Guzmán's consciousness, then Alemán's intention may be disregarded. If we disregard it, according to the operation of the Aristotelian law of probability or necessity, the repentance of Guzmán emerges as the *unrelieved extension of despair*, a further outcome of the yearning for respectability and not the commedia of a wretched man's spiritual reconstruction.[97]

The reason why Alemán's novel eludes his grasp lies, I think, in picaresque illusionism: that is, in what Carlos Blanco Aguinaga terms the "realismo dogmático o desengaño" (dogmatic realism or spiritual restitution).[98] The picaro is conditioned to a false vision of truth. His isolation enables him to see through the deception of the world, but it is also the source of dogmatism in his outlook. The reality of the self-revealed narrator cannot cast a net, as it were, beyond its artistic limits and draw in another, higher reality. Compare *Guzmán* and *Don Quixote*: Cervantes, technically concealed by means of third-person epic narration, succeeds artistically where Alemán fails. Maintaining a neutral position in relation to his material, Cervantes balances historical particularity and poetic universality against each other in a series of evolving perspectives. The reader is entertained by the illusion that Don Quixote is really the eccentric gentleman Quexana, and there to remind us of the difference is Sancho Panza, who juxtaposes an evolving point of view to his master's fluctuating sense of reality. Cervantes's realism is objective because it provides for the dual outlook: Sancho *plus* Quixote rather than Sancho as *anti*-Quixote. Thus Cervantes discovered a vehicle that could carry a large vision of life; Alemán, lacking such a vehicle, put himself in the position of an intruder.

The plot structure of *Guzmán de Alfarache* sweeps the picaro forward and downward into a desperate redemption that provides no relief. At first glance it appears that Alemán imitated the rise-and-fall duality of *Lazarillo de Tormes* and, omitting the irony in which *Lazarillo* is broiled, intended to relieve the hero's spiritual descent by a sudden reintegration in society. Closer inspection shows that *Guzmán* has a structural complication of a different kind: the rise of the hero's consciousness from nature to grace is actually an extension of his fall into antisocial asceticism. Viewed in this manner, the novel fails to make the redeemed hero's temporal present into a viable critical commentary on the past because the picaro has not discovered a new reality to oppose to the finite reality he rejects as illusion. Nothing is what it seems; all is vanity. In *Lazarillo* a certain finite reality is present as long as the hero is conscious of his own will to illusion; but in *Guzmán* all knowledge of the self has lost validity, and life has become a grotesque adventure of *desengaño*.

For convenience I distinguish four stages of the action: disobedience, delinquency, crime, and antisocial asceticism. The division is based upon the moral quality governing Guzmán's acts at each stage.

### Disobedience

Guzmán is born at Seville of the adulterous union of an adventurous Genoan usurer and a courtesan who consorts with an old knight and passes off the boy as his. The father—once a renegade Catholic and husband of a rich Algerian whom he has robbed and deserted—marries Guzmán's mother when the old knight dies; but his prodigality reduces the family to poverty. At his death the mother returns to her old profession, and the young boy runs away to seek his fortune, hoping eventually to be welcomed by wealthy relations in Genoa. Along the road to Madrid he is disheartened by the hostility of those whom he meets. At one inn he is sickened by a fricasse of hatching eggs; at another, he is robbed. On resuming his journey, he is mistakenly arrested and given a beating and is deserted in Cazalla and robbed by an ingratiating muleteer of the remainder of his money. He works temporarily as a stableboy and learns to cheat his customers. Then he begs his way to Madrid and there supports himself miserably but honestly as a porter in the piazza until taking up service with a cook.

The parental relationship is more complicated here than in *Lazarillo*. Guzmán emerges from childhood as spoiled, indolent, and abnormally sensitive of the family dishonor. Tonally his description of the parents is half-serious, half-burlesque, an attempt to uphold the Commandment in the face of disagreeable facts. He declares that his father belonged to a family of "levantiscos" who were "agregados a la nobleza" (easterners grafted onto the nobility) (1:54).[99] Although a despised usurer, "muchas veces lo oyó a sus oídos y con su buena condición pasaba por ello" (many times he heard that reproachful word yet, since he was good-natured, took no notice) (1:54). The father deceived his creditors by declaring bankruptcy, "esta honrosa manera de robar" (that honest manner of stealing) (1:59), was rumored to be effeminate, "afeitarse" (to use cosmetics) (1:67), and he could be bribed by "mujeres que solicitaban" (women who cadged gifts) (1:67). Yet, Guzmán observes, "todos somos hombres" (we are all of us only human) (1:71). Thus, like Lázaro, he blurs the distinction between honor and dishonor and shows the attempt by one in full knowledge of the facts to assert the contrary: "Por la parte de mi padre no me hizo el Cid ventaja. . . . Por la de mi madre no me faltaban otros tantos y más cachivaches de los abuelos. Tenía más enjertos que los cigarrales de Toledo." (On my father's side El Cid was no better than myself. . . . On my mother's, I was as well-descended, my great-grandfathers being men of wealth and esteem. I had more grafts than the pleasure-gardens of Toledo.) (1:97). From such statements emerges the picaro in one of his aspects as a boy accustomed to adjust his sense of honor to protect himself from feelings of shame and social inferiority. Guzmán's reactions, however, are varied. He can be gravely innocent: "Vía con la imaginación el abril y la hermosura de los campos, no considerando sus agostos." (I imagined only April and the beauty of the fields, not considering their August.) (1:166–67). Or, alone and hungry, he can viciously express self-pity full of torment and loathing: "Halléme como perro flaco ladrado de los otros, que a todos enseña dientes, todos lo cercan, y acometiendo a todos a ninguno muerde. Trabajos me ladraron teniéndome rodeado; todos me picaban y más que otro no haber que gastar ni modo con qué buscar el ordinario." (I was like a lean dog cornered by other dogs, snarling at all who approached, attacking without daring to bite. Cares closed about me, howling; things lashed out at me; but, above all, I was cursed with no money and no means to look after myself.) (2:9).

There are indeed so many compulsive and contradictory aspects of Guzmán's personality that one is tempted to question Alemán's control of his material; at the same time, Guzmán is most explicable when most nearly resembling Lázaro. Thus his aspiration to a life of wealth and ease is made ludicrous by his servility and deviousness. He knowingly rationalizes his behavior. He exalts in his work as a porter—"esta gloriosa libertad" (2:27) —snickers at the vulgar conception of honor—"¿Que frenesí de Satanás casó este mal abuso con el hombre, que tan desatinado lo tiene?" (What satanic frenzy married this foul abuse to man, making him mad?) (2:29)—and finally takes a perverse pleasure in parodying Ecclesiastes: "Todo fué vano, todo mentira, todo ilusión, todo falso y engaño de la imaginación." (All was vanity, all lies, all illusion, all false and deceiving imagination.) (2:14). During brief periods he feels guilty for running away from home, but it is clear that he has no will to return. His will seems so paralyzed by disillusionment that he marks his entry into the *picardía* of Madrid by a classical image of disintegrated mankind: "No hallarás hombre con hombre; todos vivimos en asechanza, los unos de los otros, como el gato para el ratón o la araña para la culebra." (There is no man with man. We live in ambush to prey upon one another, as the cat for the mouse or the spider for the snake.) (2:54).[100]

### Delinquency

Guzmán serves the cook in Madrid because the latter promises advancement, but irresponsibility soon earns him the distrust of his employer, and he is dismissed. Again he becomes a porter, but abandons his honesty, robs a grocer, and flees to Toledo. There he squanders some of his money on prostitutes and the remainder in an attempt to impress an army captain. Poor and humiliated, he steals and swindles to serve the captain, but this master, having taken him to Genoa, dismisses him as dangerous.

In Genoa, Guzmán approaches his relatives, only to earn their contempt for his ragged appearance: they toss him in a blanket and dismiss him as an impostor. He turns beggar on the road to Rome, and in that city is instructed by Alberto, the beggar king. Eventually, a cardinal, pitying his sham sores, has Guzmán brought home, "cured," and taken into service as a page, but an unrepentant Guzmán indulges his old passion for gambling and his new one for playing the fool. Banished for an interval by the cardinal, he is too arrogant to return until, after extreme poverty, he is too late. He is then taken up by the French ambassador, whom he serves as clown and pander. In a few years Guzmán is notorious in Rome. Ultimately he is exposed by Fabia, a matron infuriated by his advances on behalf of his master. Persecuted and reviled, he leaves service in hopes of reforming his way of life.

Sherman Eoff describes Guzmán's life from the moment he enters *picardía* as a "continuous oscillation between lower and higher social levels." In leaving the life of the street in order to serve the cook, Guzmán exemplifies the picaro's desire to gain a precarious foothold in the established social order; yet he "merely transfers his chosen norms of conduct to a higher social category."[101] His exposure to shame and ridicule increases as he climbs the ladder of success, and, consequently, he overcompensates by means of ever more clownish and degrading behavior. He conceals his wretchedness behind forced gaiety, yet his compulsiveness comes through very clearly. For example, when Guzmán buys clothes after his first robbery, he makes an explicit identification with his father, the originator of his disorder: "Parecióme, viéndome entronizado y bien vestido, que mi padre era vivo y que yo estaba restituído al tiempo de sus prosperidades." (It seemed to me, seeing myself thus enthroned and well dressed, that my father was alive and that I was restored to the time of his prosperity.) (2:119). The paternal source of Guzmán's warped sense of values, of this determination to substitute appearances for reality, is thus plainly identified. But his association with the corrupt is also a factor in his delinquency; thus he attempts to excuse his life in *picardía* in a bitter stoicism: "Este camino corre el mundo. No comienza de nuevo, que de atrás le viene al garbanzo el pico. No tiene medio ni remedio. Así lo hallamos, así lo dejaremos." (Thus goes the world: an old story that baseborn men wax proud and arrogant. There is no help, no remedy; we find it thus, thus we leave it.) (2:167). Yet for all his disenchantment, Guzmán is aware of his moral complicity. The captain dismissed him, he says, "como a miembro cancerado" (as a cancerous member) (2:161–62). He failed the cardinal through his "inclinación para lo malo" (inclination to evil) (2:288). And on the occasion of a great humiliation, he is profoundly bewildered by the moral disorder in his soul: "Ya era noche oscura y más en mi corazón. En todas las casas había encendidas luces; empero mi alma triste siempre padeció tinieblas." (The night was dark but darker still was my soul. In every house shone brilliant lights, but always in my sad soul there was darkness.) (3:163). The outsider yearning for the lives of others: here in baroque chiaroscuro is represented the same fear experienced by Lazarillo when he passed the funeral procession.

### Crime

Guzmán, now a young man about twenty, leaves Rome with an acquaintance, Sayavedra, who robs him of his trunks and divides the spoils with brigands under the leadership of one Bentivoglio. Poor once more, Guzmán soon wears out his welcome in Sienna, and en route to Florence again meets Sayavedra, pardons him, and obtains his service. From Florence they go to Bologna to denounce Bentivoglio, but Guzmán is thrown into prison for this defamation. When released, he teams with Sayavedra as a cardsharp; their fortunes improve. With criminal finesse Guzmán robs a Milanese banker of a large sum he pretends to have deposited and returns to Genoa as wealthy Don Juan de Guzmán to be received proudly by his relations, whom, however, by way of revenge, he defrauds. He returns to Spain a rich man (although Sayavedra has drowned himself out of fear and guilt), and in Madrid settles down as a businessman and marries his partner's daughter. His wife's prodigality and his own greed drive him quickly to bankruptcy. His wife dying, he decides to seek the security of the priesthood, but, after studying for seven years at

Alcalá and being within a few weeks of obtaining his degree, he runs off to marry a beautiful girl whom he presumes to be wealthy. She proves as poor as he, however, and he takes her to Madrid and there becomes her pimp. Eventually they reach Seville—where Guzmán's mother is a busy procuress—and his wife escapes with their money. Now Guzmán involves himself in clumsy swindles, in one of which he deceives a holy hermit in order to be sponsored as bailiff to a lady whom he means to defraud of all her property. In this crime he is apprehended and sentenced to the galleys for six years, a sentence extended to life after an unsuccessful prison break. Using servile tricks, he ingratiates himself with the officers of the galley and declares that he is now ready to reform. He begins his memoirs. Then one day he rescues his masters by betraying a plan for mutiny, and out of gratitude they set him free.

This episodic criminal career ends as it began, with the promise of reform, but between the promises violent spiritual unrest dominates. Consequently, the crimes are full of desperate animus toward society. For example, in the grandiose swindle of the Genoans he reveals something more than the finesse of the mature confidence man: he is violating laws of blood kinship and hospitality. Twice he profanes the marriage sacrament in order to follow his self-interest, and his effrontery is at last so cynical that he dupes the holy hermit—an act perhaps sufficient to damn him in Spanish eyes. But although this behavior suggests that Guzmán is Machiavellian—he has been compared to Bosola in John Webster's *Duchess of Malfi*—it is important to observe that Alemán's picaro is directed by no fixed policy of malevolence; rather, his actions are the manifestations of his perverted will.

Eoff summarizes the psychology of Guzmán as "that of a person who, heavily conditioned by his environment, aspires always to a comfortable and privileged position in society, resorts to subterfuge as a means of attaining his goal, rationalizes his moral disorderliness in the name of necessity and current social practices, develops pride in his expert chicanery as compensation for his inferiority, and reaches eventually a culminating point of greed, shamelessness, and buffoonery." Guzmán's good qualities, humor, vitality, intelligence, "are overshadowed by the negative, defensive reactions of one who is hopelessly shackled by his environment."[102] *Guzmán de Alfarache*, in short, is a study of social failure for which bankruptcy, Guzmán's and his father's, is a suitable symbol.

Yet the story of individual failure to achieve an acceptable socioeconomic status does not quite account for what Guzmán himself calls a "discurso de mi amarga vida" (discourse on my bitter life) (5:88). Religious despair plays a part in Guzmán's failure. Because Guzmán remains lonely and bitter after the supposed reformation of his life, he has, I contend, a continuous psychic existence between past and present times of the narrative: in other words, there is an action in the moralism of the novel that takes us beyond a culminating point of greed, shamelessness, and buffoonery.

### Antisocial Asceticism

The fourth structural stage of *Guzmán* is antisocial, that is, unrelieved asceticism.[103] In Counter-Reformation Spain, an acceptable method for escaping the misery and corruption of society was religious faith. Conformity offered a refuge to all men, regardless of class, and all men were considered deformed by original sin and able to hope for formal restitution only in supernature. Alemán intended to dramatize such spiritual metamorphosis: "El fin que llevo es fabricar un hombre perfeto." (The end I pursue is to create a perfect man.) (3:187). Yet it is to be doubted that a promised but never printed third part would have imitated the Dantean design: the novel is already coherent as the story of a picaro's disintegration and could not plausibly be changed to a story of heroic spiritual regeneration.

There are, I think, four good reasons why Guzmán may not be accepted as a regenerated hero. First, his conversion is not rendered in any dramatic sense. One day in the galleys he simply decides to accept the authority of the religious code; but there follows no rejoicing, not even an unblinking raking-in of the chips à la Moll Flanders. Second, we have grown accustomed to a Guzmán motivated by impossible dreams and driven by immediate selfish impulses. What might not a man do who has given up seven years of university training on the eve of his graduation just to marry a beautiful woman whom he can bend to his will? Guzmán, indeed, is that disturbing individual whose passion at any moment may overrule his reason, but who is incapable of recreating himself in his own passionate image. Where Don Quixote's diseased will but strengthened the affirmation of a private ideal, Guzmán has no authentic ideology to oppose to a reality in ruins. His final repentance tends to assume the quality of his other impulses gone astray. Third, his characteristic attitude toward authoritative codes is not rebellion but acceptance. He has consistently rejected the despised reality of others; therefore his repentance can be seen as action that accedes to social disorder and adds to it. He has slipped more deeply than ever into his old dilemma because now even his former pretense of honor cannot serve. Fourth, his God is not felt as a Christian God of love. *Guzmán de Alfarache* is a novel in which love and charity appear on the scene but lack all force. True, there is an Aristotelian "general sympathetic feeling" engendered by the story of a wicked man's fall into misery, but this feeling is not the same thing as pity, or even love: that is, there is no perspective of love within the novel. All is seen through Guzmán's eyes; hence all is distorted and grotesque. Significantly, there are no other "characters" in the novel except Guzmán, not even such matchstick types of charity as the cardinal. Guzmán by himself is the only character in whom we might possibly see love directing the will—as, for example, in Don Quixote's freeing of the galley slaves. But what Guzmán feels most is not love. It is, decidedly, disgust. His first experience on the road, that of being served a bad fricasse in an inn, ends in nausea; and nausea leads him to reflect later in life upon man's hopeless sickness: "Porque, como después de la caída de nuestros primeros padres, con aquella levadura se acedó, toda la masa corrompida de los vicios. . . . De allí le sobrevino ceguera en el entendimiento, en la memoria olvido, en la voluntad culpa." (For, ever since the fall of our first parents, the mass of mankind has been soured with that leaven of theirs and corrupted with their vices. . . . From hence grew that blindness in man's understanding, forgetfulness in his memory, and evil in his will.) (5:52–53).[104] The entire Creation is disrupted by original sin, which contaminates the three Aristotelian faculties of man's soul: understanding, memory, and will. But love must be a dynamic component of free will; the will being hopelessly corrupt, there can be no real love. Not love at all but animosity still rules Guzmán after his repentance: his last act, the betrayal of his mutinous fellow slaves, bears grim testimony to Guzmán's unchristian code. Nothing has happened to change his Cartesian pleasure in dramatizing human error.

Guzmán's religious problem is, in fact, insoluble. His withdrawal from the world is a form of asceticism; but his impulse to self-interest is negative and antisocial. Behind his insistence on *desengaño*—on the invalidity of human knowledge, on the vanity of ethical canons, on the frailty of the historical will—behind this catastrophic disillusion, there stretches a monotonous vista of negation. Thus Alemán's *atalaya de la vida humana* really comes to represent an epoch locked up in a tower that receives but one echo from the surrounding void: "There is no man with man."

I have now sketched in very briefly my interpretation of the formal coherence of *Guzmán de Alfarache*, and I have suggested that Alemán's intended reversal of his hero's dissolution could not take place within the meaning of the novelist's art. I have further suggested that the reason for this conflict between intention and expression lies in Alemán's intrusion on the narrative, an intrusion that doubtless has an origin in racial despair. At the same time I have briefly related Alemán's intention to some neo-Aristotelian concepts that were current in his time and of consequence to someone writing prose fiction; and I have tried to convey the impression that Alemán and his contemporaries were not necessarily aware of thematic conflict between thought and feeling. It has remained for a later age of cultural distress to speak of a "dissociation of sensibility."

On the one hand, there is Alemán's intended theme of social order; on the other hand, there is the structure of despair expressing social disintegration. Let us examine this conclusion in terms of two principles common to Spanish drama of the Golden Age, poetic justice and causality.[105] If we assume that Alemán conceived of the picaro's life as a metaphor in which a moral theme asserts its primacy over action, then we may be struck by the manner in which Guzmán is punished for his wrongdoing. Does his brief service in the galleys adequately atone for the evil in question? If to some later readers the novel seems immoral because Guzmán does not seem to be punished enough, it is probable that Alemán's contemporaries thought that poetic justice had been served because of the nature of the punishment. According to Alexander A. Parker, Spanish drama of the period gives examples of three forms of punishment: damnation, death, and frustration. While damnation and death are reserved for evildoers whose contribution to disorder seems to the writer great, frustration is related to the idea of purgatory, varying according to the quality of the sin, the nature of the individual's contribution to disorder, and the sum of his redeeming features. In *Guzmán* the father, renegade and adulterer, and Sayavedra, robber and traitor, die, the latter melodramatically possessed by a feeling that he is Guzmán himself.[106] Guzmán's fate is frustration. He is condemned to the galleys, and it is consistent with his personality that he fears exposure to public shame more than anything else. In addition, his life of maintaining appearances lies in ruins around him. Even his intellectual aspiration to orthodoxy becomes a torment because he cannot rid himself of self-interest—an anguished impasse since reason frees his will from illusion and passion enslaves it again. Under the principle of poetic justice, therefore, Guzmán suffers hell on earth. As a corollary to this principle, there would be no strict poetic justice if Guzmán were removed to a state of grace and reformed within society.

The principle of causality also immobilizes the theme of social order and supports the theme of social disintegration. As the cause of Guzmán's disorder is traced back to its source, one sees that the parents are the first cause. They have spoiled and deceived Guzmán, left him insecure, ashamed of inferiority, and obsessed with the desire for credit. Their function approximates that of the blind man in *Lazarillo*: to narrow the picaro's vision of life. Later a hostile society only confirms the dogmatism in Guzmán's outlook, and he embarks upon a course of evil that he is unable to interrupt even in ultimate degradation.[107] How, then, may we reconcile this deterministic emptying-out of cultural values with Alemán's insistence upon freedom? The stars, he declares, are not to blame, but you who "te fuerzas a dejar lo bueno y te esfuerzas en lo malo" (force yourself to leave the good and apply your energies to evil) (3:12). Guzmán has "habilidad para lo bueno" corrupted by an "inclinación para lo malo" (2:288). By the voluntaristic analysis, Guzmán's original sin, like Robinson Crusoe's, is disobedience in running away from home! On that occasion he comments: "Hice como muchacho simple, sin entendimiento ni gobierno. Justo castigo fué el mío, pues teniendo mi descanso, quise saber de bien y mal." (I acted the part of simple youth, without understanding or governance. I was justly punished for this living at ease and seeking after the knowledge of good and evil.) (1:168). Later, when he returns too late to the cardinal, he pities himself as "el hijo pródigo" (the prodigal son) (3:11). What this allusion means in terms of causality is that Guzmán's freedom leaves him guilt-ridden. In the penitent aftermath, the burden of guilt should be mercifully lifted —but it is not. In Guzmán's stoic eschatology the world goes around in an interminable cycle of becoming: "Toda ha sido, es y será una misma cosa." (All has been, is, and will be the same thing.) (2:167). This is not a redeemed man's world, but a world nearing the apocalypse. Life remains for Guzmán one of unceasing strife: "La vida del hombre, milicia es en la tierra: no hay cosa segura ni estado que permanezca, perfeto gusto ni contento verdadero; todo es fingido y vano." (The life of man is an earthly trial; there is no certainty, no permanent condition, no perfect pleasure, no true contentment: all is counterfeit and vain.) (1:161). According to the principle of causality, Guzmán is a man who ends up without *any* reality. He cannot be saved until the world is saved. He cannot ascend to supernature because the free act of accepting the social version of reality means that he accepts a reality that he consistently sees as illusion. Freedom itself comes finally to be an illusion.

To call the theme of *Guzmán de Alfarache* "disintegration" is to stress the thematic continuity of the first picaresque novels. But *Guzmán* alters treatment of the theme. The programmatic illusionism of *Lazarillo de Tormes* evolves into the catastrophic

[79]

illusionism of *Guzmán de Alfarache*. For Lázaro, freedom is intolerable; for Guzmán, impossible. Yet in both novels the picaro ends up with acquisitiveness that, not yet founded on a new conception of nature, grace, and God, cannot be appropriated as an ascetic vocation in the condemned human world.[108]

## *El Buscón*: The Autobiography of Nothing

The third great picaresque novel is *Historia de la vida del Buscón, llamado Don Pablos* (published in 1626 but composed earlier, possibly as early as 1604). Its author, Francisco de Quevedo y Villegas (1580–1645), who also wrote an equally famous satire, *Los sueños* (*The Visions*), is an artist of extraordinary genius, though it is difficult to imagine his personality without such labels as snob, anti–Semite, and bully suggesting themselves embarrassingly as if an admirer of Swift's savagery, Congreve's wit, Baudelaire's spleen, and Brecht's toughness had suddenly to explain such qualities with the biography of Ezra Pound. The analogy exaggerates, of course, for *Buscón* is not the sum of Quevedo's work. There is evidence, too, that he did not reject high-minded sentiment, both religious and patriotic. So even *Buscón* can be seen as the reaction of a basically tender mind to the horror of existence in a world where the human spirit, before his very eyes, is being uprooted and violently torn asunder. In 1604, for example, he wrote to the Flemish humanist, Justus Lipsius: "As for my Spain, I cannot speak of it without grief. If you are a prey to war, we are a prey to idleness and ignorance. In your country we consume our soldiers and our gold; here we consume ourselves. There is no one to speak out, but numbers to tell lies."[109] When Quevedo spoke out in *Buscón*, his implacably hostile attitude may well have sprung from impotent rage. He cruelly portrays all those responsible for Spain in her grief— no one is excused. He resembles Shakespeare's Mercutio crying plague on all houses or Molière's Alceste sulkily begging to be left alone *dans ce petit coin sombre, avec mon noir chagrin*. But Quevedo's energies carry him beyond cynicism and misanthropy.

Over half a century ago Quevedo's tone in *Buscón* was regarded as cynical and misanthropic. According to James Fitzmaurice-

Kelly, who was writing about Quevedo's picaro, "There are few characters so odious, so uniformly base, so devoid of any pleasing, redeeming vice. Quevedo writes the epic of famished roguery, sparing no detail however loathsome and defiling. Swift himself does not dwell more fondly on the obscene squalor of existence, and Quevedo has an individual love of the ghastly which holds him still further aloof from common humanity."[110] Dale B. J. Randall correctly says that to think thus is to miss the point: "It is almost as if one should denounce Defoe for wanting to hang all dissenters, or damn Swift for wanting to cook Irish babies. Either it is true that inhumanity, callousness, and brutality are things which Quevedo deplores, or he is a canting, two-tongued hypocrite."[111] Quevedo, according to Randall, is a satiric moralist who seeks to alert readers, through an exemplary novel, to their own vices. First, he writes from a religious and philosophical standpoint. Second, he is positive. These two propositions need to be examined.

Quevedo's religious and philosophical ideas owe much to the neo-Stoic movement of his time, as Henry Ettinghausen has recently shown. Quevedo's life was "dogged by continual reverses of fortune: ill health, penury, imprisonment, lawsuits, and a disastrously short-lived marriage to an elderly widow punctuated a brilliant career as diplomat and writer." At periodic moments of crisis of conscience, he was highly critical of Spain and life in general and depicted himself "with embarrassing self-abasement as morally reprehensible." A man so horrified by his own shortcomings would be attracted by the ideals of Stoic imperturbability and self-reliance "in direct proportion to his own need for an effective shield against adversity and to his essentially unstoical nature." At all events, neo-Stoicism plays a dominant part in Quevedo's thought, becoming fused there with a Christian philosophy laying stress on the moral life led largely through the exercise of reason and will. Stoical clichés about the deceptiveness of appearances, the misery and brevity of life, the inevitability of death, and the vanity of acquiring worldly goods inspired Quevedo from 1604, when he was still a student of theology in Valladolid, until his final imprisonment in León from 1639 to 1643, when he composed such Stoical works as *La constancia y paciencia del santo Job* and *Providencia de Dios*. For him, the aims of Stoicism were, according to Ettinghausen, "to seek virtue for its own sake, to raise one's soul above ill fortune, to live with the body but not for it, to live with a view to dying, and neither to despise nor to fear death."[112] Only sinners need fear death—for a Christian reason, the fear of hell. By the correct use of understanding, all honors of the world are stripped of their fake appearance; by the correct use of memory, a man should be reminded of his miserable state and use his will to desire eternity. The Christian sage, stoically fortified against adversity, could withstand the prevailing chaos of the times.

Quevedo's neo-Stoicism granted, is it then clear from *La vida del Buscón* that the picaro Pablos is portrayed, as Ettinghausen declares, as "the antithesis of the Stoic sage,"[113] that his moral disintegration results from his unstoical failure to distinguish reality from appearance? Is it true that the "Senecan" message in the final sentence of the novel—"Y fuéme peor, pues nunca mejora su estado quien muda solamente de lugar, y no de vida y costumbres" (But [things] went worse, as they always will for anybody who thinks he only has to move his dwelling without changing his life or ways) (*Buscón*, p. 288)[114]—is, as Randall suggests, the moral that Pablos, a sinner trapped inside himself, "may never change, but the book in which he appears is a possible means of awakening readers to the hypocrisy and viciousness which disfigure their own lives"?[115] Of course, it may be true that Quevedo pitches everything, the efficacy of a didactic intention, on the toss of an ultimate commonplace. From Aesop to Thurber, the short fable has been anchored to sententiousness. *Buscón*, however, is no short fable. It is a full-length novel, too long and too carefully written for the author's last-paragraph intrusion to exert aesthetic force. Furthermore, is there in *Buscón*, as T. E. May and Alexander A. Parker have argued, internal evidence that human conduct is presented as the struggle between good and evil? According to Parker, "The triumph of Quevedo —what helps to make *El Buscón* the peak of the picaresque novel —is that the values of morality are intrinsic to the narrative, and that it is impossible to read it correctly without reading it as a profoundly moral story."[116] Yet a correct reading of *Buscón* may lead to the opposite deduction.

Don Pablos, son of a thief and a witch, aspires from childhood to rise above his inferior position in society. Rejecting his parents' way of life, he goes to school; there, although exposed to the ridicule of other children, he ingratiates himself with a young aristocrat named Diego. This relationship provides him with some relief, but he remains morbidly sensitive, and, when he is teased about being a bastard, he confronts his mother and is deeply shocked by her cynical confession that the scandal is true. Thereafter any childish accident that occurs to Pablos is seen as persecution for the parental sins. Gladly he accepts Diego's offer to take him as a servant to boarding school; but the new school introduces Pablos to the struggle for existence. Its master Cabra —descendent of Lazarillo's blind man and prototype of Smollett's niggardly schoolmasters and of the beadle in *Oliver Twist*— systematically starves his pupils, with the result that both Pablos and Diego resort to stratagem in order to eat. Eventually Diego's father rescues them and sends them together to the University of Alcalá. But, once there, Diego lodges separately, and Pablos finds himself alone in a hostile crowd. Worst of all, student jests make him appear foolish in Diego's eyes. Pablos's response is to yearn more than ever for respectability, to avoid further persecutions, and to conform to the ways of his persecutors. He embezzles from Diego and steals in the marketplace in order to gain prestige with the students. Yet his success leads to a decisive break with Diego, who is ordered home by his father. About the same time, Pablos hears from his uncle, hangman of Segovia, that he has executed Pablos's father and that his mother awaits the same fate as prisoner of the Inquisition. Diego makes one final offer to place Pablos in service to another gentleman, but Pablos, absorbed in the news of his parents, and temperamentally anti-Stoic, refuses on the ground that he will improve his own credit in the world. Having once abandoned any idea of virtue in order to devote himself to gaining honor and wealth, he begins to cultivate a life of pretense that may obscure the past. But first he returns to Segovia. All whom he meets on the road seem to him false or absurd representatives of a society gone mad; but in the fact that he fails to recognize how much he himself has gone astray, such encounters are morally significant of his disintegrating sense of reality. Confronted by his brutal uncle, he does, however, recognize his compulsive need to reject the past. Taking the road once more, he meets a fake gentleman named Don Toribio, who becomes his new ideal. There follows a period of indoctrination into the *picardía* of Madrid. Pablos becomes increasingly despicable, associates with the utterly depraved, and slips ever further into the grip of fear. If he surrenders his pose as a gentleman, he falls back into the old situation of inferiority; but if he continues to pretend, he becomes liable to exposure. He tries to make a rich marriage. Posing as Don Felipe Tristán, he has almost succeeded in swindling an heiress into marriage when Diego, her cousin, reappears and, learning that Don Felipe is his old servant, has Pablos beaten and his face hideously disfigured. This climax of the story presents the picaro as scourged for his loss of moral identity. He sinks back into the underworld, drifts with events, and is involved with murderers in Seville. When last seen, Pablos has taken up with a prostitute and has resolved out of sheer weariness to travel with her to America.

To return now to the question of a didactic intention in *Buscón*: is it true that Quevedo depicts goodness as the picaro's alter ego, that is, as Parker claims, is Don Diego "the symbol of reality and goodness contrasted with the illusory world of delinquency"?[117] Actually, far from being a symbol of reality and goodness, Don Diego is, as Carroll B. Johnson has shown, as morally ambiguous as Pablos.[118] Both he and Pablos are meant to be New Christians. Diego is a member of the Coronel family (that is, a historically real family known by Quevedo to have *converso* background and to be constantly trying to prove their "cleanness" and worthiness as aristocrats). Diego, like Pablos, is tied to an inescapable past and is equally, if less conspicuously, committed to a life of illusion. So Diego cannot serve as a symbol of virtue. Quevedo divides the world of *Buscón*, not into good and evil, but into several facets of evil. The values of morality are demonstrably not intrinsic to the narrative.

The world of *Buscón* is totally damned, totally chaotic. Denying a didactic intention in the work, Francisco Ayala finds it the occasion for a cold display of verbal pyrotechnics:

Este nos ofrece en su novela, igual que en *Los sueños*, el mundo como mero espectáculo que el lector enfrenta con marcada distancia, y en el que no participa de manera alguna. La suerte de don Pablos le es ajena: el Gran Tacaño funciona como la percha de que su autor cuelga aquellos cuentos que ha oído o que ha inventado . . . , y no se nos presenta nunca como una conciencia individual con la que podamos entrar en relación. . . . Se advierte bien que a Quevedo no le importaba tanto su criatura como el juego del ingenio ye el centelleo de las palabras.

He offers to us in his novel, as in *Los sueños*, the world as a mere spectacle that the reader faces with a distinct distance and in which he does not participate in any way. The luck of Don Pablos is alien to him: the Great Miser functions as a perch from which the author hangs some stories that he has heard or invented . . . , and is not presented to us as an individual conscience to which we might be able to relate. . . . It is noticeable that Quevedo did not care as much for his creature as he did for the play of wit and the sparkle of words.[119]

Finally, we have been accustomed since the nineteenth century, particularly in the theory and practice of Flaubert and Henry James, to discern the moral of fiction in its realism, its truth-to-life. But is Quevedo even a realist? Although Parker concedes that *Buscón* "stretches and distorts realism into caricature, creating a grotesque world of surrealist fancy," he still insists that Pablos is "a rounded character" who "can arouse our understanding and compassion, all the more so because of the unflinching hardness of the world in which he is placed."[120] Again, Ayala opposes such a reading:

Su intención, lejos del *realismo* que le ha atribuído . . . no es la de suscitar en la imaginación del lector el ámbito de circunstancias concretas donde surge, se mueve y comienza a bregar con el mundo esa particular vida humana que va a ser objeto de la novela, sino, más bien, la de destruir, al desvalorizarlo, ese mundo: el mundo en toda, su amplitud, el mundo en sí mismo.

His intention, far from the attributed *realism* . . . is not to awake in the imagination of the reader the spectrum of concrete circumstances where appears, moves, and starts to deal with the world that particular human life that goes to its object in the novel, but, rather, the one of destruction and devaluation of that world, the world in all its vastness, the world in itself.

Ayala sums up Quevedo's purpose as "la desvalorización incondicional y definitiva de la realidad de la existencia. Quevedo se propone disolver esta realidad en el caos, la destruye, la niega." (the unconditional and definitive devaluation of the reality of existence. Quevedo decides to dissolve this reality in chaos, destroys it, denies it.)[121] On this reading, with which I agree, Pablos is not a rounded character at all, not even a Lázaro or a Guzmán. His humanity is emptied out, his autobiography comes to *la nada*.

The deceptiveness of *Buscón* lies in the fact that a reader's sympathy would normally flow to this picaro as he is first encountered, a simple child, a victim of family circumstances, and a beleaguered schoolboy with an aristocratic master and chum. But Quevedo is not the author of *David Copperfield*. If he tricks us into sentimentality, into giving the literary facts more emotion than they may deserve, he is having a joke at expense of the reader. He is not interested in Pablos's humanity but in his hybrid or "unnatural" breeding and inferior social caste. In fact, Pablos is presented as prétty much of a nonself to begin with. Were it not for our commendable inclination to pity the child victim who chooses the sinner's life, it is doubtful that we would even see a process of "becoming" in the life of Pablos: his disintegration is a foregone conclusion.

The Parker thesis that Pablos is a kind of mock-Christ seems, at first, extremely attractive. When Pablos arrives in the classroom at Alcalá, he seems to suffer a Christ-like "Passion" though he remains unredeemed by the experience. Approaching him, a student says, " 'Por resucitar está este Lázaro, según hiede.' " ('This Lazarus is ready to be raised from the dead, he stinks so much.') (*Buscón*, p. 65). The students shower Pablos with spit until, stupefied, he returns to his home, where he sees his landlord, a Morisco. Fearing another attack, Pablos whines, " 'No soy Ecce-Homo.' " ('I am not *Ecce-Homo*.') (p. 66). "Behold the Man" were the words spoken by Pilate as he brought out Christ to be shown to the people. Since Pablos repudiates any connection between himself and the suffering Christ, his words, "I am not *Ecce-Homo*," might be taken as the rejection of Christ and of, with a glance at the Lazarus reference, spiritual resurrection.

Parker reads religious significance into these references and concludes that Pablos's "links" with the sufferings of Christ represent "the grief of humanity."[122] This reading, however, has been refuted by Fernando Lázaro Carreter: the *Ecce-Homo* expression, in Quevedo's Spain, was a popular anti-Semitic joke.[123] A serious Pablos-Christ parody is not, then, evident in the text. Not in dispute, of course, is the spiritual deadness of Quevedo's picaro.

This spiritual deadness of *Buscón* has, paradoxically, the energy of great art. One critic finds the unity and structure of the work in "an orderly train of misfortunes, which connects a network of recurring motifs." C. B. Morris writes: "What is remarkable in the *Buscón* is why Quevedo disposes at regular stages throughout the novel the closely related motifs of family, filth, and legal and lawless cruelty: to remind Pablos crudely and painfully that his attempts to combat heredity must fail, and to show him that his aspirations to nobility are ludicrous because the life into which he was born is coarse and brutish."[124] Of these reminders the most crushing is Don Diego's reentry into Pablos's life just at the moment when the former servant, in the gallant guise of Don Felipe Tristán, is about to swindle an heiress into marriage and to obtain security and respectability. Diego wastes no time in getting brutally to the point: " 'No creerá v.m.: su madre era hechicera, su padre ladrón, su tío verdugo, y él, el más ruin hombre y el más mal inclinado que Dios tiene en el mundo.' " ('You won't believe this, sir, but his mother was a witch, his father a thief, and his uncle a public executioner, and he was the worst and most unpleasant man you ever saw.') (p. 231).

Quevedo was an early master at rendering the feel and texture of social experience through the inwardness of the individual. Let us consider, for example, that gruesome occasion when Pablos, returning home from the university, finds his father's remains scattered outside the walls of Segovia.

Llegué al pueblo, y a la entrada vi a mi padre en el camino, aguardando a ir en bolsas, hecho cuartos, a Josafá. Enternecíme, y entré algo desconocido de como salí, con punta de barba, bien vestido. Dejé la compañía; y considerando en quién conocía a mi tío (fuera del rollo) mejor en el pueblo, no hallé a nadie de quien echar mano. Lleguéme a mucha gente a preguntar por Alonso Ramplón, y nadie me supo dar razón dél, diciendo que no le conocían. Holguéme mucho de ver tantos hombres de bien en mi pueblo, cuando, estando en esto, oí al precursor de la penca hacer de garganta, y a mi tío de las suyas. Venía una procesión de desnudos, todas descaperuzados, delante de mi tío; y él, muy haciéndose de pencas, con una en la mano, tocando un pasacalles públicas en las costillas de cinco laúdes, sino que llevaban sogas por cuerdas. Yo, que estaba notando esto con un hombre (a quien había dicho, preguntando por él, que era yo un gran caballero), veo a mi buen tío; que poniendo en mí los ojos, arremetió a abrazarme, llamándome sobrino. Penséme morir de vergüenza; no volví a despedirme de aquél con quien estaba.

I reached the town; and there at the entrance I saw my father scattered along the way and waiting to be taken in quarters and bags to the Valley of Jehosaphat. A bit affected, I went on, feeling that I was somewhat of a stranger now and that few would recognize me. I had now grown a beard, you see, and was well dressed. I took leave of my companions; and casting about in my mind to ascertain who in the town might know my uncle best, I could not think of a soul—except, perhaps, one of those persons whose heads had been exposed publicly on pillars after their execution. I approached several people and asked them if they knew Alonso Ramplón, but no one had even heard of him. I was feeling happy to see so many honest men in my town, when I happened to hear the town crier approaching very audibly, followed by uncle enthusiastically at work. Along came a procession of culprits followed by my uncle. They were bare and without hoods; and my uncle, wielding his cowhide, played a veritable passacaglia on the ribs of five living lutes— and in this musical performance no strings were used, but only ropes. I stood watching all this next to a man whom I had told I was a great gentleman [at the time I was inquiring of him whether he knew my uncle]. When my esteemed relative's eyes fell on me, he rushed over to embrace me and cried: "Nephew!" I thought I would die from sheer embarrassment. I could not summon up enough courage even to wish my companion a good day as I hastily went away with my uncle. [p. 139]

Without the social context of this bizarre memory, the serio-comic point of the scene might be obscured. The youth sees his father, symbol of the outlaw family, literally having been torn to pieces outside his native city; his uncle, symbol of justice, has performed this deed; yet the youth, who would reject his real relationship to brutalized society, has not only that relationship exposed but also his pretense to being a great gentleman and the reason for it. Three motifs are violently yoked together in the scene: death, love, and time. A father is dead, but the son's natural affection has been blocked and corrupted at the source.

Not only has Clemente Pablo been a notorious thief, but also he is not Pablos's real father: the real father has even less of an identity than the mutilated remains. Thus Pablos's reaction is sterile and self-involved. He is at first relieved to realize that he is now virtually a stranger in Segovia. But then, too, Pablos knows he cannot love his uncle; so he goes out of his way to invent an identity for himself, feeling reasonably certain that he has escaped the oppressive past, the methods of which he has nevertheless been using in his flight from reality. Greeted by his uncle, he fails to hold his assumed identity. He has no choice but to walk off hastily with that past. At the same time, all unconsciously, he has foreseen in the scourging of the five criminals his own destiny at the hands of Diego's thugs: that is, in the autobiographical disposition of events, this scene is already remembered from a point in time after Diego's punishment, so that Pablos may with justice be said to feel the blows his uncle delivers, blows deserved, hence sardonically described as a musical performance. The grotesqueness of the scene thus serves as a kind of double metaphor, first, to depict violence in society, second, to reveal the guilt and torment of the individual entangled in that society. Society has shaped the individual, yet the individual can neither accept that society nor succeed in rejecting it. Instead, he comes increasingly to reflect the most debased aspects of that society. But it is one thing to find in the Spanish picaresque novels a dynamic relationship between individual and society and another to see how static and unchangeable the social reality remains, as a matter of spiritless belief, in the moral schemes of the writers. Nothing seems more evident to a reader today than the need for the picaro's society to change so as to prevent the negative conditioning that Pablos is subjected to. But this view was not Quevedo's. Because he assumed that social disorder was traceable to the individual, he could not change the destiny of his hero. Pablos breaks against the stasis of society and plunges downward to perdition.

Quevedo's novel about a picaro's self-destruction is even more ideological than its predecessors. What could be more soothing to people who feel impotent to change the course of empire leading to destruction than a theory that assures them that violence stems from our attempts to escape heredity and that the best we can do is to expose the dark power for what it is—the passionate attraction to what is dirty, dead, and decayed, to a world of things, of possessions, of nonpersons, of techniques without goals, of feelings without joy, a world of death? A possible measure of Quevedo's necrophilous attraction to death is the absence from his novel of a single character with redeeming features. He builds a novel as if it were a machine and markets the product with a single, final bit of sententious moralizing. There is nothing in *Buscón* that makes sense of life by mobilizing and representing vitality and integration. Quevedo's perverted vision is of life turning against itself. His aversion to Pablos's pursuit of the impossible may be accepted by some readers as consistent with didactic purpose, a call to Spain to remedy moral paralysis. But if reform begins with the knowledge of sin, if the salt of salvation is to prevent decomposition, what is Quevedo offering the sinner if not more death, more of the sacred past that rules through institutions, laws, traditions, and hierarchies? The changing of life and ways recommended by Quevedo-Pablos has no potent image from the present or of the future.

Within the historical context—*Buscón* appeared eleven years before Descartes's *Discours de la méthode* (1637)—Quevedo's picaro is unable to affirm his own existence by means of a scorching rejection of the past. Rather, his past, personified by family and fellow students, returns upon his present and with malignant aggression disfigures him. Society is violent and incoherent. Diego is a fake aristocrat; Pablos is a negative hero. When, almost two centuries later, the theme of an aristocrat's pursuit of an underdog becomes intense in the novel, as it does in William Godwin's *Caleb Williams* (1794), the underdog is a hero, the aristocrat a criminal. In *Buscón* that revolution remains a very long way off.

The Spanish picaresque novelists wrote of man's predicament within a disintegrating socioreligious order—*order* in the sense of the contemporary assumptions of the culture. Holding to the medieval theory of a divinely ordained hierarchy, in which the only transformation of personal concern was that from worldly illusion through the portal of death to the other-worldly reality, they came to regard vital change as the result of individual failures to live up to the responsibilities of office and social position. By tracing social problems to erring individuals, they were not able, when the decadence of Spanish power arrived, to formulate a new conception of man in his social relationships. The picaro whom they placed at the heart of their novels was for them a compelling *exemplum* of error. In *Lazarillo de Tormes* the picaro was an individual who sacrificed moral principle in order to survive. In *Guzmán de Alfarache* he was a typical sinner whose dim hope lay in an abject rejection of the world. In *El Buscón* he was an individual who refused to accept his class and reached a point at which he could neither support his social pretense nor return to his original status as a servant. The social attitudes of the picaresque novelists were therefore astringent. But they were not totally cynical and exclusive: the picaro was compelling because his experience conveyed the tragic sense of life. The picaresque novelists were aware that the old order was breaking apart in the sea of ambiguities. What hope was there for the ordinary individual who looked to society to teach and guide him and give him a secure start in life and who was betrayed? Values were corrupt and incompatible with existence—yet they were indispensable. The individual, meanwhile, was wandering from the pathway to salvation, seeking the byways of distrust, and bartering his soul for a crust of bread. Despite his freedom of choice, the picaro was a reflection of a certain mechanical determination of life; the mechanism was the medieval world itself, a world that could not often account for the manner in which personal identity had come to rest on credit. For this reason, I think, illusionism became functional in the picaresque novels. The picaro, who began as an innocent, good-natured child at large in a hostile society, was deformed into leading a mythic, symbolic existence. He became a confidence man, an outcast, whose reality was mere deception, whose identity was a nonidentity in process of dissolution with time itself. The Spanish picaro, then, mirrored a world no better, and no better off, than himself. He had a representational quality, moreover, that afforded him a measure of moral justification. He stood for the human condition, its distress and loneliness, and he reflected the failure of exalted ideals and absolute laws. He was satirized, but he was also a satirist. His story was told on two planes, individual and social, brought together artistically in the form of autobiographical self-revelation. On the one hand, there was the society that deformed the individual and helped to make him a stranger. On the other hand, there was the individual whose search for identity within society led to an anguished sense of failure. Crossing the fine line between adventure and exile, conformity and heresy, innocence and damnation, the disintegrating picaro of the classic Spanish picaresque novels projected, in sum, a dark predicament of his age.

The myth of the picaro is concealed in three novels that are ostensibly comic. In *Lazarillo* the soul dies and is born again without humanity or reality. In *Guzmán* the soul despairs of release from sin and loses reality. In *Buscón* the soul is devalued by the nothingness of existence.

# 3

# *The Conversion of the Natural Man*

Petrarch's *De remediis utriusque fortunae*, one of the most influential books in sixteenth-century Spain—and a decisive reading experience for Rojas—provided, Stephen Gilman writes, "a portrait of man exposed to the world in all its aggressive immediacy."[1] For those who felt helplessly subjected to adverse fortune, which they identified with continuous aggression from without, Petrarch's words meaningfully described what customary sociological idiom calls "alienation." For Petrarch, as for Heraclitus in antiquity, the constant condition of life, one consciously perverse in man, is strife. For the authors of *Lazarillo*, *Guzmán*, and *Buscón*, the myth of this metaphor that life is continual warfare is essentially their world view.

Outside Spain, however, by the middle of the seventeenth century, that world view was being projected as a decadent myth inferior to and replaceable by a myth of rational man and society. When Hobbes in *Leviathan* (1651) declares the "general inclination of all mankind" to be "a perpetual and restless desire of power after power" (p. 64), he pays his philosophical dues to Petrarchan and Heraclitan thinkers of all ages, then finds them wanting, at least according to the logical postulates of his mathematician's mythmaking. He sees the life of continual warfare as a presocial condition. His mythical natural man—a self-interested, rational competitor rather than Shakespeare's simple but treacherous Caliban—is everyman, free and equal but terrifyingly insecure because of human alienation. Presto, Hobbes waves his Prospero's wand, civil society is created via social contract, and natural man is converted into a new mythical entity.

"Manners," Hobbes declares, are "those qualities of mankind, that concern their living together in peace, and unity" (*Leviathan*, p. 63). Manners are, then, first concerned with the problems arising from the inclinations of individuals, which Hobbes went on to define as a perpetual and restless desire of power after power. Understanding of the nature of man would logically lead, Hobbes thought, to an understanding of society, thence to an understanding of the means to bring men to live in peace and unity. To have understanding at all, one had to assume that the perception of manners carried its own validity.

The novel of manners and the picaresque novel are different forms. The novel of manners depends upon realism in the social sphere. The Spanish picaresque novel stresses the illusionism of empirically observed reality: that is, it places reality in the supernatural sphere.

In a sense, this opposition of realism and picarism is that between the real and the romantic. James's distinction of these in the Preface to *The American* is useful here because he bases it upon the idea of perception:

I suggest not that the strange and the far are at all necessarily romantic: they happen to be simply the unknown, which is quite a different matter. The real represents to my perception the things we cannot possibly *not* know, sooner or later, in one way or another; it being but one of the accidents of our hampered state, and one of the incidents of their quantity and number, that particular instances have not yet come our way. The romantic stands, on the other hand, for the things that, with all the [facilities] in the world, all the wealth and all the courage and all the wit and all the adventure, we never *can* directly know; the things that reach us only through the beautiful circuit and subterfuge of our thought and our desire.[2]

Whereas the romantic stands for what we never can directly know, the real always has the possibility of being perceived; in this sense, the illusion of the picaro has a quality that makes the real unknowable. Yet to modify picarism in its "romantic" aspect is to change it altogether, to subsume the half-lights of the tragic imperceptible in the triumphant surge of the real. In such a case there remains only a picarism that, shorn of its logical development, threatens at a distance but does not destroy what is already known. In the eighteenth-century novel, I think, illusionism has been reduced from the functional to the antithetical.

[94]

## The Conversion of the Natural Man

That perpetual and restless desire of power that Hobbes took for man's general inclination is the new way of expressing the picaresque idea. In the eighteenth century, the two planes of the picaresque novel, individual and social, are frequently reduced to one, the individual's plane: it is the individual with his disruptive passions who threatens the social reality, but his individualism is not a reflection of the ultimate, mythic nature of that society. Sooner or later the individual must be integrated into society, experience the real that he could not possibly *not* know. Sooner or later in the eighteenth-century novel antisocial individualism is declared an illusion, a capitulation to Satan. Where the tension between picarism and realism is evident in the eighteenth-century novel we approach a modified "dialectical" form of the picaresque novel. Obviously, the degree of modification is a subject critics may debate. But when Maximillian Novak declares "freedom" to be "the thematic center of the picaresque," the boundaries of the subject are being expanded too far. Novak views the picaresque as a "universal mode" that "shares with the novel of manners a concern with the real world" but "represents the very opposite of that form in its organizing principles," namely, "its free movement, its free form, and its view of middle and upper-class social and political conventions through a character who, as a result of circumstances or choice, has been partially liberated from those conventions."[3] This description does not apply to the Spanish novels that express the myth of the picaro, the literary idea of disintegration, but the description does fit the eighteenth-century version of picaresque precisely because the myth is submerged or has become a threat.

Thus in eighteenth-century fiction, because the myth of the picaro is submerged, there is no longer a picaresque novel in a complete formal sense. Although books, articles, reviews, dissertations, reference works, and lectures have asserted and continue to assert that the picaresque novel is to be identified and studied in eighteenth-century European literature outside Spain, the proof has not been convincing. Critics usually start from assumptions that equate the Spanish picaresque novels with realism; there follows a teleological bias imposing an untenable pattern of growth and development upon the history of prose fiction. Other critics stress the influence of standard satiric devices such as the master-servant relationship or the confidence game, or select, as the defining of a whole, some partial aspect or mode such as freedom or delinquency or childhood rejection. Such studies of picaresque fiction, indeed of early fiction generally, have neglected to find a context, a myth. Since a novel is an act of communication between author and reading public, the structure of an eighteenth-century novel may be approached in terms of ideology, a term, as John J. Richetti defines it, that "suggests a body of assumptions and attitudes which commands immediate, emotional, and inarticulate assent, as opposed to a set of ideas which requires self-conscious and deliberate intellectual formulation."[4] The new social myth of the eighteenth century conflicts with picaresque myth. Popular criminal biographies are to the point: the criminal (or sinner or rogue) is, in the eighteenth century, both hero and antihero. According to Richetti, the criminal's career

evokes the desire for secular freedom and economic self-determination which is a real part of the outlook of the age; but this latent social aggression is, at the same time, a source of guilt and anxiety which must be severely and decisively punished. The criminal, as a type figure, is a necessary social myth whose triumphs and abasements mirror the ideological tension between the new secular world of action and freedom and the old religious values of passivity and submission. Highwaymen and whores are heroes, in that their stories are gratifying fantasies of freedom—moral, economic, and erotic. But this freedom is necessarily desperate, for the social myth includes the fear that divine surveillance and mysterious retribution are inescapable.[5]

Two opposing attitudes toward experience, individualism and moral and religious conformity, take the literary form of dramatic confrontation. Usually, as Ronald Paulson has shown in studies of the English picaresque, these narratives end in "conversion."[6] The situation whereby the conversion of Guzmán de Alfarache merely extends his despair, because his reality is illusion, no longer presents itself in the reality-constructing style of eighteenth-century fiction.

Furthermore, and especially in English fiction, the myth of the picaro is converted, like as not, into an allegory of evil. As the brilliant studies of Bernard Spivak show, the Vice of medieval morality plays had, long before Shakespeare, been a popular personification of evil. Essentially an abstraction, the Vice "is neither moral nor a person, only a homiletic formula designed to express, through his standard intrigue, the insinuation of evil into the human heart." Like the devil—but a comic con artist rather than the undifferentiated source of all evil—the Vice "is an artist in dissimulation, seduction, and intrigue; and his purpose on the stage is to display his talent triumphantly at work against the affections, duties, and pieties which create the order and harmony of humane society. His specialty is the destruction of unity and love." When he is habitually disguised as a compassionate friend to his frail human victims, his "love" is an imposture that conceals his assault upon "unity and order and the piety of love in all its forms."[7] After the morality plays, this archetypal figure reappears in a Shakespearean villain like Iago. Thereafter, the Vice's archaic nature may be present in literature, especially where a villain's central characteristic is deceit. Since his victims are mere credulous humans, though they may be disguising their own dishonesty, the fictionalized Vice is apt to be a confidence trickster—and therein lies his proximity to the picaro of the Spanish novels. If this background shows why an English picaro is easily translated into a criminal, it also points to an opposition of good and evil that differs from that presented in Spanish picaresque novels, wherein both individual and society are in error. Should evil triumph in the struggle for men's souls, picaresque chaos would prevail; that is, a Vice-picaro-confidence man paradigm is available to the moral imagination, as in Melville's in *The Confidence-Man*, where the connections are made.

No complete picaresque novels were written in the eighteenth century because the myth of the picaro did not prevail against the traditional system of social and moral limitations and their religious foundations. To demonstrate this thesis requires, *mutatis mutandis*, a negative argument. Nevertheless, in the modified form of picaresque novel, the "submerged" picaro can still be felt as a mythical figure of great significance.

What novels can show this dialectical picaresque, this conversion of the natural man?

Lesage's *Histoire de Gil Blas de Santillane* (published in installments between 1715 and 1735) is perhaps the classic example of a novel of manners with a critical reputation as a picaresque novel,[8] although, significantly, its picaresque reputation has been slight in France. *Gil Blas* was praised by nineteenth-century French critics as the preeminent *roman de moeurs*, and even when commenting adversely on Lesage's lack of a strong unifying principle, they rarely used the term "picaresque"; a modern editor describes *Gil Blas* as a *roman-revue*.[9] In England and the United States, however, the "picaresque" tag has stuck to *Gil Blas*. As recently as 1958 "picaresque novel" in the *Encyclopedia Britannica* contained this description unrevised from the edition of 1911: "Gil Blas is a creation of the gentler, sunnier French spirit; like Caron de Beaumarchais's Figaro he is a Spaniard born, reared and humanized in Paris, and these two are the only picaroons whose relative refinement has not been gained at the cost of verisimilitude."[10]

To account for its reputation as a picaresque novel, we should recall that *Gil Blas* once was the eye of a critical hurricane. Lesage stood accused of wholesale plagiarism from Spanish sources, and though he was acquitted when scholars proved that he was indebted to his sources (by no means all picaresque novels) for less than one-fifth of *Gil Blas*, there has lingered on a popular association of the novel with Spanish literature.[11] As early as 1849 the American Hispanist, Ticknor, proclaimed *Gil Blas* as the great work in the picaresque genre.[12] The next step was to treat as a picaresque novelist any author indebted to Lesage—Stendhal, for example[13]—or to take as the defining characteristics of a picaresque novel the loose structure, the happy-go-lucky pace, and the satiric multifariousness of *Gil Blas*; the journey motif alone has been taken to indicate picaresque influence, a fact that provoked Hervey Allen to write in 1937, "It will not be long before every romance in which the principal character is not completely paralyzed at birth will be 'picaresque.'"[14]

In my opinion *Gil Blas* is picaresque only in a modified form.

The English novel presents a case less critically confused than that of *Gil Blas* because historians of the English novel have used the "picaresque" tag warily, if at all, and then usually in discussions of Defoe or Smollett; yet it is probably the consensus of opinion that the English novel has a picaresque strain. The critical problem is to decide which authors and which works represent this strain.[15]

Chandler's *The Literature of Roguery* was long the only guide to the subject as a whole. Although démodé, Chandler has never been thoroughly refuted, and so his work is still today, in the non-Hispanic world, the primary source of critical confusion. In the house of "roguery" that he constructed there were big rooms assigned to Nashe, Bunyan, Defoe, Fielding, Smollett, Dickens, and Thackeray. It is quite clear that Nashe and Bunyan have no place in the structure. Twice the notion that Thomas Nashe's *The Unfortunate Traveller* (1594) is a picaresque novel has been effectively disposed of, first by Ronald B. McKerrow, who notes that the hero Jack Wilton is not a trickster, then by G. R. Hibbard, who shows that the work is not novelistic but a potpourri in half a dozen different manners.[16] Bunyan's *Life and Death of Mr. Badman* (1680), characterized by Chandler as "a Puritan romance of roguery,"[17] likewise presents neither a trickster nor a novelistic kind of society. Mr. Badman is a generic portrait of a sinner, a vile body depicted from on high. Of course, it is not unlikely that Bunyan may have known *Guzmán de Alfarache* in Mabbe's translation; if so, Alemán's moral austerity might have made its appeal. The Bible and the morality plays, in which the figure of the Vice appears, are obvious sources of Bunyan's allegorical art.

Serious consideration of the picaresque strain in the English novel begins with Daniel Defoe. The question is, which of Defoe's novels is most typically picaresque in quality? *Robinson Crusoe* presents an acquisitive man's problems of isolation rising ostensibly out of social context but actually, in terms of cultural issues, within society; therefore, *Crusoe* repeats an artistic concern of the Spanish picaresque novels, the concern with individual isolation within society. But the real question raised by Defoe in *Robinson Crusoe* involves the nature of isolation itself: is isolation a state of inward-looking that is a normal human condition, or is it solitude with a social reference, the problem of identity? Defoe leaves no doubt that the kind of isolation that interests him is the former—whereas the latter kind had been the concern of the picaresque novelists. Furthermore, Crusoe's typical acts are not deceits. But in *Roxana*, we immediately meet a heroine who goes to awkward lengths to deceive her daughter. Roxana lives a lie: but is she not in the same case with Crusoe after all? The self she conceals is always something more; her identity does not shift with her masks; so she is by no means a picara who paradoxically creates form out of nothing. Her suffering results from vanity, not from moral aloneness. Neither *Robinson Crusoe* nor *Roxana* is then very typical of picaresque quality in Defoe. *Captain Singleton* is even less typical and belongs as much to the literature of travel as to the novel. In both *Moll Flanders* (1722) and *Colonel Jack* (1722), however, there is a picaresque quality in the presentation of low life. Even here a further obvious distinction can be made. Moll Flanders, like some of her literary forebears, Petronius's Matron of Ephesus, Chaucer's Wife of Bath, Rojas's Celestina, Delicado's Lozana, López de Ubeda's Pícara Justina, Castillo Solórzano's Rufina, and Grimmelshausen's Mother Courage, is a robust antiheroine. Orphaned at an early age, when her mother is transported to the plantations as a convicted thief, Moll receives a fashionable education and aspires to be a gentlewoman. Thereafter she learns to be mercenary, since money is the asset essential to the genteel world, and, as her actions become increasingly criminal, she characteristically absolves herself of all moral responsibility. Eventually she repents of her life as whore and thief and, in the colonies, achieves her status of gentlewoman. But her rise in society is accompanied by serious moral compromise. As J. A. Mitchie observes, "Outwardly, Moll's is a success story: inwardly it is an imaginative demonstration of the way in which sin leads to more sin, and of how evil can diminish the freedom to do good."[18] Admittedly, this sort of irony—"success" at the price of an enslaved will—must recall the process of spiritual disintegration in *Lazarillo de Tormes*. Yet Defoe's presentation of moral ambiguity in *Moll Flanders* and in his mercantile society still leaves open the possibility, in his world view, of social integration. One can succeed without anesthetizing the emotions—as long as there is money. This option, I believe, is less ambiguously presented in *Colonel Jack*, which begins with a typical picaresque pattern, a young orphan's moral problems in a hostile environment. Because *Colonel Jack* may clarify, better than *Moll Flanders*, Defoe's special attitude about "necessity," I have chosen it to represent his ultimate transformation of picaresque myth.

Henry Fielding's *Jonathan Wild* (1743) is his only work with a place in picaresque tradition because on one of its levels of meaning it burlesques picaresque novels and romances of roguery. But neither *Joseph Andrews* (1742) nor *Tom Jones* (1749) is similarly related to the genre. Both were influenced by the objective, nondogmatic, and hence nonpicaresque realism of Cervantes. Both have, perhaps, a slight affinity to the picaresque novels in their adventures on the road, and Tom Jones's career as a gigolo has Spanish precedent, but, again, the journey motif is not a defining characteristic of the picaresque novel, for, if it were, one would have to include as picaresque almost every work of fiction from the *Odyssey* to *Lolita*. And young Tom, as no picaro, has love and reforms.

Tobias Smollett must be considered, but on his own merits as a novelist and not because he acknowledged his indebtedness to Lesage.[19] This supposed influence of Lesage has sometimes led to a hasty acceptance of *Roderick Random* (1748) and *Peregrine Pickle* (1751) as picaresque novels. Yet neither Rory nor Perry is a picaro (in the Spanish sense) or a rogue (in the English sense); nor does the hostile society through which they wander correspond to *picardía*. On the other hand, the hero of Smollett's third novel, *Ferdinand Count Fathom* (1753), is part confidence man, part Vice. In this novel Chandler believed he detected "the right Spanish ring."[20] *Ferdinand Count Fathom*, then, should serve to show the picaresque strain in Smollett.

Charles Dickens had an ambivalent attraction-repulsion attitude toward roguery as content. His work invariably departs from typical picaresque patterns, but, to show this departure, I will use as an example *Oliver Twist* (1838), in which deceit and crime predominate.[21]

William Makepeace Thackeray's *Barry Lyndon* (1844) was called by Chandler "altogether the most powerful in the range of picaresque fiction."[22] Certainly Thackeray felt less squeamish than Dickens about making his protagonist a scoundrel, but, like Dickens, he uses picaresque conventions only to transform their meaning. The picaresque quality of *Barry Lyndon* is more pronounced than that of *Vanity Fair* (1847–48). The scampish Becky Sharp is more or less sympathetically self-interested; but, like Moll Flanders, Roxana, or Manon Lescaut, she is not a picara.[23]

For the purposes of critical analysis the following works may be taken to represent the picaresque strain in the novel, 1715–1844: *Gil Blas, Colonel Jack, Jonathan Wild, Ferdinand Count Fathom, Oliver Twist*, and *Barry Lyndon*.[24]

In the eighteenth- and early nineteenth-century novels we may find picaresque content without picaresque form, that underlying structure determining the myth of the picaro. We need to discriminate between the archetypal and fiction residually picaresque but transformed in meaning. To be sure, we cannot overlook the irony or critical structure evident in some of the English novels. An ironic process of disintegration is evident, to a degree, in *Moll Flanders* and *Colonel Jack*. Both *Jonathan Wild* and *Barry Lyndon* show a sourly ironic attitude toward criminal passions, as do *Lazarillo* and *Buscón*. Similarly, though *Oliver Twist* shifts narrative pattern from a picaresque to a nonpicaresque perspective with what looks like deliberation, and though *Count Fathom* shifts perspectives so fortuitously that the novel's unity is destroyed, it is true that the Spanish picaresque novels are also critically structured: *Lazarillo* shows an individual sacrificing moral principle; *Guzmán* is an attempt to present the sinner's life within the structure of redemption; and *Buscón* presents worlds of evil that are scorned in the author's ultimate paragraph. Indeed, the Spanish picaresque novelists reveal in the structuring of their novels as much moral opposition to delinquency as do such strident moralists as Fielding, Smollett, Dickens, or Thackeray. Therefore, neither tone nor critically responsible structure are certain pointers away from picaresque myth.

Nevertheless, the nonpicaresque may be discerned in the assumptions of a culture where these have changed from the kind of cultural assumptions underpinning the picaresque novels. In the context of the novel form that offers trickery for content, to express the idea of disintegration is picaresque but to express an ideology of viable social order is to convert the myth of the picaro.

Were Lesage and Defoe, for example, disposed to examine the philosophical and socioreligious assumptions underpinning their novels? Perhaps they were; but the fact is that both *Gil Blas* and *Colonel Jack*, two contemporary novels quite different in scope and style, are culturally alike, both giving evidence of a deep-rooted confidence in life that by its very nature runs counter to the picaresque idea. If we take for granted (as we should) the artistic integrity of Lesage, Defoe, and the other novelists whose work I shall discuss, we are bound to conclude that they wrote about life as they saw and felt it; and it follows from an examination of their works that they took a different view of life than had the Spanish novelists. Even Dickens's *Martin Chuzzlewit* (1844), one of the most pessimistic of English fictions, represents a faith in the old paternal Christian order. When at last a novelist in the picaresque manner used the disintegration theme to express his loss of faith in that order—as Herman Melville was to do in *The Confidence-Man* in 1857—then the picaresque myth reappeared. I cannot claim to know of or to know about all the novels in various languages between the mid-seventeenth century and 1857. But the absence or near absence of picaresque myth during this period is, I believe, to be expected by the student of literary history and culture. From the middle of the seventeenth century to the middle of the nineteenth the myth of the picaro loses its force in novels.

It will be seen that this kind of critical approach largely bypasses the study of Spanish penetration of foreign literature. For example, Defoe shares the spirit of *Lazarillo*'s author in his compassion for the outcast and distressed, but he might easily have come to this feeling without a knowledge of Spanish picaresque novels. On the other hand, Smollett probably knew the Spanish novels but is alien to the spirit that they express.

English literature is studded with simple tricksters: impostors, vagabonds, beggars, jesters, thieves, pirates, rakes, and fortune hunters. The elements of picarism are frequently present in English literature, but that special catalyst of profound cultural dissent—more particularly, of religious doubt that seeks to efface itself and cannot—tends to be absent altogether.

I will now consider eighteenth-century and early nineteenth-century novels against philosophical backgrounds.[25] Even the skeptics of the seventeenth and eighteenth centuries were able to find a faith by an interpretation of reason as revelation. At one extreme of the philosophical debate was Thomas Hobbes, who argued, in effect, that art—or reason—was superior to nature. At the other extreme was the earl of Shaftesbury who argued, in effect, that nature—or reason—was superior to art. But the common factor in Hobbesian and Shaftesburyan thought is Cartesian rationalism: this was the new faith.

Among the English novelists, Defoe leans to the views of Hobbes, Fielding to those of Shaftesbury, and Smollett seeks a middle ground; all are typical rationalists and thus typically opposed to picaresque myth. Yet those novelists influenced by Hobbes, particularly by the Hobbesian myth of the natural man, do in fact begin to approach the picaresque idea, while those novelists influenced by Shaftesbury employ exceptional literary methods in the attempt to refute the myth of the natural man and thus evade any approximate myth of the picaro.

Already in Descartes's *Discours de la méthode* (1637) there appears a view of nature that breaks with the medieval world view. Descartes regards nature, not as degenerate, but as the true source of knowledge. In the first part of the *Discours* he speaks of his youthful quest for certainty in the mazes of the world and the self: in the way of a picaro, Descartes wanders forth in search of identity. Abandoning the study of letters, he declares,

and resolving to seek no other science than that which can be found in myself and in the great book of the world, I spent the remainder of my youth in travel, visiting courts and armies, in intercourse with men of diverse dispositions and callings, amassing varied experiences, testing myself in the various situations in which fortune landed me, and at all times making reflections on the things that came my way, and by which I could in any wise profit. . . . And throughout I was obsessed by the eager desire to learn to distinguish the true from the false, that I might see clearly what my actions ought to be, and so to have assurance as to the path to be followed in this life. [*Philosophical Writings*, pp. 121–22]

The picaro, too, had tried to put knowledge on a foundation impregnable to doubt, but appearance dumbfounded him, his will could not act, and his own existence came to seem pathetically unreal. But Descartes believes he has found the solution to the problem of knowledge. How do we discover that appearances are deceptive, he asks, unless we know that some are trustworthy? To believe that you are thinking is a process of thought; therefore I exist. The essence of the self is the mind, which needs no material thing or body. We have in our minds an idea of perfection that must derive innately from God and prove God. Illusion results from man's imperfection rather than from depravity: "Though quite often we have ideas which contain some falsity, this can only be in the case of those in which there is some confusion or obscurity, i.e., owing to their participation, in this respect, in nothingness; or, in other words, that in us they are thus confused because we are not wholly perfect" (*Philosophical Writings*, p. 145). But the real cause of error and suffering, according to Descartes in his *Meditationes* (1641), is the fallibility of the human will: "What then is the source of my errors? This alone, that the will is of wider range than the understanding, and that I do not restrain it within the same limits as the understanding, but extend it to things which I do not understand; and as the will is of itself, in respect of such things, indifferent, it is easily deflected from the true and the good, and readily falls into error and sin, choosing the evil in place of the good, or the false in place of the true" (*Philosophical Writings*, p. 237). In the old scheme, error had been ascribed to original sin or to nature itself. In Cartesian thought error originates in man's willing departure from his natural reason. Man, the microcosm, is potentially as perfect as the machine of the universe, the macrocosm. But, since man fails to realize his potential, there is implicit in Cartesian rationalism some vestigial reminder of the old metaphysics: God or providence has continually to intervene in human affairs in order to establish any connection of world and mind.

In Descartes, reason replaces revelation; nature becomes the principal evidence of religion; and individual art or will or passion becomes the source of error and sin.

By the time of Newton this "religion" of reason was well established. Newton shows how one cogitating mind may connect the fall of an apple with laws of the universe. As Locke writes, "The works of Nature everywhere sufficiently evidence a Deity."

Reason, Locke continues, is "natural Revelation, whereby the Father of Light, and fountain of all knowledge, communicates to mankind that portion of Truth which he has laid within the reach of their natural faculties."[26]

"The eternal silence of those infinite spaces strikes me with terror." Pascal's *Pensée* 91 indicates that the reaction to Cartesian rationalism was not always favorable. There are terrifying infinite spaces in man as well as in the cosmos. Man's powerful subrational impulses are still, to many seventeenth-century thinkers, better accounted for by the old doctrine of the will corrupted by original sin. This concern with the human predicament—a concern that distinguished the Spanish picaresque novelists—is central to the thought of Hobbes. But Hobbes believes he has found an explanation of man's nature that will synthesize the old belief with the new rationalistic dogma. In his thought the will and the reason join together in opposition to nature.

In *Leviathan* the will or art or reason becomes the necessary agent of salvation. Hobbes thinks that the social order is generated out of the agreement of individual wills. Men, to escape the anxieties of distrust and the distractions of illusion, "created" society: in effect, society is an artifact, the outgrowth of a contract. What compels men to create society is nature, the natural passions of individuals that otherwise make for chaos. Art is superior to nature.

Hobbes's argument rests on his mythical account of man's primitive condition, the state of nature. The solitary natural man regards felicity in terms of his self-interested passions and appetites. Since all individuals in this theoretical state strive equally for felicity, the state of nature is a condition of perpetual strife in which the individual's predominant passion is fear: "For as Prometheus, which interpreted, is, *the prudent man*, was bound to the hill Caucasus, a place of large prospect, where, an eagle feeding on his liver, devoured in the day, as much as was repaired in the night, so that man, which looks too far before him, in the care of future time, hath his heart all the day long, gnawed on by the fear of death, poverty, or other calamity; and has no repose, nor pause of his anxiety, but in sleep" (*Leviathan*, p. 70). As Hobbes describes it, *the State of Nature is a state of complete disintegration.*

Whatsoever therefore is consequent to a time of war, where every man is enemy to every man; the same is consequent to the time, wherein men live without other security, than what their own strength, and their own invention shall furnish them withal. In such condition, there is no place for industry; because the fruit thereof is uncertain: and consequently no culture of the earth; no navigation, nor use of the commodities that may be imported by sea; no commodious building; no instruments of moving, and removing, such things as require much force; no knowledge of the face of the earth; no account of time; no arts; no letters; no society; and which is worst of all, continual fear, and danger of violent death; and the life of man, solitary, poor, nasty, brutish, and short. [*Leviathan*, p. 82]

This coincidence of Hobbes's vision of the state of nature with the vision of Mateo Alemán in *Guzmán de Alfarache* ("No hallarás hombre con hombre") is striking and will be commented upon later. But Hobbes, of course, is not describing an existing state of affairs but a mythical state, things as they might be if man's prudence and reason are not to rescue him from the cataclysm of experience. The saving psychic conversion of man is from a state of nature to a state of reason.

The influence of Hobbes on the eighteenth-century novel has not been explored, as far as I know, but it seems to me that Hobbes's evolutionary pattern, perhaps filtered through later seventeenth-century writers, contributed to a biographical pattern that was to hold an important place in the eighteenth-century novel.[27] Quite early, in fact, Hobbes's state of nature seems to have been identified with childhood. This, for example, is the implied joke in *Mr. Hobbs's State of Nature Consider'd* (1672), a parody by the future master of St. Catherine's College:

*Philautus* [Hobbes]: Then know, *Tim*, that I have reserved a reason for such *sauciness*, as thine: and therefore I do pronounce that *children* may not only be said to be in a *state of war* merely because they cannot enter into *Leagues*, and offer and receive *Termes of peace*; but that we oftimes see that they *actually gripe* and *demand* things to which they have not the least right or title: which if denied, they presently out of fury cry, quarrell, fight, and scratch poor *Nurse*, or *Parent* it self: now this, *Tim*, does not only *demonstrate* their naturall dispositions to *war*; but that without any affront, reason or pretence of justice, they actually fall on, and have no respect at all to our *meums* and *tuums*. [pp. 45–46]

The child is born with, in Locke's phrase, a tabula rasa and develops from a prerational natural state into a reasonable social being. Life's apparent logic is a victory of reason over nature. Thus we find by the end of the seventeenth century—and fully a hundred years before Wordsworth's *Ode*—that a finicky writer such as Jean de La Bruyère confidently divides life into three stages, childhood as natural, youth and manhood as a conflict of the natural and the rational, and maturity as rational. In the essay on man in the *Caractères* he puts forward this idea of a biography:

> Il y a un temps où la raison n'est pas encore, où l'on ne vit que par instinct, à la manière des animaux, et dont il ne reste dans la mémoire aucun vestige. Il y a un second temps où la raison se développe, où elle est formée, et où elle pourroit agir si elle n'étoit pas obscurcie et comme éteinte par les vices de la complexion, et par un enchaînement de passions qui se succédent les unes aux autres, et conduisent jusques au troisième et dernier âge. La raison, alors dans sa force, devroit produire: mais elle est refroidie et rallentie par les années, par la maladie et la douleur, déconcertée ensuite par le désordre de la machine qui est dans son déclin: et ces temps neanmoins sont la vie de l'homme.

> There is a time when reason has not appeared, when one lives only by instinct, like an animal, and when as yet memory leaves no trace. There is a second time when reason develops, is being formed as an active power neither obscured and constrained by fleshly vices nor enchained to the passions that soon follow one after the other and lead up to the third and final time, a time when reason, in full maturity, should be productive. But years, sickness, and sorrow combine to deaden and slow the reason down, and finally it is disconcerted by declining powers. Nonetheless, these times are man's life. [*Les Caractères*, 2:75]

It is not my purpose to show here how this three-stage biographical pattern actually corresponds to the fictional life of Lesage's character, Gil Blas; suffice it to say that Gil Blas evolves from a more or less natural state as a young man, through a period of conflict, to a rational maturity. In the same way, but more generally, Defoe describes childhood as a state of nature and manhood as a state of alternating reason and nature.

Among the latitudinarian divines of the seventeenth century runs an optimism quite contrary to the pessimism of Hobbes, and in the eighteenth century the earl of Shaftesbury incorporated their ideas of charity and benevolence into his own.[28] In the essays collected in *Characteristics* (1711) he sets out to discredit Hobbes by showing that the subrational part of human nature is driven by more than fear, that the creation of civil society rests as much on altruism as on self-interest. Once more, as with Descartes, nature and reason are aligned in opposition to the will or art of individuals.

To Shaftesbury it is not only reasonable but also natural that men should love their fellows. "This we know for certain," he writes, "that all social love, friendship, gratitude, or whatever else is of this generous kind, does by its nature take place of the self-interesting passions, draws us out of ourselves, and makes us disregardful of our own convenience and safety" (*Characteristics*, 1:281). The man of feeling replaces the natural man. Expressing his innate benevolence, man may strive for perfectibility. The state of nature is now not one of strife and warfare but one of primitive simplicity and innocence, days now lost because of the artfulness and passions of men, but recoverable by a return to nature, or, in other words, by approved social behavior. Thus it is humanly normal to be virtuous, the Shaftesburyan proposal "that to be well affected towards the public interest and one's own is not only consistent but inseparable; and that moral rectitude or virtue must accordingly be the advantage, and vice the injury and disadvantage of every creature" (*Characteristics*, 1:282). This proposition is to be better known in Pope's couplet:

> That REASON, PASSION, answer one great aim;
> That true SELF-LOVE and SOCIAL are the same.
>
> ["An Essay on Man"]

In this best of all possible worlds, whatever is, is right. Evil seems unnatural and not truly willed at all.

Here was a paradox. Virtuous behavior is normal, yet the majority of men lead abnormal lives and defy their own natures. Some are so abnormal or maladjusted that they are what we would call criminal psychopaths. Thus, in spite of his optimistic outlook, Shaftesbury was troubled by the failure of men to measure up to the ideal: "Man in the mean time, vicious and unconsonant man, lives out of all rule and proportion, contradicts his Principles, breaks the Order and Oeconomy of all his Passions, and lives at odds with his whole Species, and with Nature: so that it is next to a Prodigy to see a Man in the World who lives NATURALLY, and as a MAN."[29] The more rational the explanation of man, the more desperate man's predicament came to seem!

Among the English novelists whom I have selected to represent the picaresque strain were a number who believe with Shaftesbury in the inherent good nature of man or who are at least inclined to apotheosize the man of feeling. These novelists are violently opposed to picarism. Thus Fielding describes trickery in words of sardonic irony, Smollett turns with sudden revulsion against one of his own heroes, and Dickens broods darkly about the pathologically self-interested world.

Religion was involved in these philosophical contexts. Paralleling the rise of rationalism in the seventeenth and eighteenth centuries was a shift in the social teaching of the Christian, and particularly the Protestant, churches. As summarized by Max Weber, Ernst Troeltsch, and R. H. Tawney, this shift was in essence an acceptance of capitalist economics. My analysis of the Spanish picaresque novels has shown that there was no comfortable place in the doctrine of the medieval church for the acquisitive man. By the beginning of the eighteenth century, the acquisitive man was no longer a social outcast. Supporting him was a new conception of grace that made conscience the rule for conduct and good works in the world the sign of salvation; a new conception of nature as an inward and essential expression of God that led to the acceptance of the worldly "calling" as an act of obedience and self-restraint; and a new conception of God and man that made filial trust in God an inherent element in human nature. As long as the vaguely defined conscience or God or nature or light or reason or providence was there to intervene, there was little apparent necessity to check individual economic drives.

What were the implications of these philosophical trends for the myth of the picaro? According to the Cartesian dualism of mind and matter, man possesses in his faculty of understanding the counterpart of the divine reason governing the vast machine of the universe. Erring man, however, fails to act rationally; therefore, a continual intervention of the divine power is needed to bridge the void between mind and matter. This situation in effect meant that man should seek his salvation by listening to the voice of reason within. The new conception whereby no man is denied salvation meant that the mythical picaro, who had been so denied, lost his significance as a socioreligious outcast. Man's acquisitive instincts, once the despised sign of his degeneration, had become acceptable to society. His pretenses in the social sphere had lost—except by way of admonition against sin—their religious significance. Man could still live on the periphery of society, insinuate himself into positions of honor, be educated in adversity, and then excuse his selfish conduct by cynical reference to the self-preservation law of nature; but now he could always, sooner or later, abandon moral vagabondage, listen to the voice of reason, convert himself from natural man, and enter into human community. A persistent failure to enter in came to be construed as unnatural and irrational. Thus the English trickster tended more often than not to be transformed into a hardened criminal or a psychopathic gangster whom the eighteenth century seemed best to comprehend in terms of the subrational "Hobbesian" passions. This self-condemned monster—the center of the *Jonathan Wild* tradition—was beyond the range of social sympathy. Nevertheless, criminals, unlike picaros, assumed a firm identity, and, significantly, no Wild or Fagin desired to enter the community because, by his own code, he was already in.

When the eighteenth-century novel seems to present a picaro, as in Defoe and Smollett, it is presumably because the author is concerned with Hobbes's myth of the natural man. The state of nature as described by Hobbes resembles the condition of social disintegration revealed in the picaresque novel. To this theoretical resemblance another may be added: the picaro and the natural man are both in a sense artists struggling to overcome the anxieties of the human condition through a search for order and meaning. Where the picaro as socioreligious outsider is forced to create himself and act the role he is denied, the natural man "creates" both society and his identity within it. Nonetheless, the picaro and the natural man are distinguishable mythic concepts, the difference involving interpretations of the will. The picaro, a myth shaped during the breakup of feudal society, has no will of his own apart from society: he is free to act, but society defines the meaning of responsibility. The natural man has powers of responsible action as a birthright. The voice of reason frees natural man and persuades him to contract his will to other wills in the formation of collective social security. The apparently picaresque myth of the natural man actually differs from it because the will of natural man may convert illusions into a new social reality. The way out of the picaro's tragic dilemma is open.

## *Gil Blas* and the Sane Society

Had it repeated the spiritual crisis of the Siglo de Oro, the pre-revolutionary conditions of the France of Louis XIV might have prepared the way for a French picaresque novel to appear. But the disillusionment of certain French writers from about 1688 was not based upon tragic despair but upon suppressed rebelliousness. "Tout est dit," sighed La Bruyère in beginning his *Caractères*. Any ambitious probing of the deep emotional responses of life was undesirable. On the national level, overreaching ambition had led the king to the point of bankruptcy. Versailles, so grand in appearance, was in reality an archbaroque symbol of despotism. The disillusioned La Bruyère seemed to say that man had, rather like Molière's Alceste, no "character" at all, only a mask to wear and a role to play. A writer's task was to rip away the masks, to observe manners—but not to observe too closely. La Bruyère could only hint at the dangers of telling the whole truth: "Les grands sujets," he said, "sont défendus."[30] Two decades later, in the final years of the reign, there appeared in the person of Alain-René Lesage a student of La Bruyère who could speak more boldly.

The France in which the Crippled Devil[31] gained his freedom, tilted up the roofs, and irreverently laid bare the mediocrity of mankind was weighed down by defeat, poverty, and corruption.[32] No moral lesson was more deeply implanted in Lesage than that of pride going before a fall. The armies of France had been humiliated at Blenheim, Ramillies, Turin, and elsewhere. Defeat, famine, and religious and economic oppression proved the fruits of ambition. There was, consequently, a serious social content in Lesage's major novels and plays from *Le Diable Boîteux* (1707 with a Spanish origin in Vélez de Guevara's *El diablo cojuelo*), *Crispin rival de son maître* (1707), *Turcaret* (1709), to *Gil Blas* and its continuations (1715–1724 and 1735); one of his constant themes is the use and abuse of power.[33]

The world the Crippled Devil shows Cléophas is a carnival of fraud and error, while Crispin has the arrogant aggressiveness Molière's valets had not possessed:

—Mon maître? Fi donc! Violà un plaisant gueux pour une fille comme Angélique! Je lui destine un meilleur parti.
—Qui donc?
—Moi.

—My master? Come now! There's a pleasant rogue for a girl like Angelique! I have in mind a better match for her.
—Who then?
—Me. [*Crispin rival de son maitre*, I, iii]

Beaumarchais's Figaro, the revolutionary, can already be heard. Then there is Turcaret the financier, perhaps the first caricature of a capitalist tycoon: violent, vain, infatuated, yet withal a shrewd and merciless businessman. As in the picaresque novels, in *Turcaret* society around the central individual is as vicious as he: "J'admire le train de la vie humaine! Nous plumons une coquette; la coquette mange un homme d'affaires; l'homme d'affaires en pille d'autres: cela fait un ricochet de fourberies le plus plaisant du monde." (I admire the process of human life! We pluck a coquette; she devours a businessman; the businessman pillages others: that makes for the most pleasant give-and-take of tricks in the world.) (*Turcaret*, I, x). Thus speaks the cynical valet Frontin. The only honest man in *Turcaret* is a drunkard.

There is in *Turcaret*, however, an implicit sense of order. Comparing the play with, say, *Les Corbeaux* of Henri Becque shows how remote was the social realism of a classic eighteenth-century *comédie de moeurs* from the deterministic naturalism of the late nineteenth century. Lesage's subject is not doom but folly, and he questions the means rather than the ends of capitalist economics. Thus the character of Turcaret, representing the type of tax-farmer who exploited people in the name of the king, really looks back to Molière's Jourdain, the uneducated parvenu engineering his social rise by a series of odious pretenses. To the educated *honnête homme* of the upper bourgeoisie for whom Lesage, like Molière, was writing, Turcaret was simply the man who did not know his place.[34]

Lesage, I suggest, was himself an *honnête homme* whose typical concerns were not altogether different from those of the picaresque novelists but whose point of view differed fundamentally. The function of the bourgeois artist was to keep the flock pointed in the right direction. In a long narrative such as *Gil Blas* there are frequent excursions to right and left of the plot line but always a movement that is centrifugal, away from a psychologically complex central personage and toward life in all its multifariousness. The realism remains objective and not, as in the picaresque novels, dogmatic: "Je ne me suis proposé que de représenter la vie des hommes telle qu'elle est," Lesage declares.[35] Even at that, *Gil Blas*, as the Marxist critic Georg Lukács points out, lacks a concrete sense of time and place and accepts the contemporary world as something given.[36] With all its diversified social realism, *Gil Blas* comes through as an arithmetical demonstration of society's unreasonableness, the life of the protagonist being less a vehicle for conveying the feel and texture of the eighteenth century than a device for advancing principles of the same society. Environment, lacking specificity, comes to mean *l'école du monde*; character is a more or less fixed integer; and the story (though progressively more inward in the later books) can be regarded as a paradigm of bourgeois man. For this reason the adventures of Gil Blas, unlike those of the picaro, are often detachable, passing before the view, as Thomas Holcroft observed in 1780, "for no other purpose than to amuse by their peculiarity."[37] The unities of the work are stylistic. Lesage's classical prose, pure, flexible, unhurried, is perfectly adapted to a narrative intended to convey the general truth of human life. Whereas the reality-destroying style of the picaresque novelists has a pictorial complement in El Greco's haunted luminosity or in Goya's savage line, the style of an eighteenth-century French rationalist conveys the insulated calm of a Watteau. Tonally, there is a certain symphonic orderliness in *Gil Blas* as one moves from the lightheartedness of the 1715 books (I–VI) through the contrived *Sturm und Drang* of the 1724 books (VII–IX) to the resigned melancholy of the 1735 books (X–XII). The Spanish picaresque novels, pitched in a singularly minor key, suggest, so to speak, the simple guitar accompaniment.

Lesage's place in literature is not with the picaresque novelists but with the spacious novelists of social realism, with Cervantes and Fielding, and, in his way, with Tolstoy.

What is the relation of *Gil Blas* to the Spanish picaresque novels? During Lesage's lifetime (1668–1748) Spain was a fashionable topic, and Lesage rode the crest of fashion, imitating and adapting Spanish drama and fiction. That he was thoroughly familiar with the Spanish novels there can be no doubt. Yet when he published a version of *Guzmán de Alfarache* in 1732, it was a "traduction purgée des moralités superflues" placing emphasis on Alemán's "tableaux de la vie civile": characteristically, he converted a picaresque novel into a novel of manners.

Although Lesage does not share the literary purpose of the picaresque novelists, he does imitate their conventions. By means of autobiographical form he narrows the spatial plane of *Gil Blas* to a self; he satirizes manners and institutions; he shows a lively concern with society on the brink of economic ruin; he dramatizes the encounters of life in terms of appearance and reality; and he pictures life as a chronic succession of ups and downs of a more or less edifying nature.

Missing from *Gil Blas*, however, is the heart of the picaresque novel, the picaro. From the first chapter it is evident that Gil, who comes of poor but honest stock, is to be formed rather than deformed by experience. The picaresque parental humor, once a purposive convention, has been replaced by an amiable portrait of Uncle Gil Perez (an embryonic Uncle Toby). When Gil Blas leaves home, it is not because he feels inferior but because he restlessly seeks adventures. Nor is he much of a trickster in his youth: although he steals some of his uncle's cash before leaving, he is not dishonestly inclined, as proved in the central episode of the first book, his captivity in Roland's cave. Here all his intelligence and trickery aid him to escape from the bandits as deliverer of the romantic Donna Mencia, thus showing that there are right as well as wrong ways of being a confidence man (anticipating *Huckleberry Finn*). After a series of reversals governed not by antisocial acts of the hero but by his innocence and credulity, there develops, instead of a picaro's determination to live parasitically off society, a stoical refusal to give in to adversity. Always the world of experience remains open. Underlining this nonpicaresque aspect of his adventures is the appearance of Gil's schoolfriend, Fabrice, in the last chapter of the first book. Fabrice is a trusted companion, the first of a series of good-natured friends and benefactors—Laura, Don Alphonse, Seraphine, Scipion, Antonia, Dorothea—who form a bulwark against the corrupt majority of mankind. In later books, as Gil Blas comes more and more under the influence of friends, the story diminishes in picaresque atmosphere, and the reader has no doubt that Gil Blas will master his selfish and licentious impulses. The final impression is that Gil is a pragmatic, energetic, sympathetic person, neither too good nor too bad, drifting with the tide and learning gradually to place his irrational impulses under the wise restraint of an *honnête homme*'s reason. He ambitiously seeks credit and position, and this social-rise motif has its Spanish origins; but he is also launched on a quest for responsible individuality that leads eventually to a renunciation of the power obsession.

This inward story of the quest for reason becomes more pronounced as the novel progresses. In Book III, Gil reveals his bourgeois disgust with the disorderliness of theatrical life:

Je cedai au torrent pendant trois semaines. Je me livrai à toutes sortes de voluptés. Mais je dirai en même temps qu'au milieu des plaisirs je sentais souvent naître en moi des remords qui venaient de mon éducation, et qui mêlaient une amertume à mes délices. La débouche ne triompha point de ces remords: au contraire, ils augmentaient à mesure que je devenais plus débauché; et, par un effet de mon heureux naturel, les désordres de la vie comique commencèrent à me faire horreur. Ah! misérable, me dis-je à moi-même, est-ce ainsi que tu remplis l'attente de la famille? N'est-ce pas assez de l'avoir trompée en prenant un autre parti que celui de précepteur? Ta condition servile te doit-elle empêcher de vivre en honnête homme? Te convient-il d'être avec des gens si vicieux? L'envie, la colère et l'avarice règnent chez les uns, la pudeur est bannie de chez les autres; ceux-ci s'abandonnent à l'intempérance et à la paresse, et l'orgueil de ceux-là va jusqu'à l'insolence. C'en est fait; je ne veux pas demeurer plus longtemps avec les sept péchés mortels.

For three weeks I surrendered to the storm, giving myself over to all kinds of voluptuousness. But I would say that even in the midst of pleasure I felt stirring within me, mixing bitterness with delight, a remorse derived from my upbringing. Debauchery did not win out over this remorse: on the contrary, it increased as I became more debauched; and by an effect of my natural good spirits, the confusions of theatrical life began to horrify me. Ah, wretch, I told myself, is this the way you fulfill the hopes of your family? Is it not enough to have deceived them by not becoming a tutor? Your servile condition, must it prevent you from living as a man of honor? Does it profit you to live among debased people? Envy, rage, and greed rule some, others banish modesty; these are abandoned to intemperance and laziness, while those proud ones become insolent. Consequently, I no longer wish to dwell with the seven deadly sins. [*Histoire de Gil Blas*, bk. III, chap. 12]

*De vivre en honnête homme*: the phrase, occurring in a context without irony, sums up the aspiration of Gil Blas as character and Lesage as moralist. From this point in the novel life defines itself as the problem of knowing one's place. The carefree social climber of the early books gives way to the morally reprehensible bureaucrat of the middle, but, even while serving as the selfish confidential clerk of the Duc de Lerme, Gil Blas struggles to remain honest with himself, observing just before his disgrace and imprisonment, "Avant que je fusse à la cour, j'étais compatissant et charitable de mon naturel; mais on n'a plus là de faiblesse humaine, et j'y devins plus dur qu'un caillou." (Before coming to court, I was naturally compassionate and charitable; but, there, one no longer entertains such human weakness, and I became harder than a stone.) (bk. VIII, chap. 10). His fault lies in having stepped out of bounds. By the end of Book IX, therefore, the quest-for-reason pattern supersedes the search-for-credit pattern: fittingly, Gil retreats from the great world to seek the therapies of country life. The final books work out a compromise between the two patterns. It is not enough for an *honnête homme* to cultivate his own garden. Returning to court to serve the Comte D'Olivarès, Gil can put his knowledge to good use while being safely purged of extravagant desires. The world is accepted as the proper field for asceticism. Even the servant Scipion—whose autobiography tiresomely reincarnates the youthful Gil Blas—has been socially redeemed: "Si dans son enfance," beams Gil, "Scipion a été un vrai *Picaro*, il s'est depuis si bien corrigé, qu'il est devenu le modèle d'un parfait domestique." (If in youth Scipion led the life of a true picaro, he has corrected himself so well since then as to become the perfect model of a domestic servant.) (bk. x, chap. 12). Smug pastoral contentment fills the last years of Gil Blas's life. Once more at Lirias—that typical eighteenth-century formal extension of urban culture—Gil looks back upon the vicissitudes of his life, conscious that straightforwardness, tolerance, and charity are qualities necessary to preserve a sane society. Unlike the picaro, Gil Blas is so integrated into society that he emerges as its representative type, the *honnête homme*: he is, culturally regarded, one of the converted.

*Gil Blas*, with its tension between picarism and social realism, submerges the myth of the picaro. The defective manners that have threatened the working out on the individual level of orderly social process have been corrected and made an exemplification of the growth of good from limited evil. Lesage was indebted to the Spanish novelists for certain narrative conventions. Padre Isla, in translating *Gil Blas* into Spanish, claimed to have restored it to its original tongue; but Lesage's protagonist is an *honnête homme*, not a picaro, and his rationalism represents a nonpicaresque view of life.

## The Idea of Progress in Defoe's *Colonel Jack*

Although there is a singular lack of evidence that Defoe knew or was attracted by the Spanish picaresque novels, Daniel Defoe's notes from underground might tend to place him in picaresque tradition. One must be wary, though, of attributing the presence of trickery in Defoe's novels to a picaresque source because Defoe's attitude toward his material is difficult to spot; of submerged allusions, ironies, and moral judgments the critic of Defoe is never perfectly sure, although occasionally, dramatic irony may be sensed in his spiritual autobiographies.

In 1924, when Arthur W. Secord's studies in Defoe's narrative method appeared, there were four conventional accounts of the novels: they (1) continued picaresque traditions, (2) were extensions of Defoe's journalistic methods, (3) expanded biographies, criminal and otherwise, or (4) grew out of moral considerations and treatises. The last, Secord showed, was probably most influential in shaping Defoe's novels because the mass of his writings had been directed to moral and religious problems of the rising middle class.[38] Least influential was probably the picaresque tradition. Recent Defoe scholars, confirming Secord's approach, have broadened the field of investigation to include the general cultural background of the novels as well as Defoe's own idiosyncratic and often radical contribution to it. While navigational hazards remain, it is now possible for the critic of Defoe's fiction to steer by fairly reliable compass.[39]

The arrow points to Defoe's puritan individualism. This was not, of course, the hellfire-and-damnation puritanism of the American colonies. In Defoe the old moral austerity has been softened by humanitarianism, the brooding mist of sin scorched in the light of reason. There is still belief in the need for salvation, but the old force has gone. Defoe is both a severe critic of bourgeois capitalism and an exponent of salvation by success. He knows the mystery of destructive impulse yet supports a behavioristic, pragmatic morality. He quotes approvingly the earl of Rochester's "Hobbesian" couplets—

> Be Judge your self, I'le bring it to the test,
> Which is the basest *Creature*, *Man*, or *Beast*?
> *Birds*, feed on *Birds*, *Beasts*, on each other prey,
> But Savage *Man* alone, does *Man* betray—
> ["A Satyr against Mankind"][40]

then, with no sense of contradiction, dedicates a long poem "To the Most Serene, Most Invincible, and Most Illustrious Lady REASON" ("Jure Divine"). The essence of Defoe's thought is perhaps a loose synthesis of potential opposites, puritanism and rationalism. As Hoxie Neale Fairchild summarizes, Defoe believes "that every man possesses within himself a guide, a light, a voice which shows him the truth and directs him toward virtue."[41] This inner light—Locke's Candle of the Lord—is variously expressed in Defoe's works as providence, God, nature, reason, or conscience, and the novels are about this inner light that searches the retreats of the restless and the lost, the innocent and the guilty, but tantalizingly, rarely with a certain beam. The contradictions, the precarious ups and downs of life, become part somehow of a providential plan, awareness of which is the first duty of man. Sometimes the light is denied, as in the case of Captain Jack the vicious highwayman, but often as not Defoe's characters escape the punishment of men and heaven because they learn to bear witness to the light. Thus in the midst of one of the most venomously satiric periods in English letters—if the acerbities of Swift are any indication—Defoe stood steadfastly tolerant.

It is probable that Defoe's own experiences confirmed his tolerance. He knew poverty and humiliation and the terrors of isolation and of man's inhumanity to man. When he was pilloried in 1702, his sense of isolation was exacerbated, and, according to Bonamy Dobrée, he never again felt "that he was a full, and fully free member of the society he so fervently wished to benefit."[42] In writing about the socially insecure, Defoe projected his own feeling. Sudden reversals of fortune were to him but a fact of life, their occurrence a sign of spiritual trial, especially for the weak and exposed.

It might therefore be said that Defoe shares the spirit of the picaresque novelists. Like Alemán and the author of *Lazarillo*, he breathes into his narratives a quickening sense of individual predicament, of, in William Faulkner's memorable phrase, "the heart divided against itself." Defoe observed, as they did, that personality is largely shaped by society, that life is full of the dilemmas of flesh and spirit, and that the lonely or persecuted are not to be denied compassion. Particularly in his behaviorism, Defoe seems to have been anticipated by the Spanish picaresque novelists. But it is difficult to draw a line between personal experience and literary convention, especially when, as with Defoe, the novelist is a puritan and rationalist accustomed to looking within. The likely hypothesis is that Defoe always looked within, there discovering instinctively some secrets of other men's lives.

Defoe regarded inwardness as an essence of human nature.

Thus he has Crusoe reflect on solitude in terms that are unmistakably influenced by the Hobbesian analysis: "Something we may be touched indeed with by the power of sympathy, and a secret turn of the affections; but all the solid reflection is directed to ourselves. Our meditations are all solitude in perfection; our passions are all exercised in retirement; we love, we hate, we covet, we enjoy, all in privacy and solitude. All that we communicate of those things to any other is but for their assistance in the pursuit of our desires" (*Serious Reflections . . . of Robinson Crusoe*, pp. 2–3). The man who, like Crusoe on his island, is utterly alone is prey to the intolerable anxieties of the natural man: Crusoe's island belongs to myth as well as to Alexander Selkirk. Man by himself without society cannot master his soul. It is "in the midst of the crowds and hurry of men and business that man, though continuing in solitude, masters his soul" (*Serious Reflections*, p. 2). Striving to rid himself of natural fears, the Christian seeks his salvation within society despite the fact that he continues to bear the natural state with him into the social situation and that he may therefore tend to fluctuate back and forth between nature and reason in the very midst of the soul's progress.

The idea of solitude in Defoe is no longer the picaresque idea of disintegration. For the picaro, there was no survival outside society but there was also no salvation in society. Defoe's heroes, on the contrary, suffer outside society but are positively dependent upon society for their salvation. Defoe's dramatization of inwardness by means of the autobiographical form leads to a nonpicaresque conception of the self existing in time. Resolution, not dissolution, proves to be the outcome of temporal duration. Experience for Robinson Crusoe, Moll Flanders, Colonel Jack, and Roxana is positive and defines the self and puts it in the way of a realization as right reason. Defoe's heroes, too, are free of the picaro's anguished sense of failed identity. Roxana, for example, dreads that her daughter will discover the scandalous past, but her suffering has a social rather than a spiritual consequent. I would conclude, therefore, that the form of Defoe's novels derives from the inwardness of a puritan and rationalist and not from an imitation of picaresque autobiography. But I think that Defoe has a feeling for the lonely individual that is quite in the spirit of Alemán and the author of *Lazarillo*, if not of Quevedo.

Arnold Kettle places Defoe in the picaresque tradition on the grounds of his "anti-romantic, anti-feudal realism" and "his lack of pattern";[43] I do not agree. I think that it may be shown that Defoe is nonpicaresque in both realism and pattern. First, Defoe's realism differs from the so-called "realism" of the picaresque novelists, antiromantic and antifeudal as they may be. The novels of Defoe, unlike the picaresque novels, never question the validity of experience. The picaresque novels contain the kind of realism that comes from painting things as tangible, but, in the philosophic sense, the real is very much in doubt. The myth of the picaro presents the failure of identity, shows the confidence man playing his socioreligious role because dependable reality is absent, and insists finally that nothing is what it seems. Defoe's heroes are sometimes deceivers and sometimes deceived, but the nature of deception in his novels fails to hold in this philosophic sense. For example, Moll Flanders and her Lancashire husband mutually deceive one another about the extent of their fortunes, but their deceptions and self-deceptions do not destroy the concept of real identity. Indeed, far from threatening the individual identity, realism in Defoe is the essential proof of it. Crusoe on his island is literally saved by the reality of gunpowder and nails, emblems of the far-off civilization. Again, Defoe's characters know things because things are real. Moll, Singleton, and Jack are, significantly, foundlings, propelled into the world with blank souls and learning gradually what real experience teaches them through its impact on the consciousness.

Second, Defoe's novels have a rudimentary pattern of Christian redemption that—regardless of whether it convinces the modern reader—is diametrically opposed to the disintegration pattern of the picaresque novels. Lazarillo's rise to prosperity accompanies his moral dissolution. Guzmán's orthodox conversion extends the hopelessness of his fall. The illusions of Don Pablos remain indispensable to him in defeat. Thus the typical disintegration pattern of the picaresque novels traces the growth and alienation of an individual and shows him finally cast out while still seeking the social values he knows to be false. The first part of Defoe's *Colonel Jack* (1723) looks as if it might develop into such a picaresque pattern. Jack, a poor orphan, is early introduced to a picaro's experience. He falls among bad companions and learns to steal because, he innocently thinks, thieving is what he should do to keep alive. For a brief spell he, like the picaro, is the victim of a false teaching. Jack also has a picaro's obsessional desire to become a gentleman and seeks to obtain this goal by dishonorable means. But as time passes, Jack begins to have doubts about his bad education. After adventures in Scotland and Virginia, he becomes a successful planter, meanwhile growing, in the knowledge of what gentlemanly honor really is, through the kindly tutoring of a reformed convict. Following this period of moral growth, Jack makes a series of impulsive marriages and veers off into a long and irresponsible military and commercial career. Finally he feels truly repentant and tries to restrain his impulses by unselfishly helping his Virginia tutor and his first wife.

The curious fact about Jack's picaresque childhood is that it does not contribute to a picaresque pattern of the whole story. Does this mean that Defoe was imitating a picaresque novel and then abandoned the idea? I think not, because Jack's childhood can be otherwise accounted for. If his childhood is seen in the context of the myth of the state of nature, then it can be seen as the first stage of a puritan-rationalist's progress along the Christian road of innocence, guilt, and salvation, or, expressed another way, up the spiral of form from nature to reason. By the time of his first marriage Jack has become a gentleman. Yet at this point he begins to see that being a gentleman and a successful planter is not enough. Here he commences what he calls his "search after religion" (*Col. Jacque*, p. 211). Like Gil Blas he is not for a long while contrite, and he returns to a life of moral vagabondage but now as a rational adult without the natural man's excuse of ignorance or necessity. Having overcome earlier ignorance, he must now develop control of his selfish impulses. Therefore at last he becomes obedient to the dictates of conscience and, as a sign of regeneration, remarries his first wife. The pattern of *Colonel Jack*, in other words, is consistently nonpicaresque.

A third nonpicaresque aspect of Defoe's fiction is his treatment of the problem of necessity. In *Lazarillo de Tormes*, necessity had been treated as an inescapable first cause, an innocent child having been forced into antisocial behavior to preserve himself from death by starvation. The picaro's misfortunes were traced, in part, to social causes, his malfeasance was partially justified, and his damnation, the outgrowth of necessity, was a signal plea for social reformation. Defoe treats necessity, generally speaking, in the manner of *Lazarillo*'s author. His heroes confront necessity early and harshly. Their crimes, if caused by innocence and poverty and not by vice, are morally justified, and society is reproached for having brought about the conditions of necessity. But for Defoe there is a way out for the guilty individual once necessity has ceased to make its demands.

In his works Defoe sympathizes with individuals whose crimes were motivated by instinctive self-preservation. Crusoe states the theme in his *Serious Reflections*: "Necessity is above the power of human nature, and for Providence to suffer a man to fall into that necessity is to suffer him to sin" (p. 35). In his *Review of the Affairs of France*, Defoe sides with the radical views of Hobbes: "I firmly believe, there was never a man so Honest, but would *Steal*, before he would *Starve*, and if he did not, it was want of Opportunity. . . . Distress removes from the Soul, all Relation, Affection, Sense of Justice and all the Obligations, either Moral or Religious, that secure one Man against another." But Defoe also argues that necessity does not remove guilt: "*No, No, Gentlemen,* you will see the Crime lyes deeper than the Fact; *Necessity* will make us all thieves, *but the Crime is in the Cause of that Necessity*; and he that will impartially examine his Circumstances, and place things in a True Light, will see, that the *Methods to bring him into that Necessity*, Govern the Case."

Maximillian Novak (who cites the above examples) shows that Defoe's heroes do not first fall into necessity through vice and therefore are not guilty of their original crimes; but later, after they lose their innocence, they assume moral responsibility for their acts, and Defoe punishes or rewards heroes as the case may be.[44] Defoe treats necessity in *Colonel Jack* according to this formula. Young Jack says of his first robbery, "I knew no good and had tasted no evil" (*Col. Jacque*, p. 48). Abandoned by both parents, bred up with the vicious Captain Jack, and forced to sleep in the glasshouse ashes, Jack has a right to steal from society what it owes him. When, however, he robs an old woman who is poorer than he, he is guilty and must make restitution. Eventually he is freed from the necessity of the state of nature, but, because it is impossible to restore all the stolen property he has acquired, he has a residue of punishable guilt. Accordingly, he looks upon his kidnapping to Virginia as a sign of divine retribution. Yet in *Colonel Jack* necessity has also its positive value. Just as Lazarillo sympathized with the starving squire, so Jack comes to love his tutor and wife because they, too, have been victims of necessity. Lazarillo and Jack differ in their responses to freedom from necessity, the picaro sacrificing moral principle to avoid a relapse into want, Jack earning moral potentiality and relief from worry: "How happy I was that I could live by my own endeavours, and was no more under the necessity of being a villain and of getting my bread at my own hazard and the ruin of honest families" (p. 196). Jack's progressive escape from necessity is, then, a definite pattern that may be understood in terms of Protestantism, capitalism, the idea of progress, and Hobbes's philosophy rather than in terms of the picaresque myth. The picarism often attributed to Defoe is submerged in the individual and not in the society he represents; in realism, pattern, and necessitarian doctrine Defoe contributes antitheses to the myth of the picaro.

## Fielding's *Jonathan Wild* as Mock-Picaresque

In "An Essay on the Knowledge of the Characters of Men," included with *Jonathan Wild* in the *Miscellanies* of 1743, Fielding expresses a nonpicaresque faith in the benevolent powers of nature, at the same time acknowledging that the world sometimes appears to be a masquerade of evil: "While the crafty and designing Part of Mankind, consulting only their own separate Advantage, endeavour to maintain one constant Imposition on others, the whole World becomes a vast Masquerade, where the greatest Part appears disguised under false Vizors and Habits; a very few only shewing their own Faces, who become, by doing so, the Astonishment and Ridicule of all the rest. But however cunning the Disguise be which a Masquerader wears: . . . if closely attended to, he very rarely escapes the Discovery of an accurate Observer; for Nature, which unwillingly submits to the Imposture, is ever endeavouring to peep forth and shew herself" (*Miscellanies*, 1:184–85).

Similar acknowledgment and faith appear in *Jonathan Wild*. In that fable Fielding sets out to demonstrate how the apparent triumph of evil is in reality a miserable defeat, that goodness, although superficially ridiculous, is actually heroic.[45] A melodramatic fable becomes a vehicle for an indictment of the self-interested leaders of English society; Fielding gears the whole story to an irony so mordant that he seems to have feared that he would be misunderstood and that his odious hero would be thought to reflect some misanthropy of his own. Fielding therefore protests in the Preface: "I do by no means intend in the Character of my Hero to represent Human Nature in general. Such Insinuations must be attended with very dreadful Conclusions; nor do I see any other tendency they can naturally have, but to encourage and soothe Men in their Villainies, and to make every well-disposed Man disclaim his own Species, and curse the Hour of his Birth into such a Society" (*Miscellanies*, 1:xix). Fielding wants it well understood that he has no mimetic intention. "Roguery, and not a Rogue," he declares, "is my Subject" (*Miscellanies*, 1:xviii).

Here, where we are only concerned with the relation of *Jonathan Wild* to picaresque myth, Fielding's protest is suggestive. Did he perhaps have in mind the most pessimistic and misanthropic of the Spanish picaresque novels, *Guzmán de Alfarache*? Jonathan Wild's favorite book is "the Spanish Rogue" (*Life of Mr. Jonathan Wild*, bk. I, chap. 3). A typical eighteenth-century English Protestant and rationalist such as Henry Fielding might believe that Mateo Alemán had, cynically and hypocritically, allowed long moral discourses to come as if from the picaro himself. Moreover, Alemán had clearly tried to represent human nature in general in the character of the picaro. To one with the ethical sensibilities of Henry Fielding, this was impertinence that might well tend "to encourage and soothe Men in their Villanies" by removing customary distinctions of good and evil. By assuming the aloof distrust of the cynic, the picaro was apparently left free to enjoy the very crimes against which he railed. Alemán, of course, had not intended that such a construction should be placed on his Christian doctrine, but Fielding regards the picaro as a cynical hypocrite.

Fielding includes the cynic along with the conqueror under the heading of greatness. In "A Dialogue between Alexander the Great and Diogenes the Cynic" Diogenes condemns the "greatness" of bloodthirsty tyrants but is forced by Alexander to confess to his own "Hobbesian" lust for power. "Come, come," chides Alexander, "thou art not the poor-spirited Fellow thou wouldst appear. There is more Greatness of Soul in thee than at present shines forth. . . . Pride will not suffer thee to confess Passions which Fortune hath not put it in thy power to gratify. It is therefore that thou deniest Ambition: for hadst thou a Soul as capacious as mine, I see no better Way which thy humble Fortune would allow thee of feeding its Ambition, than what thou hast chosen: for when alone in this Retreat which thou hast chosen, thou may'st contemplate thy own Greatness" (*Miscellanies*, 1:334). His antiheroism exposed as envy, Diogenes eagerly accepts Alexander's offer to burn Athens in his behalf! To Fielding, a cynical rogue and a murdering tyrant differ mainly in opportunity. Conventional ideas of hero and antihero were caused by a confusion of goodness with greatness, but only in rare cases, in a Socrates or a Brutus, did the two combine to form "the *True Sublime* in Human Nature" (1:xxviii). More often a man was good but not great—"Our Wonder ceases; our Delight is lessened; but our Love remains"—or great but not good. "This Bombast Greatness" (1:xxx), as Fielding calls it, was to be held up to ridicule in *Jonathan Wild*. It is not unlikely therefore that Wild's favorite book, *Guzmán de Alfarache*, was to Fielding an example of Bombast Greatness.

Fielding worked out his comic theory either just before or just after composing *Jonathan Wild*. In the Preface to *Joseph Andrews* (1742) he defines burlesque as "ever the exhibition of what is monstrous and unnatural, and where our delight . . . arises from the surprising absurdity." Affectation is "the only source of the true ridiculous," and vanity and hypocrisy are the sources of affectation: "Vanity instigates men to affect to be something more than they really are, in order to win applause; hypocrisy incites them to affect to be something quite the reverse of what they are, in order to avoid censure."[46] Under terms of this moral theory no picaro would pass Fielding's muster. Whereas originally the picaro pretended to be other than he was because he was tragically thrust down the road to perdition, the criminal whom Fielding portrays in *Jonathan Wild* is engaged in a mock-picaresque comedy of damnation. The "apotheosis" (*Wild*, bk. IV, chap. 15) of a rogue (cynic, hypocrite, and great man) was— Tyburn. To emphasize this implacable "natural law" Fielding avoids the autobiographical form and reserves ethical authority to himself, thus creating the literary possibility of a burlesque of picaresque tradition.

Specific allusions to the picaresque novels (as distinct from criminal biographies and other rogue anatomies) are far from certain in *Jonathan Wild*. Wild's ancestor, the pickpocket Langfanger, "the first of his family who had the honour to suffer for the good of his country" (bk. I, chap. 2), reminds one distantly of Lazarillo's father who died in exile. In school Wild, like Pablos, is envious companion to an apparent moral superior.[47] Later, Count La Ruse, the conventional bad companion of picaresque tradition, suggests to Wild a way of life recalling the picaro's in *Guzmán de Alfarache*: "Is it less difficult, by false tokens, to deceive a shopkeeper into the delivery of his goods, which you afterwards run away with [cf. Guzmán as a thieving porter in Toledo], than to impose upon him by outward splendour and the appearance of fortune, into a credit, by which you gain, and he loses twenty times as much [cf. Guzmán's swindle of the Milanese banker]? . . . Is not as much art, as many excellent qualities, required to make a pimping porter at a common bawdyhouse, as would enable a man to prostitute his own . . . wife [cf. Guzmán's prostitution of his second wife]?" (bk. I, chap. 5). Like Guzmán and Pablos, La Ruse is a cardsharp; like Guzmán, he substitutes paste jewels for real; like Sayavedra, he robs his associate of ill-gotten wealth. Other possible echoes of

*Guzmán* are Wild's miserable marriage, the swindle of Heartfree, and Wild's cynical adroitness in dodging moral issues, as in the ironic "Of Hats" chapter.

But it is enough to observe that Fielding consistently mocks contemporary ideas of the morality, characters, and situations of the picaresque novels and of the rogue anatomies. The essence of his approach to the subject is summed up in the mock-heroic simile he uses to describe the picaresque journey:

> [Wild] began to enlarge his views with his prosperity: For this restless amiable disposition, this noble avidity which increases with feeding, is the first principle or constituent quality of these our *Great Men*, to whom, in their passage on to Greatness, it happens as to a traveller over the Alps, or if this be a too far fetched simile, to one who travels over the hills near Bath, where the simile was indeed made. He sees not the end of his journey at once; but passing on from scheme to scheme, and from hill to hill, with noble constancy, resolving still to attain the summit on which he hath fixed his eye, however dirty the roads may be through which he struggles, he at length arrives at—some vile inn, where he finds no kind of entertainment nor conveniency for repose. [bk. I, chap. 14]

Fielding's conviction that the picaresque hero leads a wretched existence and travels downward to damnation while apparently journeying to the summit of happiness is quite within the moral scheme of the Spanish picaresque novelists whether he intended it so to be. His mockery would therefore seem to indicate that he saw no such morality in the picaresque: picarism was unnatural and monstrous. Rationalism, which Fielding saw as the natural and benevolent, was forced to defend itself against the picaresque idea.

As a "Shaftesburyan" fable, *Jonathan Wild* has a desperate tone that tries to counter the violently antithetical by means of supercilious privileged comedy, which assumes the right to ridicule what it has not made the effort to understand. *Jonathan Wild* fails as comedy, I think, precisely because it grows exasperated with, and mocks, the tragic sense of life.

## The Picaro as Satan: Smollett's *Count Fathom*

Smollett may be the first major English novelist to attempt a serious study of the criminal mind. A Colonel Jack or a Moll Flanders is always less expressive of criminal mentality than of what Ian Watt calls "the dynamics of economic individualism."[48] Jonathan Wild is a monstrous abstraction, a totem of the criminal class. Indeed, as we have just seen, Fielding did not think the subject suitable to the novel form: to release a vicious protagonist from the bonds of ironic allegory was to risk making him sympathetic. But Smollett, in his interesting but neglected third novel, *Ferdinand Count Fathom* (1753), drew a criminal to human scale, and sympathy for the confidence man becomes possible. "You hero of rogues, Count Fathom!" Herman Melville pointedly exclaimed.[49]

Novel form gave *Count Fathom* a seriousness that *Jonathan Wild* lacked. It was Smollett's novelistic concern, indeed, that led Sir Walter Scott, a shrewd critic of novels, to prefer *Fathom* to *Wild*:

He was, like a pre-eminent poet of our own day [Byron], a searcher of dark bosoms, and loved to paint characters under the strong agitation of fierce and stormy passions. Hence, misanthropes, gamblers, and duellists are as common in his works as robbers in those of Salvator Rosa, and are drawn, in most cases, with the same terrible truth and effect. To compare *Ferdinand Count Fathom* to the *Jonathan Wild* of Fielding would be perhaps unfair to the latter author; yet, the works being composed on the same plan (a very bad one, as we think), we cannot help placing them by the side of each other, when it becomes at once obvious that the detestable Fathom is a living and existing miscreant, at whom we shrink as from the presence of an incarnate fiend, while the villain of Fielding seems rather a cold personification of the abstract principle of evil, so far from being terrible that, notwithstanding the knowledge of the world argued in many passages of his adventures, we are compelled to acknowledge him absolutely tiresome.[50]

It was Smollett's achievement in *Count Fathom* to prefigure the rebellious satanism of a Byron. Smollett seems to have known he was attempting something new in the novel. In the apologetic Dedication to *Count Fathom* he seems to be reaching for precedent in Shakespearean drama. He knew the Spanish picaresque tradition and was probably writing in reaction to it when, in the first chapter of *Count Fathom*, he refers to readers "who delight in following Guzman d'Alfarache, through all the mazes of squalid beggery." But, if I surmise correctly, the probable influence on Smollett is the tradition of the Vice, from English morality plays to such Shakespearean villains as Aaron, Richard, Don John, and Iago, who are, as Spivak says, "neither human nor moral" and for whom evil is "solely an organic function and an artistic pleasure."[51]

Since the influence of the Vice tradition is but conjecture, it would be well to discuss a variety of other possible sources for *Count Fathom. Jonathan Wild* and *Tom Jones* are two. From *Gil Blas* Smollett possibly derives the structural motif of a double rise and fall. Other sources suggest themselves, among them *Guzmán de Alfarache, El Buscón,* and Grimmelshausen's *Der Landstörzerin Courasche*.[52] Smollett, in declaring that his purpose in portraying a confidence man is "to set him up as a beacon" to warn the unwary echoes the subtitle to *Guzmán,* "Atalaya de la vida humana." But the parallels between *Fathom* and *Buscón* are more formidable.[53] Both Fathom and Pablos are unscrupulous confidence tricksters, both satirize the society on which they prey, both are finally exposed and systematically reduced in circumstances, and yet both survive, shattered, to begin again elsewhere, Pablos in the New World, Fathom in the North of England. Both characters are psychologically motivated by shamefully weird origins. Pablos is the son of a witch; Fathom's mother is a murderous camp follower. More striking still is the similarity of the two novels in the presentation of character contrast if we assume that Smollett would see in Quevedo's aristocrat Diego no *converso* ironies. Fathom, like Pablos, becomes protégé of a noble family and school companion of the goodhearted and unsuspecting heir, and in both novels this apparent juxtaposition of good and evil forms the basis of the whole story. It is possible, then, that Smollett drew upon at least two Spanish picaresque novels in order to give depth and plausibility to his protagonist, with the result that Count Fathom seems half a Spanish picaro as well as half a romantic Satan.

But it is well to remember that Fathom is related to the earlier not-always-pleasant heroes, Roderick Random and Peregrine Pickle. In the novels (1748 and 1751) that bear these names the influence of Lesage on Smollett is great. Lesage, wrote Smollett in the Preface to *Roderick Random*, had furnished him with a model for the satiric novel, showing not only how to introduce satire "occasionally, in the course of an interesting story, which brings every incident home to life," and how to represent "familiar scenes in an uncommon and amusing point of view, invest-[ing] them with all the graces of novelty, while nature is appealed to in every particular" (1:iii), but also how to unify narrative and satire with a central adventurous hero:

The reader gratifies his curiosity, in pursuing the adventures of a person in whose favour he is prepossessed; he espouses his cause, he sympathizes with him in distress, his indignation is heated against the authors of his calamity; the human passions are inflamed; the contrast between dejected virtue, and insulting vice, appears with greater aggravation, and every impression having a double force on the imagination, the memory retains the circumstance, and the heart improves by the example. The attention is not tired with a bare Catalogue of characters, but agreeably diverted with all the variety of invention; and the vicissitudes of life appear in their peculiar circumstances, opening an ample field for wit and humour. [1:iv]

Smollett admires a novel in which the protagonist is exposed to the hostility of the world for the dual purpose of entertainment and satire. *Roderick Random* is to the purpose. "I have attempted," said Smollett of this novel, "to represent modest merit struggling with every difficulty to which a friendless orphan is exposed, from his want of experience, as well as from the selfishness, envy, malice, and base indifference of mankind" (Preface to *Roderick Random*, 1:viii). An orphan struggling against adverse circumstances was a typical picaresque scheme. But Rory, like Gil Blas, is not a picaro. He—as later, Perry—is an egoist and man of feeling, proud, defiant, passionate, persecuted by society but also superior to society. Often lonely, he is never an outcast. He makes friends—Bowling, Strap, Narcissa. His will, pitted against the hostile world and assisted by other wills sympathetic to it, is valuable in itself and comes to represent the opposition of nature to convention. Smollett's typical hero, then, may be described as a rebel. But the picaro lacked this romantic quality in that his rebelliousness contributed to social evil. The will of the picaro is so diseased that he cannot act successfully against the world. Indeed, Smollett believed some of the picaro's weakness had infiltrated the character of Gil Blas; he complains that Lesage had permitted Gil's transitions from distress to happiness to occur too suddenly, preventing "that generous indignation, which ought to animate the reader, against the sordid and vicious disposition of the world" (Preface to *Roderick Random*, 1:viii). The hero, through whose eyes the vicious world was to be seen, must be a trustworthy agent with whom the reader could identify; the protagonist had therefore to be actively and naturally opposed to worldly evil.

The character of Count Fathom, although morally the obverse of Rory's and Perry's, retains in some degree this natural function, their glory as rebels, by the very fact that novels cannot present human beings as altogether unnatural. By Smollett's own definition of a novel, Fathom is a legitimate novelistic hero: the novel, he writes in the Dedication to *Count Fathom*, "is a large diffused picture, comprehending the characters of life, disposed in different groups, and exhibited in various attitudes, for the purpose of a uniform plan, and general occurrence, to which every individual figure is subservient. But this plan cannot be executed with propriety, probability or success, without a principal personnage to attract the attention, unite the incidents, unwind the clue of the labyrinth, and at last close the scene by virtue of his own importance" (*Adventures of Ferdinand Count Fathom*, 1:v). Two types of novelistic hero, Smollett continues, are possible, "characters of transcendent worth" and those who are "object of our detestation and abhorrence." The former give us the pleasure of seeing virtue rewarded; the latter leave "a deep impression of terror upon the minds of those who were not confirmed in their pursuit of morality and virtue" (*Fathom*, 1:v). A new Gothic kind of catharsis justifies the depiction of a criminal hero. A criminal hero may continue the virtuous hero's function as satirist, subjecting "folly to ridicule, and vice to indignation" (*Fathom*, 1:viii). Thus Count Fathom, like Smollett's rebel heroes, is a satirist, at the same time that he is, more than they are, the object of satire. He denies the good in the name of nature and makes nature a power bent on destruction. Rebellion and resentment join in him, but the logic of resentment involves self-resentment, a subtlety beyond Smollett's power, so that the novel splits down the middle and Smollett declares revulsion with his hero.[54]

Obviously, my short description does not prove matters beyond a doubt, but it may suffice to show the direction in which Smollett was going. By inverting his usual plan and making his hero in *Count Fathom* a criminal, he did not recreate the picaro; rather, he extended the moral potency of his own earlier heroes whom he modeled after Gil Blas. *Count Fathom* must be examined more closely in an effort to account for Smollett's use (or probable use) of such a picaresque source as *El Buscón*.

Until Chapter LVII, when Smollett wrests ethical authority away from Fathom, the curve of Fathom's fortunes is not unlike that of a picaro's. Born during the insecurity of war, the cheerless but intelligent Ferdinand is adopted by Count Melvil as a servant and companion to his son Renaldo. Ferdinand soon learns to triumph over his good-natured master by means of stratagems that place his actions in a good light and Renaldo's in a bad (Chapters I–X). Despite a limited success, however, Ferdinand welcomes a chance to attend Renaldo in the wars in order to put himself beyond the fear of exposure to the count. He finds means to desert Renaldo, sets up as a cosmopolitan gambler and adventurer, assumes the title of count, and rises to the top of the English beau monde until his ambition overreaches itself and he is disgraced (Chapters XI–XXXVIII). At this point he is rescued by Renaldo, but, after attempting to ruin Renaldo and seduce the latter's fiancée Monimia, he is again disgraced (Chapters XXXIX–LVI). Now Smollett steps in, rejects Ferdinand as hero, and establishes Renaldo in that role. Renaldo has penetrated Fathom's disguise; he and Monimia are reunited; and in the last scene they forgive Fathom, by now reduced to poverty and the despondency of awakened conscience. Fathom is last seen commencing his atonement by marrying Elinor, a girl whom he had earlier seduced (Chapters LVII–LXVII).

The abrupt structural change in Chapter LVII—perhaps be-

cause of slavish imitation of dramatic form or of *Jonathan Wild*—
is all the more puzzling because of inconsistencies of tone. In the
early chapters there is a Quevedo-like irony, in some middle
chapters there is fine Gothic terror, and the novel ends as sentimental melodrama. But when, at one point, Smollett exclaims,
"Perfidious wretch! thy crimes turn out so atrocious, that I
half repent me of having undertaken to record thy memoirs!"
(*Fathom*, 2:91), we are curious to know why Smollett chose for
his story an unsympathetic hero. There are, perhaps, four explanations: (1) the biographical: Fathom projects something deep
in Smollett himself; (2) the picaresque: Fathom is an uncritical
extension of the picaro; (3) the satiric: Fathom is more a device
than a character; and (4) the philosophic: Fathom and Renaldo
represent abstract principles.

Lewis M. Knapp, Smollett's biographer, believes that Smollett
was in a peculiarly introspective frame of mind when he wrote
*Count Fathom*. He conjectures that "Doctor xxxxx" to whom
Smollett dedicates the novel is none other than Smollett himself. This could mean that in this novel Smollett unearthed and
reproved some of his characteristic weaknesses—coldness or resentment or impulsiveness, perhaps. "There were in Smollett,"
Knapp concludes, "two powerful forces, at times mutually an-
tagonistic, but, in the long run, essentially interlocking and com-
plementary. In many respects Smollett aspired to be, and was, a
typical rationalist, a typical satirist, and a conventionally aristocratic gentleman of the mid-eighteenth century. At the same
time, he was, in many respects, a man of ebullient and violent
feelings which often escaped from the leash of reason."[55]

The character of Fathom (the name implies depth and conceal-
ment) may, then, express something deep in his creator. What
makes Fathom particularly unpleasant is not his cunning or vice
but his lack of warmth and spontaneity, his brooding envy, and
his pointlessly exasperating sexual energy—in a word, his satanism. More than once Fathom is called Satan or "the devil himself" by victims, a meaning reinforced by recurrent images of
artfulness, acting, insinuating, practicing, deceiving, and disguising.[56] Was Smollett giving himself psychotherapy? Certainly
there is in *Count Fathom* a seething undercurrent of unexplained

emotion, almost, one might say, as in Conrad, a fascination with the abomination. This undercurrent flows in scenes that in the picaresque novels would have been matter-of-factly sardonic about evil but in Smollett subdue humor with strong suggestions of perversity. Seduction scenes in particular hold this quality. These vary in extravagance from Fathom's attempt to seduce Renaldo's sister with aphrodisiacs and pornography to his conquest of a credulous fifteen-year-old by means of a wicked Aeolean harp. Fathom takes no ordinary pleasure in his trickery and seems actively to dislike virtue. Thus he refrains from debauching a drunken country girl because "his appetite demanded a more perfect sacrifice than that which she could yield in her present deplorable situation, when her will must have been altogether unconcerned in his success" (1:225). Yet precisely the uncontrollable demoniac element engenders the structural control Smollett thought he had found when he switched the point of view from Fathom to Renaldo. In other words, the eighteenth-century rationalist stepped in to assert the nonpicaresque supremacy of order.

*Count Fathom* seems to draw upon picaresque tradition for psychological content. Ferdinand is born illegitimately during the upheaval of war and thus has a picaro's disturbed personality. He bitterly resents the heroic goodwill of Count Melvil and Renaldo because, one surmises, the Melvils remind him of his inferior origins. He overcompensates for his shame by means of elaborate trickery, and overexposure and disgrace follow. Yet he is unable to change until reduced to misery. But does this picaresque psychology of Fathom necessarily mean that Smollett drew critically from picaresque tradition? Too much, it seems to me, would be left unexplained if this were true. Fathom is not opposed by a cruel environment, but rather has no reason to doubt the existence of charity because he is often the object of it. The Melvils, Don Diego, Monimia, Madame Clement, and the good Jew Joshua contradict Fathom's misanthropy. *El Buscón* also could have been seen to present the existence of the good within the picaro's consciousness; unlike the picaro, however, Fathom may easily secure for himself a dignified place in society on condition that he conform his actions to reason. The picaresque psychology appears, then, to be taken over uncritically from picaresque tradition. As in *Colonel Jack*, so in *Count Fathom* an apparently picaresque hero is probably a version of the natural man whose subrational impulses lead him astray.

Another explanation of Smollett's choice of an unsympathetic hero is that Fathom is both a satirist and an object of satire.[57] In the Spanish picaresque novels, the concern was with the breakup of feudal society, thus giving the picaro a right to judge because social dissolution inevitably implied his own. In the eighteenth-century novels a typical hero such as Gil Blas judged society from his vantage point as representative of a social ideal. Smollett follows this practice in *Roderick Random* and *Peregrine Pickle*, novels in which the adventurer wanders forth as an exploitable object. But in *Count Fathom* the satiric elements are submerged in the hero and serve a double purpose: to expose the satirist as pathologically malcontent and his victims as dangerously sentimental. Smollett aims to satirize, not fundamental social disorder, but extravagance. Fathom is cold and selfish: he must learn to be less so. His victims are naive: they must learn to be wary. Both critiques are appropriate because Fathom's trickery is unnatural while his exposure of sentimentality is natural.

It is probable that Smollett sought in *Count Fathom* a middle ground between the philosophies of Hobbes and of Shaftesbury. Accordingly, Fathom is the natural man and Renaldo the man of feeling. There is in Fathom "a most insidious principle of self-love, that grew up with him from the cradle, and left no room in his heart for the least particle of social virtue" (1:25–26). Fathom's point of view is Hobbesian: "He had formerly imagined, but was now fully persuaded, that the sons of men preyed upon one another, and such was the end and condition of their being" (1:59). But self-love carried to extremes is, to Smollett, wrong. Equally wrong is social love carried to the sentimental extreme, as with Renaldo. Smollett is explicit. Referring to doctors who regard a bad reputation as a sign of success, he comments: "Success raised upon such a foundation would, by a disciple of Plato, and some modern moralists, be ascribed to the innate virtue and generosity of the human heart, which naturally espouses the cause that needs protection; but I, whose notions of human excellence are not quite so sublime, am apt to believe it is owing to that spirit of self-conceit and contradiction, which is, at least, as universal, if not as natural, as the moral sense so warmly contended for by those ideal philosophers" (2:125–26). If, then, we may accept Smollett's "spirit of self-conceit and contradiction" as indicative of his own philosophy,[58] it becomes clear that his literary purpose is nonpicaresque because Smollett believes that even a satanic picaro may yet become a man of feeling. When, in the final scene, Fathom sheds tears of gratitude, it is a characteristically eighteenth-century sign of grace. As Smollett states elsewhere in the novel, "There are some remains of religion left in the human mind even after every moral sentiment hath abandoned it" (1:43). Fathom, in short, suffers remorse but not the picaro's anguish.

A composite portrait of *Ferdinand Count Fathom* emerges from these four explanations of Smollett's choice of an unsympathetic hero. Preromantic and rationalist, Smollett sought to reconcile in this novel some standard contrarieties of his age. He may have borrowed from Spanish picaresque novels, but he was a nonpicaresque novelist. He was indignant at the follies and vices of mankind yet introspectively knew that the satirist could be deplorably wrong. And he observed in life how many fell short of happiness because of an imbalance of head or heart.

Artistically *Fathom* fails because of Smollett's uncertain attitude toward his material. Nevertheless, this novel presents in its protagonist an interesting link between the picaro and the romantic Satan. By opposing art to nature, Fathom already shows art in process of becoming natural, an intellectual transformation completed in the nineteenth century when the artist as satanic-and-Promethean hero emerges as champion of human liberty.

## The Escape of *Oliver Twist*

In the Preface to the Third Edition of *Oliver Twist* (1838) Dickens states that his intention had been to write a protest against romances of roguery: "I had read of thieves by scores—seductive fellows (amiable for the most part), faultless in dress, plump in pocket, choice in horseflesh, bold in bearing, fortunate in gallantry, great at a song, a bottle, pack of cards, or dicebox, and fit companions for the bravest. But I had never met (except in Hogarth) with the miserable reality. It appeared to me that to draw a knot of such associates in crime as really do exist: to paint them in all their deformity, in all their wretchedness, in all the squalid poverty of their lives . . . would be to attempt a something which was greatly needed" (pp. xvii–xviii). Hogarth had not been exceptional, however, and in the same preface Dickens declares that Cervantes, Defoe, Fielding, Smollett, Richardson, Goldsmith, and MacKenzie had also shown the "false glitter" (p. xx) of roguery.

Dickens had a thorough knowledge of picaresque novels and anatomies of roguery, judging by the catalogue of books in his library at the time of his death. Side by side with *A Select and Impartial Account of the Lives, Behaviour, and Dying-Words of the most remarkable Convicts* were English translations of *Lazarillo de Tormes*, *Guzmán de Alfarache*, *El Buscón*, and Cervantes's rogue anatomy, *Rinconete y Cortadillo*.[59]

There are significant parallels between *Rinconete y Cortadillo* and *Oliver Twist*. Cervantes describes how two idle young rogues, one a proficient pickpocket, the other a cardsharp, journey to Seville to join the monkish Monipodio's gang of thieves. Here are prototypes of Artful Dodger, Charley Bates, and Fagin. But one significance of these parallels is that both Cervantes and Dickens center interest on *picardía*, not on the picaro: both are anatomizing the objectively observed world of roguery.

This is not to say that Dickens lacks interest in the literary character of the picaro. One of the typical picaresque patterns had been the struggle of an unwanted child against a hostile environment, and this, as Sherman Eoff has shown, is an evident pattern in the early chapters of *Oliver Twist*.[60] Oliver, a lonely orphan reminiscent of Lazarillo, is born into a hostile and brutal world. He is systematically starved by Mr. Bumble, as Lazarillo had been by the priest of Maqueda and Pablos by the schoolmaster Cabra. Potentially a picaro, Oliver, "a parish child—the orphan of a workhouse—the humble, half-starved drudge—to be cuffed and buffeted through the world—despised by all, and pitied by none" (*Oliver Twist*, chap. 1), takes to the road, falls in with evil companions, and is well on his way to delinquency when the story takes a sudden nonpicaresque turn with the appearance on the scene of benevolent Mr. Brownlow. Then, having learned from Mr. Brownlow what charity is, Oliver has his natural rebelliousness fortified against corrupting influences, and eventually he escapes from *picardía*.

Dickens, although interested in the picaresque novel, was determined to prevent his hero from becoming a picaro. "I wished to show, in little Oliver," he declared, "the principle of Good surviving through every adverse circumstance, and triumphing at last" (*Oliver Twist*, p. xvii). Probably this antipathy to picarism had a source in Dickens's own childhood. When his father was jailed for debt and Dickens was put to work in a blacking warehouse, his sensibilities were deeply disturbed. He felt, he revealed to John Foster, a "secret agony of my soul as I sunk into this companionship," his hopes crushed "of growing up to be a learned and distinguished man"; he never forgot "the sense I had of being utterly neglected and hopeless." So bitter was the memory, in fact, that Dickens virtually locked it out, revealing it only in his art. He, too, he thought, might have been a picaro. "I know that I have lounged about the streets, insufficiently and unsatisfactorily fed. I know that, but for the mercy of God, I might easily have been, for any care that was taken of me, a little robber or a little vagabond."[61] Haunted by fear and loathing —and also, perhaps, by the attraction—of *picardía*, Dickens made certain that Oliver Twist would make a similar miraculous escape.

## Thackeray's *Barry Lyndon* as Deluded Gentleman

Luck is to Thackeray's *Barry Lyndon* (1844) what greatness is to *Jonathan Wild*. Whereas Fielding had been alarmed by the popular confusion of greatness with goodness, Thackeray was upset by the bogus morality of "good luck" and "bad luck." Both writers derived their moral positions from what they understood to be the observable truth in human nature.

Programmatic disgust with romanticizing roguery is evident in Thackeray's career. At the close of the first chapter of *Cath-*

*erine*, his "Newgate novel" of 1839, he declares: "Now, if we *are* to be interested in rascally actions, let us have them with plain faces, and let them be performed, not by virtuous philosophers, but by rascals. Another clever class of novelists adopt the contrary system, and create interest by making their rascals perform virtuous actions. Against these popular plans we here solemnly appeal. We say, let your rogues in novels act like rogues, and your honest men like honest men."[62] Thackeray's was a rigid, eighteenth-century concept of personality according to which every man would have a ruling passion. Along with Fielding, Thackeray probably would have thought the moral ambiguity of the Spanish picaresque novels hypocrisy.

This eighteenth-century orientation of Thackeray's art is evident in *Barry Lyndon*. Human nature is absolute. If Barry's life has a moral, Thackeray sermonizes in the final chapter,

it is that honesty is *not* the best policy. That was a pettifogger's maxim, who half admits he would be a rogue if he found his profit in it, and has led astray scores of misguided people both in novels and in the world, who forthwith set up the worldly prosperity or adversity of a man as standards by which his worth should be tried. Novelists especially make a most profuse, mean use of this pedlar's measure, and mete out what they call poetical justice. Justice, forsooth! Does human life exhibit justice after this fashion? Is it the good always who ride in gold coaches, and the wicked who go to the workhouse? Is a humbug never preferred before a capable man? Does the world always reward merit, never worship cant, never raise mediocrity to distinction? . . . Sometimes the contrary occurs, so that fools and wise, bad men and good, are more or less lucky in their turn, and honesty is "the best policy," or not, as the case may be. If this be true of the world, those persons who find their pleasure or get their livelihood by describing its manners and the people who live in it are bound surely to represent to the best of their power life as it really appears to them to be. . . . Who knows, then, but the old style of Molière and Fielding, who drew from nature, may come into fashion again, and replace the terrible, the humourous, always the genteel impossible now in vogue? Then, with the sham characters, the sham *moral* may disappear.[63]

Things as they are: this, above all, is what a post-Cartesian rationalist and realist sets out to describe because there is always the assumption that there is an order of reality open to the observation of truthful men. To an early Victorian such as Thackeray there is a name for this truth-seeking man of reason, the gentleman, lineal descendent of the *honnête homme*, the man who knows his place. And it comes about that Thackeray's Barry Lyndon represents the degraded ideal, the bogus gentleman, the self-deluded and unnatural scoundrel finding room at the top in spite of the fact that real gentlemen disapprove of him.

If *Barry Lyndon* be placed in evidence, there lingered on into the nineteenth century some ugly vestiges of the eighteenth-century code of honor. Dueling, gambling, heavy drinking—urbane vices urbanely fobbed off on an Irish pariah—may still have survived as honorable. And in any case the code of the gentleman suffered from the ambiguous ethics of industrial society to which the snob, humbug, or scoundrel found ready access. Thackeray used the old novelistic theme of appearance and reality. By upholding his bogus gentleman as honorable, he achieves a rhetorical effect akin to Mark Antony's oration, irony cries havoc, and then proceeds to create it unpleasantly on all sides. What remains, however, is not the manly Brutus but rather the rhetoric imposing itself between the reader and the self-revealing and self-deluding brute who cannot know his ideals are obsolete. (Stanley Kubrick's motion picture based upon *Barry Lyndon* omits most of the rhetoric and makes Barry sensitive and sympathetic.)

Cervantes is the great progenitor of the novel in which the hero is deluded. But whereas Don Quixote mistakes appearances for reality yet really sees in appearances a higher spiritual reality—the soul of the deluded hero dignifies his delusions—Barry Lyndon merely boasts the wrong kind of gentlemanly dash and reveals crude egotism. Barry is a brutalized Quixote.

But is a brutalized Quixote a picaro? At times Barry seems to have the picaro's heritage. Born into a seedily aristocratic Irish family that prides itself on dubious royal descent, Barry does have a picaro's perverted education. Spoiled by grandiose pretensions, he comes to see virtues in his brutish actions that in others he condemns as vices. He is incapable, however, of learning from experience, whereas the picaro found in experience a confirmation of the dogmatism in his outlook. From juvenile duels to the vicious life of a Prussian soldier, from swindler and

gambler to fortune hunter and rakish English landlord, Barry
steers an increasingly odious course, but stupidly defends himself
as honorable or, at worst, motivated by necessity. Thus after an
ugly scheme of blackmail proves lucky, he comments: "I say
that anything is fair in love, and that men so poor as myself can't
afford to be squeamish about their means of getting on in life.
The great and rich are welcomed, smiling, up the grand staircase
of the world; the poor but aspiring must clamber up the wall, or
push and struggle up the back stair, or, *pardi*, crawl through any
of the conduits of the house, never mind how foul and narrow,
that lead to the top. . . . What is life good for but for honour?
and that is so indispensable, that we should attain it anyhow"
(*Barry Lyndon*, p. 146). The passage reveals in style and morality
a critique of struggle-for-existence principles that has been met
with before in *Lazarillo de Tormes*; and in a sense the critique
maintains itself in the pattern of characterization when Barry's
principles effect his reduction to a simpering fool. Barry therefore recalls the picaro in three of his aspects: he has the sense of
illusion about his disreputable past; his will constructs honorable
appearances by dishonorable methods; and he rationalizes the
failure to achieve membership in approved society as a misfortune caused by the corrupt ways of the world. Nevertheless,
in this instance a brutalized Quixote is not truly a picaro: the
illusions are delusions. Barry does not develop or reveal that
kind of honesty with himself that might permit him to escape
convention. He *is*. Thackeray presents Barry's insatiable craving
for wealth and title, not as the plausible outgrowth of a false
ideal in the mind of an unwanted child, but as ruling passion.
Barry's dishonorable actions originate, not in the picaro's frustrated attempt to gain a recognized social standing, but in his
own belief that he is, in fact, honorable. And thus, unlike the
picaro in symbolic deceptiveness, Barry, believing in his own
pretensions, never seriously passes himself off as other than he
thinks he is. He is one of the possessed. Finally, the lack in *Barry
Lyndon* of the double plane of the picaresque novel whereby
both picaro and society disintegrate makes it clear that Thackeray's brute could be integrated into the good were he not, by
nature, evil. The reality of goodness comes out in the novel by

means of the Fieldingesque irony that good people may be silly but may also be right. Since his seedy family is not impoverished or unkindly, Barry earns no sympathy by pleading necessity. Barry Lyndon, by this analysis, is not a picaro.

Thackeray's novel, called by Chandler "altogether the most powerful in the range of picaresque fiction,"[64] transforms some conventions of the picaresque but does not continue the myth of the picaro. Such power as this novel has would derive, it seems to me, from Thackeray's realism—realism that is nonpicaresque because, by treating picarism as brutal delusion, it permits truth, somewhere in this world of vanity, to exist.

From this short analysis of novels representative of the picaresque strain in the eighteenth and early nineteenth centuries, I conclude that picarism was at most an antithesis to, and within, realism and that the myth of the picaro does not form the underlying structure of novels in France or England during the period. But, hesitant to dismiss the notion that the picaresque idea may have become a submerged element in the novel, particularly the English novel, I have proposed that we could criticize these novels as a dialectical form of the picaresque. I have tried to account for the shift in the literary fortunes of the picaro by reference to the intellectual history of the period from the middle of the seventeenth century to the middle of the nineteenth. The rise of rationalism, Protestantism, and capitalism took from the picaro his role as religious outcast and created for the individual a new worldly salvation. This new idea of order achieves expression in those very novels that seem, on the surface, to be the most picaresque. Further, I have argued that the myth of the picaro, the literary idea of disintegration, carries over into another myth, Hobbes's myth of the natural man; yet even here, where it is possible to trace in the English novel a tragic awareness of disintegrating forces, it is also possible to see how natural man exists, through conversion, in a manner contrary to the picaro's literary existence. The idea of disintegration looms as a threat—I noted some of these threatening aspects particularly in Defoe and Smollett—but it remains as an idea incapable of overthrowing period assumptions about the nature of man and the universe.

# 4

# The Symbolic Confidence Man

In discussion of the Spanish picaresque novelists I noted that their creative imagination foundered on an empirical approach to reality. The truth of the inherited medieval world seemed remote from actual life. The moral and spiritual inadequacy of the picaro was more pathetic than that of Quixote and less ridiculous and less winning because the picaro's reality was not elevated by delusion. The imagination could not guide its problem child, the picaro, into saving relation to the dogmatic truth. The social order could not save one who had been pressed toward inner stagnation by the hostility of the order itself.

In eighteenth- and early nineteenth-century novels the protagonist, no longer a true picaro, once more moved within a social reality because an author's creative imagination could accept society as the human imitation of universal truth. The protagonist might travel, go adrift morally—but sooner or later his innate powers of reason could return him to the community. With new confidence an author's imagination could now journey outward into a world giving back the rich and regenerative life of appearances. Yet faith in a religion of reason did not last. Not only would the nature of reality come under skeptical scrutiny but appearances would become impenetrable masks, the world a stage, and the existence of truth so dubious as to eliminate any difference between it and fiction.

As more and more writers observed a world grown abstract and material, their imaginations broke away from empirical limitations and engaged themselves in a quest for higher truth. The mind became a symbol, engaged in symbolic activity, the journey of vision, the personal quest for transcendent order away from the indeterminate appearances of history. And thus the symbolist writer stood for a vision that at any given moment might fuse for him the real world and the represented world, the world as nature and the world as idea. In the nineteenth century the creative imagination assumed a new relation to the truth and became the special instrument for its revelation.

But the art of the symbolist was precarious. In the words of Charles Feidelson, it was an art that walked "a thin line between [the symbolist's] theoretical premises and certain practical conditions which, if fully admitted, would render his premises null and void."[1] The self became the locus of meaning, the world the locus of meaninglessness. But to lose confidence in the self was to sink the imagination back into the world and to make the meaningful and the meaningless, God and devil, seem one, and reality, or this imminent loss of meaning, a version of hell. In other words, there was a Nemesis in the symbol-making activity itself: too much faith was bound up in the powers of the poetic genius, the reality-destroying artist. If for some art was superior to life, for example, Henry James's assertion, "It is art that *makes* life"[2]—for others, art was less to be worshiped than feared. Some writers saw in the artist a limited human being who, in his attempt to disenchant the material world, might in fact be leading it, and himself, further astray. Such a skeptical and disillusioned writer, particularly, it would seem, toward the middle of the nineteenth century, felt a crippling—though possibly comic—sense of self-distrust that mocked as a hoax the claim that in art all-reconciling truth could be found and whispered that all cultural enterprise was a joke, a great confidence trick of civilization; it was a sense that might assert at last that there was evil, the evil of the world, of nihilism, of the devil, at the heart of existence.

The potential subversion of imagination by latent ambiguities in its activity gave rise, I think, to a situation not unlike that felt by the Spanish picaresque novelists—a situation of spiritual frustration. Certainly at this time the myth of the picaro reestablished itself in writers' minds as an image or symbol of disintegration, expressed as the confidence man.

The symbolistic picaresque or part-picaresque writers I will discuss—Herman Melville, Mark Twain, Nicolai Gogol, and Thomas Mann—all, in one way or another, seem to be concerned with the disintegration theme in one or all of its projections as the disintegration of reality (the problem of knowledge), the disintegration of goodness (the problem of morality), and the disintegration of trust (the problem of faith). But where the Spanish picaresque novels show disintegration as a process, as a human happening in time, as a movement of spiritual death, the symbolic picaresque novels take disintegration as symbol, as a state of being in some way nonhuman. The symbolic confidence man may represent a universal paradox, a "something that is nothing," and, when he appears, his character is unreal or at least opaque and impenetrable because reality has become endlessly contingent; and if ill will enters into his con game, he is also grotesque. Indeed, as a creature of nihilism the symbolic confidence man seems to be at times actively engaged in the destruction of whatever reality, goodness, and trust remain in the living world. If the Spanish picaro is the victim of an atomizing process, the symbolic confidence man is the atomizer, incarnate destructiveness, devil, man, or civilization.

In one restrictive sense the new symbol-making picaresque novelists do not write "novels"; that is the sense in Lionel Trilling's assertion that the "classic intention" of the novel is "the investigation of the problem of reality beginning in the social field."[3] The tradition—perhaps the great tradition of the English novel—supports the assertion and provides the restriction. To Fielding, Jane Austen, George Eliot, or Anthony Trollope the individual is interesting in relation to history and society, and the novel form is concerned with the richness of nuance and tone that the social field provides. But the novel form may obviously do more, while remaining, by and large, novel form. The new, like the old, picaresque novelists looked inward, away from social rootlessness or cultural catastrophe. And they appeared in countries where the traditionally historical commitment of the novel was not, at the time, the easily authentic form. New forms, responsive to passions and ideas as well as to manners, were called for—and the forms found by Melville, Twain, Gogol, and Mann tended to be antihistorical. These new picaresque novelists created mythopoetically, not denying the agony of historical man, but seeking a peace revealed within, behind, or around him. Accordingly, their ideas of the novelist's art and function tended to be religious, even mystical, a rhetoric of fiction that was also a metaphysics. Melville declares (perhaps too playfully) that readers of fiction look "for more reality, than real life itself can show" (*The Confidence-Man*, p. 206). Gogol claims that the poet should live apart from the marketplace: "Like a silent monk he lives in the world without belonging to it and his pure, spotless soul speaks only to God."[4] Twain tried to express the comfort of the ineffable beyond history, as in this passage from *Huckleberry Finn*: "When it was dark I set by my campfire smoking, and feeling pretty satisfied; but by-and-by it got sort of lonesome, and so I went and set on the bank and listened to the currents washing along, and counted the stars and drift-logs and rafts that come down, and then went to bed; there ain't no better way to put in time when you are lonesome; you can't stay so, you soon get over it" (p. 34). Thomas Mann writes of the search for a schema of myth in every human life: "For the myth is the foundation of life; it is the timeless schema, the pious formula into which life flows when it reproduces its traits out of the unconscious. . . . What is gained is an insight into the higher truth depicted in the actual."[5] It is evident that these writers attempted to represent through novel form an inner vision that yearned for the continents of thought and feeling beyond reason. Sometimes their feeling for life is a feeling for the episodic, life as serial encounters rather than as a historical problem. Giving structure to their works is symbolism—a symbolism that, from one point of view, is antihistorical, antirealistic, and perhaps antinovelistic.

Nor did the new picaresque novelists merely dissent from the contemporary cultural milieu. There can be a certain romance in dissent; it can appear as satiric content, as in *Tom Jones* or *Hard Times*, and yet make of the protest indulged some traditional appeal to reason. But in the picaresque novelist's world that appeal, too, looks pretentious; skepticism, disillusionment, spiritual torment hold sway; satire simply dissolves all. And when there is some form of reconciliation with an objective world, there is its eccentricity.

Although the symbolic picaresque and part-picaresque novels were achieved by writers sensitive to Spanish literature, this is not to claim that direct influence of *Lazarillo*, *Guzmán*, *Buscón*, or *Quixote*, although possible, was necessary to their writing. Melville, for example, owned *Guzmán* and *Quixote* and borrowed *Lazarillo*. Gogol, Twain, and Mann possibly knew Spanish novels other than *Quixote*. There is some room for speculation that the confidence man as presented by Gogol and Melville, representing self-love, derives from an inversion of the character of Quixote, regarded as a symbol of idealism. Mann has left a curious note concerning such inversion: "What," he wondered while reading Cervantes in 1934, "would a Don Quixote at the other extreme be like? Anti-idealistic, sinister, a pessimistic believer in force—and yet a Don Quixote? A brutalized Don Quixote? Even Cervantes, with all his melancholic humour, had not gone so far as to conceive that."[6] Directly influenced or not, the new picaresque novelists have been apt to feel attracted to a literature of free design, ironical temper, and, above all, religious or metaphysical idea and myth.

## The Picaresque Archetype in America

American literature of the nineteenth century offers the possibility of a more-or-less spontaneous development of picaresque myth.[7] First, the archetypal American of literary myth is a lonely, rootless Adam with some natural resemblance to the picaro—the solitary feudal outcast—of Spanish novelistic myth. Second, an acquisitive American trickster not unlike the Spanish picaro appears in the oral and journalistic humor of the growing nation, a trickster who may be accounted for as the literary outgrowth of life on the American frontier. Scholarly evidence assembled in recent years supports the idea of the spontaneous appearance of the American trickster. Folklorists have pointed to the existence of an indigenous trickster hero.[8] Specialists in American humor have traced the development of a popular antihero, the Yankee, from his appearance on the stage and in newspaper sketches of the late eighteenth and early nineteenth centuries to his emergence as a poor white squatter in the conscious literature of the Old Southwest during the period from the triumph of Jacksonian democracy in the early 1830s to the Civil War.[9] Third, both Melville's *Confidence-Man* (1857) and Twain's *Huckleberry Finn* (1884), major novels in which American tricksters appear, may be seen as closely related to the tradition of southwestern humor.[10]

The note of desolation that appears in American literature in such diverse works as Poe's *Fall of the House of Usher* and Eliot's *The Waste Land* has wilderness for a theme. For, from the beginning, the American is a lost person faced with the necessity of creating durable selfhood out of conflict with nature and time. He is—as Cooper's saga of Leatherstocking makes particularly clear—a solitary innocent, an Adam emancipated from history, from the Europe of the mind, and existing morally prior to the world, yet endlessly moving into the world that provides experience.[11] His natural home, as Melville wrote in *Moby-Dick*, is "that unfallen, western world, which to the eyes of the old trappers and hunters revived the glories of those primeval times when Adam walked majestic as a god, bluff-browed and fearless" (p. 188). Significantly, the heroic view is already fading into nostalgia. If, at first, the encounters between the radically self-reliant outsider and the alien world seemed heroic, in time the mood of some writers responding to the American experience shifted to the tragic. Leatherstocking, who begins as a comic Yankee, Natty Bumppo, and then acquires heroic stature, is last seen as a broken outcast of a hostile, encroaching civilization. Just so, Melville's Captain Ahab is both heroic and tragic: carrying to extremes the assault of self against the world, Ahab destroys not only himself but all but one of his crew. Ahab is Adam desolate: "I feel deadly faint, bowed, and humped," he cries to Starbuck, "as though I were Adam, staggering beneath the piled centuries since Paradise" (*Moby-Dick*, p. 535).

Questions were being raised by the middle of the nineteenth century that persist today in the aftermath of foreign wars: how innocent is this American Adam? Is self-reliant individualism a partially inadequate democratic faith? Is there not a great truth in that Calvinistic "power of darkness,"[12] that lingering puritan suspicion that Adam himself may be leagued with the devil? Melville, in particular, raises such questions in his work, and they rise from the sense that there are two Americas striding· forth in Adam's guise, the one creative and Promethean, the other destructive and satanic.

The general historical analysis is that there is what Marius Bewley, following others such as Frederick Jackson Turner, calls a "basic split or tension in American experience,"[13] antagonism between Europe and America (later, East and West), aristocracy and democracy, city and country, opportunism and other-world-liness or idealism. The man who went West was both civilizer and destroyer. And thus, as Thomas P. Abernethy has observed, the first offspring of the West was not democracy, but arrant opportunism; and further: "The frontier spawned other evil off-spring as well. While it gave men freer play for the exercise of individualism, at the same time it took them out of contact with cultural influences and established the crass and superficial equalitarianism of the Jackson period for the relatively conserva-tive but constructive ideas of Thomas Jefferson."[14] Individual-ism passed over into commercialism and from there to Manifest Destiny: expansionism was God's plan for America, for had not God been called upon to uphold the inalienable rights of 1776? Pushed to defend itself, the American mind would always affirm the mystical apprehension of God. But a critical minority saw in such American idealism an ambiguous reality. One such was Melville, who had been at sea during the heyday of expansionism and had observed the havoc wrought by· Western civilization among the primitive Polynesians. In book after book Melville declared that God was past finding out—a private declaration of independence from the shallow democratic faith of his era.[15]

Thus there could be two versions of Adam, both appearing in classic American literature. In *The Confidence-Man* Adam is trick-ster and tricked, the gullible and the tempted, or the misanthropic devil masquerading as Promethean civilizer. In *Huckleberry Finn* Adam as radical innocent takes Huck's form, but all along the frontier he encounters those other Adams, the destroyers. Both

Melville and Twain see American civilization tottering on the brink of collapse because of self-inspired illusion. The ideals of justice and brotherhood, they find, are being undermined by persons devoted to selfish and material ends. Yet the grand deception is a pretentious belief in fugitive and cloistered virtue: Adam, protesting innocence and benevolence but engaged in or because of corruption, might not be a radical new person emancipated from history, but might instead be history personified. And thus the disintegrated picaros in *The Confidence-Man* and *Huckleberry Finn* are multiform cosmopolitans, symbols of corrupt civilization. They wear the masks of American idealism; behind their masks they seek to bring about its collapse.

The literary symbol of the American was Adam; the popular symbol was the Yankee, that sharp-witted Brother Jonathan who tricked old John Bull. The Yankee trickster appeared in cycles of short tales, fables, and plays, and he was consistently mythical: all efforts to reach his inner character failed. He was, as Constance Rourke has written, "a symbol of triumph, of adaptability, of irrepressible life—of many qualities needed to induce confidence and self-possession among a new and unamalgamated people."[16] But conspicuously missing from the Yankee's typical qualities was any hint of moral grandeur, as, for example, in General David Humphrey's *The Yankey in England* (ca. 1815). This is Humphrey's stock description: "Made up of contrarieties —simplicity and cunning; inquisitive from natural and excessive curiosity, confirmed by habit; credulous from inexperience and want of knowledge of the world; believing himself to be perfectly acquainted with whatever he partially knows; tenacious of prejudices; docile, when rightly managed; when otherwise treated independent to obstinacy; easily betrayed into ridiculous mistakes; incapable of being awed by external circumstances; suspicious, vigilant and quick of perception, he is ever ready to parry or repel the attacks of raillery by retorts of rustic and sarcastic, if not original and refined wit and humor."[17] The "contrarieties" planted in Humphrey's homespun yokel—the juxtaposed innocence and cunning—are the seeds of a double transformation of the Yankee into trickster and victim. As to the trickster aspect, the Yankee soon appeared as that vagabond sharpster, the Yankee peddler.

To judge by the sober words of President Timothy Dwight of Yale, the real Yankee peddler did not fall far short of legendary proportions:

All the evils, which are attendant upon the bartering of small wares, are incident to this, and every other mode of traffic of the same general nature. Many of the young men, employed in this business, part, at an early period, with both modesty, and principle. Their sobriety is exchanged for cunning, their honesty for imposition; and their decent behavior for coarse impudence. Mere wanderers, accustomed to no order, control, or worship; and directed solely to the acquisition of petty gains; they soon fasten upon this object; and forget every other, of a superior nature. The only source of their pleasure or their reputation is gain; and that, however small, or however acquired, secures both. No course of life tends more rapidly, or more effectually, to eradicate every moral feeling. [*Travels in New England*][18]

The legend had grown by 1833 when Thomas Hamilton, a foreign observer, wrote *Men and Manners in America*: "The whole race of Yankee peddlers in particular are proverbial for dishonesty. They go forth annually in the thousands to lie, cog, cheat, swindle, in short, to get possession of their neighbour's property in any manner it can be done with impunity. Their ingenuity in deception is confessedly very great."[19] The unsavory reputation of the Yankee peddler did not attend James Fenimore Cooper's character of Harvey Birch in *The Spy* (1821), but it was singularly present by the time Thomas Chandler Haliburton described Sam Slick of Slickville, Connecticut, in the *Clockmaker* series of 1836.

Haliburton, a conservative Nova Scotian judge who wished to warn his countrymen about their base democratic neighbors, portrayed in Sam Slick, the clock peddler, a shrewd, garrulous parasite with an inherent love of barter. Although Haliburton introduced a secondary character, the squire, as mouthpiece of his own opinions—and thus elevated himself by making the Yankee peddler appear correspondingly low—the sayings and doings of the Yankee trickster were responsible for the great vogue of the *Clockmaker* series in the United States and Great

Britain.[20] Haliburton made the Yankee peddler a symbol of American culture and tried to find in the squire a point of view for his dissent. Both the symbolism and the point of view were to turn up in later American literature.

The Yankee peddler, real and fictitious, traveled South, and in the frontier region between the southern Appalachians and the Mississippi, then called the Southwest, the acquisitive, amoral Yankee underwent a literary transformation as the poor white squatter.

Suddenly in the 1830s conservative lawyers, doctors, and journalists in the southwestern region began to write local-color sketches for the widely distributed New York sporting paper, the *Spirit of the Times*.[21] These relatively cultured writers, aware of the older tradition of the East, were roused to fear and laughter by the rampaging frontier environment. On one side were the gentlemen (themselves) and on the other were the rogues. The contrast was evident in what the Virginia-born lawyer Joseph G. Baldwin wrote of the "flush times": "Superior to many of the settlers in elegance of manners and general intelligence, it was the weakness of the Virginian to imagine he was superior too in the essential art of being able to hold his hand and make his way in a new country, and especially *such* a country, and at *such* a time. What a mistake that was! . . . All the habits of his life, his taste, his associations, his education—everything—the trustingness of his disposition—his want of business qualifications—his sanguine temper—all that was Virginian in him, made him the prey, if not of imposture, at least of unfortunate speculations" (*Flush Times of Alabama and Mississippi*, pp. 66–67).

Gentlemen and rogues: the contrast was basic to the humor of the old southwestern stories. But the situations of humor were a matter of anxious concern to the writers themselves, largely for political reasons. According to Kenneth Lynn, the most important fact about the best-known southwestern writers—August B. Longstreet, William T. Thompson, T. B. Thorpe, Joseph G. Baldwin, Johnson J. Hooper—is that they were all opposed to Andrew Jackson. They were professional men, conservatives, either planter-aristocrats or Whigs or both. Fearing the encroaching national power of the Jacksonian "rabble" and exposed to the competitive scramble of the new country, they seized on the cunning and clownish folk hero as symbol for the mob of poor whites and made him an outrageous, indeed demoniac, stranger to social order.[22]

The southwestern rogue developed rapidly in the pages of the *Spirit of the Times.* Appearing first as a loafer and pickpocket at country race tracks, he then began to emerge as a cardsharp, actor, impostor, and confidence trickster. A favorite stage for acting his roles became the deck of a Mississippi steamboat— soon to be the stage for Melville's *Confidence-Man.* By the 1850s the American rogue was well entrenched in the popular consciousness.

One southwestern writer stands out above the others as the creator of an American rogue with a dimension as symbolic picaro: Johnson J. Hooper. Johnson Hooper was a cultured North Carolinian with a distinguished background. His great-uncle was a signer of the Declaration of Independence; his mother was directly descended from Jeremy Taylor, "the Shakespeare of divines." Because of a decline in the family fortunes Hooper moved as a young man to the Alabama frontier in 1835, there to practice law, champion the Indians against white man's fraud, edit a weekly paper devoted to Whig politics, and eventually become a leading figure in the Confederate government. Hooper's sketches started appearing in the *Spirit of the Times* in 1843; two years later these were collected in book form as the *Adventures of Captain Simon Suggs,* a work that, in more than one of its chapters, equals *Huckleberry Finn* in comic art.[23]

*Simon Suggs,* though not completely novelistic, is a considerable artistic achievement. In it for the first time in southwestern humor the author all but removed himself from the narrative as a mediating influence between the confidence man and the reader. The gentleman retired behind a curtain of irony and left the stage, for the most part, to the rogue. The result—comparable in its way to Quevedo's removal of Alemán's direct moralizing and reminiscent of Rojas's Celestinesque irony—is that the world represented through the warped mind of Simon Suggs, forerunner of Faulkner's Flem Snopes, seems dark and degraded. Moral standards are dissolved in Simon's favorite motto, "It's good to be shifty in a new country" (*Adventures of Captain Simon Suggs*, p. 12). Simon, while clearly symbolic of wild and diabolic Jacksonian equalitarianism, nevertheless wins the reader's partial sympathy when he outsmarts the gross, greedy world.

Hooper fashioned his collected stories as a parody of political campaign biography. Simon Suggs, explains the ironically reverent biographer, is running for office. Voters must be familiarized with his features; thus, for example, Simon is said to have a four-inch mouth on which "an ever-present sneer—not all malice, however—draws down the corners" (p. 11), as well as those stock features of the Yankee trickster—today of the cartoon Uncle Sam—a long, sharp nose and hard, bright eyes. But later these details of Simon's appearance add to the symbolism of his character. Defending the usefulness of campaign biographies, the narrator declares that they enable "all the country [to keep] in its mind's eye, an image of a little gentleman with a round, oily face—sleek, bald pate, delicate whiskers, and foxy smile . . . [called] Martin Van Buren; and future generations of naughty children who will persist in sitting up when they should be abed, will be frightened to their cribs by the lithograph of 'Major General Andrew Jackson,' which their mammas will declare to be a faithful representation of the Evil One—an atrocious slander, by the bye, on the potent, and comparatively well-favoured, prince of the infernal world" (p. 9). Later still, there is a reference to "the nation's Jackson and the country's Suggs" (p. 82),[24] and thus, while it is apparent that Hooper's parody biography is something of an afterthought, the symbolic suggestiveness of the confidence man is built up.

*Simon Suggs* unfolds as the story of civilization running amuck. Son of an itinerant frontier preacher, Simon takes early to cards, tempts his father to "cut jack," secures the family horse—which closely resembles Don Quixote's Rocinante—and hits the trail. When Simon next appears, he is married, the father of a large pinewoods family, and known all over Tallapoosa County as an unscrupulous speculator in Indian lands. His specialty is the confidence trick. In successive episodes he outwits greedy strangers by posing as a rich planter, a senator, and a wealthy Kentucky hog-drover. But he has a certain quixotic delusion: he is convinced that he can beat the faro machine in spite of consistent losses. The first few episodes of *Simon Suggs* are thus concentrated upon the characterization of the confidence man. But in the latter part of the book the social landscape is broadened to include the whole morally degraded frontier. With his fellow citizens Simon joins in a cruel swindle of the Creek Indians; then, as rumor spreads that the Creeks plan revenge, Simon, privately informed of the rumor's falsity, fans the fears of the ignorant villagers into a drunken blaze, has himself named captain, declares martial law, and turns the hysteria to his own profit by fining those who stumble across the sentry lines. The hysterical and, of course, Jacksonian mob is even more grotesquely presented when Simon attends a revivalist meeting. Singled out by the ecstatic congregation as a well-known sinner, he twitches, grovels in the dust, and screams "Gloree!" to signify his sudden miraculous redemption. To the tearful crowd he confesses that he has just overcome Satan, who had appeared to him in the shape of an alligator; then, having won confidence and passed the collection plate, Simon disappears into the swamps. It is not his last, but it is his most memorable trick, and forty years later Mark Twain imitated the camp-meeting scene, for similar reasons, in *Huckleberry Finn.*

The *Adventures of Captain Simon Suggs* combines several elements of the picaresque idea. In its limited fashion, it is concerned with the disintegration of reality, goodness, and trust. The limitations are that it is too episodic to be a novel and too concerned with local politics to be serious. The fascinating picaresque aspect is that evil is represented on two planes, individual and social, for the confidence man fulfills the degraded desires of society and in this "benefit" appears ironically as the people's true representative. In short, Simon Suggs comes across more as a symbol than as a person, even as the Yankee had before him. And what he symbolizes ultimately, through the references to Simon as Jackson and as devil, is a violent splitting apart of society from culture and of materialism and opportunism from the control of an older order of American democratic ideals.

Although Simon's camp-meeting trick recalls the scene in *Lazarillo de Tormes* when the pardoner's cohort faked epileptic seizure in order to gull a superstitious congregation, it is difficult to know whether Hooper knew the Spanish picaresque novels. He did, apparently, admire *Don Quixote*,[25] and there are hints of Cervantes's influence in *Simon Suggs*, such as the lean appearance of Simon, the touch of delusion, the withered horse. But in the absence of proof it may be assumed that Hooper drew his symbolic confidence man mainly from a knowledge of life on the frontier and of American humor.

It is axiomatic that a myth may be spontaneously reborn. Out of native folkloric and literary materials, a trickster hero emerged in the United States. When narrative structures fused this content with the idea of disintegration, the myth of the picaro surfaced once more.

## Melville's Picaresque Myth: *The Confidence-Man*

Herman Melville went to Illinois in the summer of 1840, and in the light of his portrayal of the West years later in *The Confidence-Man*, the date is significant.[26] The 1840s were the heyday of the democratic faith, the expansionist ethics, and the Transcendental philosophy that Melville came to satirize; they were also the heyday of the native American humor that was to provide Melville's novel with its comic key. The western trip—to Galena, Illinois, and probably thence to St. Louis and Cairo, Illinois, by steamboat—proved of short duration. Seeking to restore his family fortunes elsewhere, Melville took ship for the South Seas, and the genius who might have wasted in the fever-ridden West took hold of life at sea, lost provincialism, and gained deep insights into human nature far from the national heartland. But Melville was no common seaman. Well-born and well-educated, earnest and sensitive by nature, Melville might easily have figured as the hero in a contemporary romance.[27] To an extent aware of this himself, his first works were semiautobiographical: *Typee* (1846), *Omoo* (1847), *Redburn* (1850), *White-Jacket* (1850), and, above all, *Pierre* (1852). Yet even sensitive Pierre Glendenning is not completely a Herman Melville, for Melville was too high-minded to accept a sentimental version of himself as a child of misfortune. Refusing to sentimentalize himself, he was also skeptical of the self-righteous sentimentalism that seemed to blind his countrymen to American realities. From the start of his literary career in 1846 to his withdrawal from the public view ten years later, Melville never feared to be outspoken in his criticism. *Typee* and *Omoo* revealed unpleasant truths about the missions in Polynesia; *Mardi* (1849) canvassed the creeds and cultures of history, including Christianity, and found all wanting; *Redburn* called attention to the appalling suffering of the poor in Liverpool; *White-Jacket* was intended to promote the abolition of flogging in the American navy; and *Moby-Dick* (1851) was, on one of its planes of meaning, a vote of no confidence in the nineteenth-century cult of individualism. With *The Confidence-Man* Melville brought his spirit of criticism boldly to focus on the American heartland.

Melville's is a spirit of criticism rather than of satire, I think, because satire implies the upholding of widely shared moral standards—and the moral standards of his contemporaries were being called into question. Certainly a major theme of Melville's works after *Mardi* is the soul's quest for unity. That part of him that drew for inspiration upon European and American thought of the Enlightenment came into conflict with that part of him that was romantic and inwardly compelled to seek for some vision of the whole. The result was tension, even anguish; but, of course, the degree of Melville's spiritual anguish remains debatable. Thus for a long time Melville's biographers tended to baptize him in the name of the devil. D. H. Lawrence saw Melville as the white destroyer of the Dark Gods,[28] and some others saw Melville as a bitter Timonist, Captain Ahab himself.[29] Precisely what is omitted from such accounts—Melville's humor, warmth, love of life and letters, earnest and responsible conduct of public and private affairs—makes Melville an admirable and compelling man of letters. That "fine-hammered steel of woe" (*Moby-Dick*, p. 422) he admired in the words of Ecclesiastes was no desperate image: steel could mean strength and durable structure.

Ahab, Melville tells us, had his "humanities" until monomania destroyed the balance of his head and heart. I believe that Melville, an Ahab with all humanities intact, stood between two worlds. That is how Hawthorne saw him. Hawthorne's famous notebook entry on Melville's visit to Liverpool in 1856—immediately after the composition of *The Confidence-Man*—reveals that Melville informed his closest intellectual companion that he had "pretty much made up his mind to be annihilated." But, Hawthorne added, "still he does not seem to rest in that anticipation; and, I think, will never rest until he gets hold of a definite belief. . . . He can neither believe, nor be comfortable in his unbelief" (*The English Notebooks*, pp. 432–33). Hawthorne shows a man in torment—but torment contained and not abnormally vulnerable—and of a man who could be Ahab but was closer to Ishmael.

A brief review of some of Melville's major novels shows both tragic and comic perspectives. In *Moby-Dick* Melville accepts good and evil as so ambiguously intertwined that he grants heroic grandeur to the man who, like Ahab, sees "all visible objects" as "pasteboard masks" (*Moby-Dick*, p. 161) and dies in the attempt to strike through them; yet, at the same time, Melville recognizes a saving sanity in Ishmael's speculation that life is a hoax: "There are certain queer times and occasions in this strange mixed affair we call life when a man takes this whole universe for a vast practical joke, though the wit thereof he but dimly discerns, and more than suspects that the joke is at nobody's expense but his own" (p. 225). In *Pierre* Melville again expresses a complex vision. Pierre is a young author who tries to make moral absolutes fit the practical conditions of everyday life and who ends by destroying himself. Melville allows the tragic aspect of this story to make its appeal, then indicates, as if from a cosmic point of view, the absurdity of the whole. Thus at one moment the tragic Pierre struggles to reconcile world and soul: "Hereupon then in the soul of the enthusiast youth two armies come to the shock; and unless he prove recreant, or unless he prove gullible, or unless he can find the talismanic secret, to reconcile this world with his soul, then there is no peace for him, no slightest truce for him in this life." But Melville continues the passage in comic vein:

Now without doubt this Talismanic Secret has never yet been found; and in the nature of human things it seems as though it never can be.

Certain philosophers have time and again pretended to have found it; but if they do not in the end discover their own delusion, other people soon discover it for themselves, and so those philosophers and their vain philosophy are let glide away into practical oblivion. Plato and Spinoza, and Goethe, and many more belong to this guild of self-impostors, and with a preposterous rabble of Muggletonian Scots and Yankees, whose vile brogue still the more bestreaks the stripedness of their Greek or German Neoplatonical originals. That profound Silence, that only Voice of our God . . . ; from that divine thing without a name, those impostor philosophers pretend somehow to have got an answer; which is as absurd, as though they should say they had got water out of a stone; for how can a man get a Voice out of Silence? [*Pierre, or, The Ambiguities*, p. 244]

Pierre's tragedy is that he does not recognize life as a comedy of thought: the danger is that good men may be trapped in the great confidence game of idealistic philosophy. In the "Chronologicals and Horologicals" chapter of *Pierre*, Greenwich time and heavenly time never coalesce; man, therefore, Melville argues, "hitherto, being authoritatively taught by his dogmatical teachers that he must, while on earth, aim at heaven, and attain it, too, in all his earthly acts, on pain of eternal wrath; and finding by experience that this is utterly impossible; in his despair, he is too apt to run clear away into all manner of moral abandonment, self-deceit, and hypocrisy (cloaked, however, mostly under an aspect of the most respectable devotion); or else he openly runs, like a mad dog, into atheism" (p. 252). Christian civilization, Melville feels, is apt to promote the nihilism it professes to eliminate. And thus he has Pierre's sense of reality destroyed in the end: " 'It is all a dream—we dream that we dreamed a dream' " (p. 322). Nevertheless, Melville was not to forget the artistic possibility of a baleful comedy about man's confidence in gods that fail: *The Confidence-Man: His Masquerade*, written five years after *Pierre*, is dominated by just such a comic point of view.[30]

The ingenuity of *The Confidence-Man* is that Melville discovers a way to reexpress his familiar tragic themes in a picaresque schema. Part of the wit of that vast practical joke envisaged by Ishmael is that the great supernatural jokers are no more than petty con men—Yankee peddlers made cosmic. One is tempted to find a certain playful irony in Melville's description of a novel as showing "more reality, than real life itself can show" (*Con-*

*fidence-Man*, p. 206)[31]: the higher reality might be comically considered lower. Then, too, the wit of this multistructured *Confidence-Man* might be a joke at the reader's expense. The picaresque blends with satiric allegory, Lucianic dialogues, anatomies of folly, Job-like parables, ironic sermonizing based upon the Sermon on the Mount and I Corinthians, and, doubtless, other forms. But beneath this kaleidoscope of inspired melancholy moves the symbolic action of picaresque myth in which a not entirely ignoble world heads blindly toward annihilation.

Melville's complex vision gives him the last word. *The Confidence-Man* presents the world by means of symbolism, not of *is*, but of *if*.[32] If the human world persists in justifying its ways as God's ways, then it is deceived and damned: this, I believe, is essentially what Melville is saying. If men convert an inscrutable silence into a voice, then the voice they hearken to will not be God's but Satan's, respectable, confiding, solacing. I think it may be fairly said that Melville's attitude remains conditional. However, the total effect of *The Confidence-Man*, in form and content, is painful: human reality seems to hang very precariously near the abyss, as it did in the Spanish picaresque novels.

In recent years *The Confidence-Man* has come to be accepted as Melville's most nearly perfect work. "We must look at every word, every object, every action as though it represented an ultimate meaning," declares H. Bruce Franklin, though adding that "every word, every object, and every action in the book is almost endlessly meaningful," and that the work is Melville's "most comic," "most appalling," and "most puzzling."[33] I agree and add that critical decisions about *The Confidence-Man* can often be subverted so as to seem gratuitous impulse. There is, for a start, no general agreement that the work is a novel. Variously described as satire, allegory, and myth, its fictive status as primarily that of a novel depends upon our willingness to accept it as adapted to plausibility and to respect and discover in it a sense of an inscrutable reality. If *The Confidence-Man* is a satire, then it is one that fails to meet much of a minimum requirement for a perspective or standard of judgment. If the work is an allegory, it is one without fixed points that embody precepts. Is it myth, then, as Franklin, one of the most perceptive critics of

Melville, contends, when he finds certain Hindu myths the main subject matter and structural principle of the work? I prefer to regard *The Confidence-Man* as a novel with a mythological motif. That is, the mythological parallel is suggested as an analogy or contrast to the contemporary world and extended as a motif. Perhaps the most significant function of Melville's novel is to demythologize aetiological myths of Creation and apocalypse. A prefigurative technique, providing a shorthand system of symbolic comment on modern moral and intellectual events, would seem likely, even though Melville, like authors today, may have reckoned that few readers would be familiar with the relationship of myth and realism.[34] Whereas, according to Frank Kermode's distinction, a myth "presupposes total and adequate explanations of things as they are and were," fictions "are for finding things out."[35] In *The Confidence-Man* life is no longer being experienced as a biblical narrative. Instead of finding eschatological hopes confirmed, the readers are forced to share an experience of multidimensional fragmentariness in which the sense made of reality —our wholeness as humans at stake—has its paradigm in the creative myth of the picaro in a fiction called *The Confidence-Man*.

One way to approach the problem is to put oneself in the place of a novelist who has or thinks he has an idea for a new novel to be called *The Confidence-Man: His Masquerade*. There is popular subject matter, a Mississippi riverboat full of contemporary Americans and the popular tradition of the American trickster. The most important literary fact about *The Confidence Man: His Masquerade* is the title. From it the reader anticipates deceits, and he expects the deceiver's actions to effect counteractions from his victims, exposure, and punishment. This is the first stage. At the second stage the rules are changed, suggesting that the reader is to look, not for a lone operator, but for a specified number of suspects, any or all of them up to tricks. At this stage the reader is still expected to believe in a distinction between the confidence man and his victims. By the third stage the reader is disabused of this comfortable notion. Now the entire world of the ship called *Fidèle* comes under suspicion. From seeking to learn *who* the confidence man is, the reader must turn to consider *what* he is. That is, if all mankind is identified as the swindler, what inward character or quality of mankind constitutes the swindling element? Faiths of all kinds being the human cargo of the *Fidèle*, the reader will answer the question: man's myth-making powers deceive us. So far, it is an intellectual game only. Now, stage four, the reader is caught in the act of conning himself. The author tries to convince him that the gods have come down, as in a myth. The reader is given, if just for a moment, his ageless, idiotic illusion that gods are made in man's image, then —*April Fool*! Until now the structure of the story has been essentially linear, though simultaneity of allegory or pseudoallegory has pressed the reader outward from the line and from himself on the trail of false clues. In the final stage, the linear structure is changed by a peripeteia in which the reader at last crosses from his so-called real world into the so-called fictional world and sees himself as the confidence man (*mon semblable, mon frère*). Now that the reader is participating, not in a game but in his own life and death, he is left to test the validity of his knowledge against nothingness, annihilation, or at any rate a version of apocalypse. His confidence in God, man, and nature thoroughly shaken, he will have to readjust his expectations of the "end" to a new version of his "origins" in the cosmos, origins equivocally atavistic, loveless, and demoniac—a heart of darkness. With the nonheroic universe stripped of all tragic potential, with all hope betrayed as futile, then the implied need for human charity becomes desperately clear.

I am not pretending to have described Melville's actual strategy, but I think the approach points up several possibilities of a consistently novelistic vision. First, if supernatural beings are actually represented as mingling with mere mortals aboard the *Fidèle*, then Melville has no respect for our sense of reality; if on the other hand, gods do not come down but are mirrored projections and distortions of human perspective, then picaresque comedy—the picaro and *picardía* as reflections of each other—is a feasible novelistic plan. Second, if *The Confidence-Man* leads to a rectilinear rather than a cyclical view of the world, then the work is consistent with a modern novelist's, as opposed to a mythographer's, way of ordering events. Is there no moment in this work when author and reader can cooperate in the making of a meaning? Most readers have assumed that all the events about the *Fidèle* occur on April Fool's Day and hence that everything is unreliable and probably a hoax, including the events of the ultimate chapter in which the cosmopolitan, a diabolic confidence man, seems to extinguish the last lamp of faith. But if there is a novelistic peripeteia in this final chapter, then there needs be some unmasking, some return to conventional reliability. Though little noted by commentators, Melville, in the last chapter, almost certainly advances the clock *beyond* April Fool's Day. In Chapter XLIII, the cosmopolitan signs an agreement "at a quarter to twelve o'clock, P.M.," but when we next see him in Chapter XLV, he tells a passenger of this event "not a half-hour since." In this novel of concealed clues, we cannot overlook the high probability that the time is now just *past* midnight—in other words, the day of licensed foolery is over, and we can seriously consider where we are. Significantly, Chapter XLV is entitled, "The Cosmopolitan Increases in Seriousness." And though the final sentence suggests that "this Masquerade" continues, the author has at last established the kind of community with his reader that we call irony and that reassures us he is finding something *real* for us. What that reality amounts to, whether we call it silence or the absurd, is less significant than the dramatic structure of vision. By this account, Melville's practice as a novelist may be at least as much illuminated by that of James, Conrad, and Faulkner as by the *Bhagavad-Gita*.[36]

The action of *The Confidence-Man* takes place from sunrise to midnight on April Fool's Day—and slightly beyond—aboard the Mississippi steamer *Fidèle*, bound from St. Louis for New Orleans. The passengers are "a piebald parliament, an Anacharsis Cloots congress of all kinds of that multiform pilgrim species, man" (*Confidence-Man*, p. 8). They are world pilgrims on the Ship of Faith bound for salvation. And the sustained rhythm of the voyage is that of history, a constant coming and going between the "life" of the river and the "death" of the shore. But river life has been sullied; as a rejected fragment of the novel indicates, the once "sacred" river has mixed with an evil element at St. Louis.[37] Indeed, since action occurs on the *Fidèle*'s lower deck or in the purgatorial cabins, it is easy to recognize that Melville's Ship of Faith is also hell.

The probability that the lower deck represents hell increases when a man in cream-colors, "in the extremest sense of the word, a stranger" (p. 1), comes aboard at sunrise. His dress and the fact that simultaneously with his "advent" we learn of a placard offering a reward for the capture of "a mysterious impostor, supposed to have recently arrived from the East" contribute to the impression that he is a savior figure or type of Christ—but Christ descending to hell (where He falls asleep) before the Resurrection. Whether the man in cream-colors is a confidence man is for the moment left in doubt. He is a deaf-mute—the God of silence in *Pierre*—and circulates about the deck with a slate on which he scribbles verses from I Corinthians such as " 'Charity thinketh no evil.' " But the passengers do think evil, and their opinion is succinctly expressed by a "No Trust" sign near the barber shop.

While the man in cream-colors falls asleep, there appears his seeming opposite, a crippled Negro beggar named Black Guinea, in his hand "an old coal-sifter of a tambourine" (p. 9) suggesting infernal origin. His minstrel antics, his allusion to "der good baker's oven," and the stress upon his dark, doglike appearance (connoting misanthropy as in *Timon of Athens*) increase the suspicion that he, at least, is a confidence man. A naive Episcopalian and a violent Methodist urge that Black Guinea be given charity; but a wooden-legged man retorts: " 'To where it belongs with your charity! to heaven with it! . . . Here on earth, true charity dotes, and false charity plots' " (p. 14). This announces a proposition—similar to that in the "Chronologicals and Horologicals" chapter of *Pierre*—that the novel as a whole will discuss. But Melville does not employ the wooden-legged man as his spokesman: symbolically one-sided, this minor character is the first of several Timonists in the novel, with no one of whom may Melville be associated. In fact, the text gives the misanthrope away because "dotes," that suggests weakness or folly, does not belong with "true charity."

Black Guinea stumps out of sight, and next we meet a man in

mourning who, in a series of encounters, preaches the virtues of sentimental feeling and of optimism. Producing a copy of Akenside's *Pleasures of the Imagination* from his pocket, he warns a collegian to destroy a volume of Tacitus on the grounds that such writers are "ugly" (p. 28). This Shaftesburyan definition of evil, taken together with the graveyard sentimentality, indicates that the man with a weed is a confidence man whose swindling faith is eighteenth-century optimistic philosophy.

Next appears one whose countenance reveals "little of sorrow, though much of sanctity" (p. 31). He diddles the Episcopalian (marked earlier as a dupe by Black Guinea) and jeers at the wooden-legged man: "Money, you think, is the sole motive to pains and hazard, deception and deviltry, in this world. How much money did the devil make by gulling Eve?" (p. 36). But since we are by now accustomed to converting the words of the various confidence men into their opposite meanings, it is soon apparent that the man in a gray coat and white tie combines an air of sanctity with the economic motive; he is a spurious advocate of enlightened self-interest. "For what creature but a madman would not rather do good than ill, when it is plain that, good or ill, it must return upon himself?" (p. 45). He appeals for donations to the Seminole Widow and Orphan Asylum (Wilberforce-like comfort for a people then recently crushed by the white man) and promises to organize a World Charity "with the Wall Street spirit."

Elizabeth Foster observes that the first three "avatars" of the confidence man represent ironic reference to the Sermon on the Mount. Black Guinea is one of the meek and poor in spirit; the man with a weed is one of those that mourn and shall be comforted; the man in a gray coat hungers and thirsts after righteousness; and each character is spurious. The next three confidence men, continues Foster, dramatize the last verse of the chapter from I Corinthians with which the man in cream-colors began the novel: "And now abideth faith, hope, and charity, these three; but the greatest of these is charity." The man with a big book is faith; the herb doctor is hope; the man with a brass plate and the cosmopolitan are charity; each, again, is spurious and without faith, hope, or charity.[38]

The new avatar of the confidence man sells stock in the Black Rapids Coal Company. His stock "transfer book" tempts more than one passenger to speculate; it represents the Bible, the validity of which is accepted on trust by many Christians. The coal image, however, has appeared earlier in the Black Guinea episode and carries here the same connotation of diabolism.

When the man with a big book descends to the "purgatory" (p. 81) of the emigrants' quarters in order to defraud a sick old miser, there appears a stock comic character, a medical quack or Yankee peddler specializing in the sale of remedies. The herb doctor, as his name implies, sells "natural" remedies. In him Melville satirizes the nature cult of the eighteenth and nineteenth centuries and also such Emersonian doctrines as "From evil comes good. Distrust is a stage to confidence" (p. 94).

Two misanthropes with intimate knowledge of nature resent this confidence man. One is an "invalid Titan in homespun" (p. 96), a yellowed Leatherstocking of the swamps who is accompanied by his puny half-Indian daughter. The other is Pitch, a bristling "Missouri bachelor" (p. 120). The feverish giant readily identifies the doctor with the devil: "'Profane fiddler on heartstrings! Snake!'" (p. 100). Pitch's milder, "'I have confidence in distrust'" (p. 137) is also proof against the temptations of the doctor. However, neither character represents goodness in this novel: both characters are seriously flawed. The Titan—once, perhaps, a heroic Leatherstocking—has been darkly united with natural evil, a union for which the child is symbol. And Pitch is a bachelor, a term that in *Moby-Dick* and elsewhere in Melville connotes a frivolous mentality.[39]

Pitch has informed the doctor that he is going to New Orleans to purchase a machine to replace the crew of dishonest boys working on his plantation. This odd (and prophetic) plan to mechanize American agriculture is the signal for the next confidence man, the man with a brass plate, agent of an employment bureau named the Philosophical Intelligence Office. The positive-thinking agent persuades Pitch by turning Pitch's scientific faith against him. He claims that a sinful child "scientifically viewed" (p. 137) grows into a saintly man—Augustine is the supreme example. This "science" proves that vices are transient.

Pitch agrees to employ one more boy—but later, upon realizing that he has been tricked, he becomes more distrustful and soulless than ever. Meanwhile, the P.I.O. man lands near a bluff named the Devil's Joke.

The most prominent avatar of the confidence man is in many respects the sum of all the others. He is a philanthropic "citizen of the world" who professes to enjoy "that good dish, man" (p. 151) and whose theme is brotherly love: "I am Philanthropus, and love mankind" (p. 261). As might be expected, the cosmopolitan's statement is a spurious inversion of Timon's "I am Misanthropus, and hate mankind." Claiming that "no man is a stranger" (p. 151), the cosmopolitan is in fact at furthest remove from the man in cream-colors who had been "in the extremest sense of the word, a stranger." In successive episodes the cosmopolitan overmatches a genuine Mississippi sharper but meets his match in a Yankee mystic (Emerson) and his "practical disciple" (probably Thoreau).[40] While the Transcendentalists preach friendship and harmony, the cosmopolitan finds them so soulless that he gives them a shilling; his protest about their "under ice of the heart" (p. 253)[41] is in this instance Melville's own protest against Transcendentalism.

Throughout the novel Melville has stressed that a surplus or deficiency of head or heart weakens the good in men and cripples their humanity. But William Cream the barber, the cosmopolitan's last major victim, has both head and heart, mind and passion; the barber comes disconcertingly close to meeting Melville's representation of normal, though fallible, humanity. The barber's name links him to the man in cream-colors, the Christ-like stranger of the first chapter who has seemed—again, *seemed*—no confidence man. The "No Trust" sign outside William Cream's shop does oppose the deaf-mute's call for absolute charity, but, since the novel has demonstrated how the called-for charity is either inapplicable as an absolute to human life or perverted to selfish ends, the "No Trust" sign may simply symbolize a relative, wary distrust. The man in cream-colors belongs to the realm of absolutes, William Cream to the relative, practical life of the world. Melville stresses the barber's humanity. He is the "honest barber" (p. 254), a dreamy tippler who mixes shaving cream as if it were whiskey punch, a "sociable" being who is "almost as pleasantly garrulous as the pleasant barbers in romances" (p. 261). His sign, William Cream admits, spares him work that does not pay and gives him relative freedom of choice. This flexibility baffles the cosmopolitan, who asks: " 'Now, what I would ask is, do you think it sensible standing for a sensible man, one foot on confidence and the other on suspicion? Don't you think, barber, that you ought to elect?' " (p. 259). But experience has shown the barber that freedom is always relative. Twenty years in his trade have taught him "facts": " 'What, sir [he replies] can one be forever dealing in macassar oil, hair dyes, cosmetics, false moustaches, wigs, and toupees, and still believe that men are wholly what they look to be?' " (pp. 262–63). On the other hand, when the cosmopolitan accuses him of " 'the spleen of Thersites,' " the barber bristles and says misanthropy " 'is not exactly in my line' " (p. 255). It is difficult for the cosmopolitan to trick in the usual ways this man who is neither absolutely trustful nor absolutely distrustful. The cosmopolitan is forced to resort to black magic, thus revealing himself as Vice or devil. Even at that, the barber, whose will has not actively confided in the devil, soon recovers composure.

William Cream is both dupe and cynic. Representing, as Frank Jaster has shown, "middle ground between blind faith and an absolute self-reliance," he has erected his "No Trust" sign as "the buffer between his trusting nature and those who would take advantage of it."[42] To be sure, he is actively employed aboard the Ship of Faith, and his partial identification with the man in cream-colors indicates a nature flawed by confidence. But when the cosmopolitan tricks him, William Cream quickly recovers "his self-possession and senses" (p. 269). He functions, then, however ambiguously, as *l'homme moyen sensuel* and serves to underscore mankind's tragicomic predicament, namely, that without confidence there would be no humanity. He has another, related function: he is sufficiently reliable to be given the role of challenging and almost unmasking the confidence man. He refers, without irony, to the "True Book" and from Melville's favorite Ecclesiastes quotes a telling passage, " 'An enemy speaketh sweetly with his lips' " (p. 267). The enemy, of course, is truly archaic, the evil or destructive principle, the devil, or Vice. "But in after days, telling the night's adventure to his friends, the worthy barber always spoke of his queer customer as the man-charmer—as certain East Indians are called snake-charmers —and all his friends united in thinking him *Quite an Original*" (p. 269). Not previously noted by commentators is the barber's virtual identity with the disembodied voice that speaks (as it were) for Melville in the final chapter. For, there, when the cosmopolitan ponders the passage from Ecclesiastes that the barber had quoted defiantly, an unseen, sleepless man defiantly spells out the connection between "enemy" and "confidence-man" —the first and only such direct unmasking in the entire novel and all the more authoritative for its probable occurrence on 2 April.[43]

The introduction of the humanity of the barber occurs immediately before the cosmopolitan extinguishes the lamp of faith and the universe of man. The scene is extraordinary, an apocalyptic vision. The confidence man enters the gentlemen's cabin where burns a "solar lamp" surrounded by "other lamps, barren planets, which had either gone out from exhaustion, or been extinguished by such occupants of berths as the light annoyed, or who wanted to sleep, not see" (p. 272). By the light of the lamp an old American reads the Bible: he is quickly confused by the cosmopolitan and then duped by a savage young peddler with "leopard-like teeth." Franklin has noted that this boy and the man in cream colors are the only passengers without a place to sleep and that the boy's bedraggled yellow coat seems to be all that is left of the lamblike man's cream-colored clothes.[44] Given, as Watson C. Branch has shown, that the first and last chapters of the novel were planned as a frame,[45] the implication that the boy is the Christ-like man unmasked is pretty much confirmed. Just as in Chapter XVIII knaves and fools are subsumed under the concept of "original genius," and as in Chapters XLIII–XLIV "original" signifies the confidence man, so now apparent opposites are united. The destroyers are both devil and Christ. Indeed, these mythic types, like the cosmopolitan and the boy, act as accomplices. The old man is led out, and the confidence man extinguishes the solar lamp. All is dark; but Melville's promise that

"Something further may follow of this Masquerade" (p. 286)[46] points less to a literary sequel than to the Day of Judgment.

*The Confidence-Man* is a masquerade of swindling faiths, the swindler a cosmic picaro. The deeper symbolic significance of the masquerade is, moreover, underscored by three variations in the narrative pattern that I have just reconstructed: (1) parables that show the omniscience of evil, (2) elaborate punning on the "original" powers of the confidence man, and (3) the first chapter.

The three parables of Goneril, Moredock, and China Aster express the idea that human evil is omnipresent and inexplicable. The first two are tales of morbid passion; the third is a version of Job.

Goneril, like her namesake in *King Lear*, is a diabolical wife and mother. She has an "Indian figure" (*Confidence-Man*, p. 65) —in *The Confidence-Man* Melville, whose tolerance is beyond doubt, categorically symbolizes Indians as depraved—and she chews sticks of clay.[47] She is utterly sadistic. When she torments her child, her husband abandons her and takes the child; she, undeterred, gains custody of the child and ruins her husband in the legal process. The parable ends with the husband an outlaw desperately fleeing Goneril's threat to commit him as insane.

Moredock is an Indian-hater, a terrorist against evil. Son of a woman thrice widowed by the tomahawk, he attains manhood only to witness the massacre of his family. Thereafter, he is to Indians "a Leatherstocking Nemesis" (p. 170),[48] although to his fellow citizens he remains gentle and responsible. Unlike Goneril, Moredock is essentially noble, but he has lost his soul in the wilderness.

China Aster (= star, delicate flower) differs from Goneril and Moredock in passion and fortune. He is a "subordinate Prometheus" (p. 234),[49] a poor honest candlemaker. When his rich friend Orchis (= luxury) tempts him to accept a loan to improve the business, he accepts. But hard times come, debts accumulate, the friends fall out, and both are ruined. Aster dies, followed by his wife; the orphaned children remain to suffer. The story ends as three of Job's comforters, Old Plain Talk, Old Prudence, and Old Conscience, erect a tablet commemorating the pitiful man of light, whose trifling dream of success lured him into annihilation.

One way of regarding these parables in the manner of Hawthorne is to see that Melville confronts Milton's epic theme with the Book of Job: how justify the ways of God to man when good people suffer and evil ones prosper? Melville's justification is Protestant but not Miltonic: God, in his view, is past all finding out. Nor is man any less enigmatic than his God: "Upon the whole it might rather be thought, that he, who, in view of its inconsistencies, says of human nature the same that, in view of its contrasts, is said of the divine nature, that it is past finding out, thereby evinces a better appreciation of it than he who, by always representing it in a clear light, leaves it to be inferred that he clearly knows all about it" (p. 77). This statement by Melville in his own person occurs in Chapter XIV of *The Confidence-Man* and is, I think, though often overlooked by commentators, the key passage in the novel. If God and human nature are past finding out, then all dogma, philosophy, and myth that present them in clear light are fraudulent pretense and also, to the degree that man's Promethean creativity is endangered, criminal. The clear light is ironically a great fog behind which lurks not God but the devil. Hence the man who is tricked by rational explanations of the universe is soon apt to believe that God *is* the devil.[50]

When William Cream the barber realizes that the confidence man has cheated him of the price of a shave, he exclaims, " 'Quite an Original!' " (p. 269).[51] The exclamation recalls to memory the mysterious impostor for whom reward was offered in the first chapter and who was said to be "quite an original genius in his vocation, as would appear, though wherein his originality consisted was not clearly given" (p. 1).[52] By means of punning on "original" Melville calls attention to the cosmic, mythic ambiguities of origin. Who is the original, God or the devil? Melville gives no categorical answer; rather, he toys with the question by reference to the artist's attempts to achieve a sense of the primitive and organic in life. Few artists, he claims in Chapter XLIV, have successfully created "original" characters. He names Hamlet, Don Quixote, the Satan as "original" in the sense that their creators comprehended in them "original instincts" (p. 270).

(Earlier, in Chapter XXXIII, Melville theorized: "It is with fiction as with religion: it should present another world, and yet one to which we feel the tie" [p. 207]). The original character in fiction, he continues, gives the reader an insight into the powers of the universe: "The original character, essentially such, is like a revolving Drummond light, raying away from itself all round it—everything is lit by it, everything starts up to it . . . so that, in certain minds, there follows upon the adequate conception of such a character, an effect, in its way akin to that which in Genesis attends upon the beginning of things" (p. 271). Melville (wittily) implies that the "original" confidence man gives us an understanding of Creation. And this is one reason why *The Confidence-Man* is ingeniously picaresque: the archetypal picaro always pretends to an ancestry and credit he does not possess. Melville's picaro, accordingly, has cosmic pretensions, and is indeed a kind of Drummond light, appearing and reappearing in regular sequence throughout the novel. If I interpret Melville's irony aright, an adequate conception of the picaro is attended by an insight into the cosmos as chaos. The confidence man takes his origin from the divine will. To the diabolic suggestiveness of this Melville adds by claiming "but one such original character to one work of invention," which is to say that life is no Manichean struggle of good and evil forces but unitary, evil apparently part of good. This Job-like or Blakean reflection is traditionally tragic; therefore, the context of Melville's novel as comedy is significant. For he is not writing about the devil as epic hero; he is, on the contrary, making the devil a cosmic picaro, an impostor, a usurper of identity, an utterly nonoriginal character.

The obverse of the irony is to present absolute goodness as a nonoriginal imposition. This helps to explain the ambiguous advent of the Christ-like stranger in the first chapter. The deaf-mute impostor appears "suddenly as Manco Capac" (p. 1), the Inca sun-child apparently come down to earth. He has no luggage (= no sin), his gospel is absolute love, and he is the supreme stranger in the world of relative values. Like the wanted criminal, he has recently arrived from the East (= the Orient, but also Down-east, home of Sam Slick and the Yankee tricksters). Melville's Christ figure is unheroic if not antiheroic. He is not the manly, self-assured historical Jesus, the Jesus of the Sermon on the Mount. As the man in cream-colors he is ineffectual and effeminate: "His cheek was fair, his chin downy, his hair flaxen . . . of an aspect singularly innocent . . . his whole lamb-like figure" (pp. 1–5). The *Fidèle* passengers take this weak Christ with Uncle Sam's features "for some strange kind of simpleton, harmless enough, would he keep to himself, but not wholly unobnoxious as an intruder" (p. 2). He thus lacks the potential power of the returned Christ, in Dostoevsky's "Legend of the Grand Inquisitor," who was told that there was no need for Him because people had traded freedom, faith, and love for mystery, miracle, and authority. The man in cream-colors, good inasmuch as he is passive, is then a kind of confidence man, of the same genus as the other avatars of the confidence man, but not of the same species. Melville's emphasis upon the crowd's reaction to the deaf-mute "good" impostor points an obvious moral: the world's Sunday-school idea of goodness is inadequate to protect it from its own debased desire to put confidence in evil.

Thus, I think, Melville's narrative variations—parables of evil, puns on "Original," and ambiguous Christ symbolism—elaborate a theme of moral relativism. Evil in the world threatens the faith of those who insist that God is good. Human goodness is apt to be spurious; but, on the other hand, spurious goodness cannot be thought of as God's; and the world's attempt to reconcile its concept of absolute love with experience actually weakens the idea of goodness into evil.

Melville leaves the voyage of the Ship of Faith unfinished and enchanted. In one of the rare lyrical passages of *The Confidence-Man* he suggests that the enchantment is not without beauty and benevolence: "The sky slides into blue, the bluffs into bloom; the rapid Mississippi expands; runs sparkling and gurgling, all over in eddies; one magnified wake of a seventy-four. The sun comes out, a golden huzzar, from his tent, flashing his helm on the world. All things, warmed in the landscape, leap. Speeds the daedal boat as a dream" (p. 86). The "daedal" boat does not fit the impersonally lovely world of nature. It—faith—is winged for freedom by means of human artifice and craft. It is man-created out of an inherent need for confidence in life—yet the very human aspiration of faith represents its greatest danger. What is created by man may be destroyed by man; a swindling faith may lead to the disintegration of reality, goodness, and trust; and such a disintegrating world is the picaro's, conceived in the image of the confidence man, loveless and unreal as a dream.

In that final apocalyptic scene when the cosmopolitan extinguishes the solar lamp appears a barefoot peddler boy in vagabond's clothing who tries to cheat an old miser—as Lazarillo once tried. Melville presents this young trickster in a Spanish context. His multicolored rags "flamed about him like the painted flames in the robes of a victim in *auto-da-fe*" (p. 277). Laughing, he bares "leopard-like teeth, like those of Murillo's wild beggar-boy's." These hints of heresy and savagery are joined to the boy's cynicism. He talks of unmarried fathers, housebreaking, and picking pockets. He is quick to blame necessity for his premature worldliness. And, like Lazarillo, he knows at least as much as the devil himself. It may be farfetched to see in this Mississippi trickster Melville's recollection of Lazarillo and Guzmán. But the presence of a wily lad in the cabin with the diabolic confidence man does offer a suggestive kinship between the Spanish picaro and the symbolic confidence man.

*The Confidence-Man* is a picaresque novel in a nonautobiographical symbolic form. Some of its characteristics relate it to the central picaresque tradition and demonstrate its continuance of picaresque myth. *The Confidence-Man* (1) parodies heroic and epic literature, specifically the Bible from Genesis to apocalypse; (2) presents life as a series of encounters between the picaro and society; (3) presents picaro and society, as well as good and evil, as mutually reflective aspects of the same reality; (4) shows reality functioning as an illusion; (5) is structured to reveal disintegration into chaos and spiritual death; (6) makes the world's lack of love desperately apparent; and (7) has a picaro for protagonist. This last feature may not be quite as obvious as it seems from the ubiquitous confidence man's resemblance to a trickster and to a devil or Vice who takes artistic pleasure in deceit. Is the confidence man similar to the Spanish picaro who is a failed identity and a half-outsider? Certainly this confidence man is both. Behind his masks, he is neither a true god nor an adequate human. Through the world's lack of Pauline charity, he has become deformed in a shifting, dehumanized nonself. He is another dead soul, another invisible man. Nevertheless, he has a kind of character as a stranger who seeks by means of imposture to enter in to the human community. In terms of his function vis-à-vis his victims, he yearns to be accepted by and necessary to them. An insider in respect to humanity's need for confidence, he is doomed to the outside because, like the mature Lázaro of *Lazarillo de Tormes*, he hides a heart of stone.

## Confidence Men in *Huckleberry Finn*

The brilliant but eccentric design of Melville's *Confidence-Man* demands a brief recapitulation of the historical view that shaped *Lazarillo de Tormes* and *Guzmán de Alfarache* and made these the epicenter of picaresque narratives. In them, modern man is emerging as simultaneously committed to and detached from culture. The past, which has hitherto been sharply delineated in Creation myth, no longer assures men of divinity in the scheme of things. The past is no longer the sanction of authority. It is losing, in Lionel Trilling's word, "authenticity," becoming inauthentic.[53] The new man—the picaro of the narratives—has become historically weightless and transparent, so he wanders forth in search of a new authenticity in the experience of the here and now. His quest fails, of course, but life irresistibly begins to gather meaning as a perspective of free individuals aware of civilization as oppression. Outside Spain and for several centuries the picaresque narratives are transformed—come no closer to the epicenter than the novels of Defoe—because life in civilization is still tractable to reason. And then, quite suddenly, the prophetic vision of Melville again reveals a world without authentic roots and sanctions, a world in which the past is dying and becoming a rubbish heap and a swindle. In *The Confidence-Man* divinity, whether good or evil, is imposture. Such a death of the past implies, for Melville, a present of stern encounters lived at the contingent edge of human annihilation.

## The Myth of the Picaro

In Mark Twain's *Adventures of Huckleberry Finn* (1884) there is no such clear evidence of continuation, at the core, of picaresque myth. The thrust of the narrative is nonpicaresque in the sense that I have attributed to eighteenth- and nineteenth-century novels such as *Gil Blas* and *Oliver Twist*. But Twain is aggressively antihistorical. He has made an uncomfortable alliance with the new methods of life in scientific and industrial society— witness *A Connecticut Yankee*. But, again, because culture is complacently, implacably, and intractably determined, in his view, by the corrupt past, his presentation of a life of freedom, love, and moral choice seems an unacceptable indulgence. As in *Lazarillo de Tormes*, so finally in *Huckleberry Finn*, readers are deceived into approval of the protagonist and of his apparent social success and moral regeneration. How deliberate Twain's deception was may never be known, for much depends upon our acceptance, however reluctantly proffered, of Tom Sawyer's evasion, those chapters in which Huck seems to negate his humanity and to approximate the deformed identity of the confidence men, the King and Duke.

On the surface, *Huckleberry Finn* is a novel in which an apparent picaro discovers right uses for his trickery and comes to oppose the confidence men, the symbolic picaros, with whom he becomes involved. Some earlier critics, avoiding this distinction, judged *Huckleberry Finn* as a picaresque novel. Thus Martin Hume wrote: "One sees in Mark Twain's *Huckleberry Finn* a transparent intention to experiment with an American picaro, as near as circumstances could make him to Lazarillo, Guzmán de Alfarache, and the rest of the goodly company of sharp-witted youngsters with pockets as light as their hearts, who sprang from the Spanish genius as a reaction from the wandering knights of chivalry."[54] Chandler corrected this impression by contrasting Huck, "a matter-of-fact rogue," with the King and the Duke, "arrant picaros equal to any swindle."[55] In my view, Huck's relationship to the confidence men is the key to interpretation of Twain's novel as picaresque.[56]

It is known that Mark Twain had in mind a dialectical form of picaresque novel, *Gil Blas*, when he first thought of the book that was to be *Huckleberry Finn*. In 1875, after Howells had urged him to write a story about a boy who grows up, Twain replied: "I have finished [*Tom Sawyer*] & didn't take the chap beyond boyhood. I believe it would be fatal to do it in any shape but autobiographically—like *Gil Blas*. . . . By & by I shall take a boy of twelve & run him on through life (in the first person) but not Tom Sawyer—he would not be a good character for it."[57] *Gil Blas* conveyed to Twain two important aspects of the future *Huckleberry Finn*: autobiographical angle of narration and a central character who is "low" but capable of growth and good-natured but not priggish.

Beneath the surface appearance of *Huckleberry Finn* there is evident interest in the picaro as a lonely child confronted by and trained by an unsympathetic society. Huck has some of the picaro's sensitivity about inferior social status. He is alienated from home and tends to become involved with persons existing precariously on social frontiers. On the surface, however, Huck, seeming not to be a picaro, retains innocence, humanity, and freedom. For a while, he fosters charitable actions, is loving and loved, and finds a true father in Jim the runaway slave. Eventually he matures sufficiently to make moral decisions that apparently isolate him still further from society yet turn him away from a life of trickery and imposture. On this narrative surface, Huck is therefore closer to Gil Blas, Colonel Jack, or Oliver Twist than to the picaro; he is integrated, if not, like them, in present society, then in himself and in society of the immediate future. His tricks serve the causes of justice and brotherhood. Huck is a "good" confidence man, a down-to-earth version of Melville's messianic deaf-mute and neither passive nor destructive.

Because Huck is presumably a "saved" person, it is interesting to note how the introduction into the narrative of two confidence men, the Duke and the King, affects this final outcome. In the sense that a literary hero's fate needs to be worked out in terms of relationships, the con men are indispensable to Huck's apparent salvation—or so it would seem from the evidence of Twain's composition of *Huckleberry Finn*. According to Walter Blair, the novel was composed in several stages between 1876 and 1883.[58] The first sixteen chapters, describing Huck's escape from

Miss Watson and Pap, his meeting with Jim, and his loss of Jim in the steamboat collision, were written rapidly in the summer of 1876. There Twain stalled, perhaps because the freedom theme was frustrated by the fact that Huck and Jim had drifted too far downriver to escape the slave states. If we judge by the later development, it would seem that the story needed a shift in narrative pattern toward some panoramic *Gil Blas* type of survey of social conditions and toward a symbolic structure counterpointing the life of the river and the life of the shore. In 1879–80 Twain felt his way toward the new pattern when he added the Grangerford episode (Chapters XVII–XVIII). The Grangerfords represent much that Twain considered good in the antebellum South. But they are fanatics and sentimentalists damned by mindless belief in the codes of Cloud-Cuckoo-Land. Huck must escape their doom, find again the sanctuary of the raft. At this critical moment in the narrative the Duke and King are introduced. They provide a dramatic contrast to Huck and Jim, bring evil aboard the Edenic raft, and lead the story forward into a series of satirical excursions into the corrupt civilization of the shore.

Twain's confidence men take their literary origin from southwestern humor.[59] Between 1879 and 1882 Twain busied himself selecting stories for inclusion in the work published in 1888 as *Mark Twain's Library of Humor*. In his younger days as a printer-journalist Twain had steeped himself in the writings of such newspaper comedians as Haliburton, A. B. Longstreet, and Johnson Hooper; now he was rereading them and noting how they had achieved a survey of frontier life and manners by linking episodes through the agency of a trickster hero. Significantly, then, the episode that follows the Grangerford chapters is drawn from the camp-meeting scene in Hooper's *Simon Suggs*. The King's first confidence trick is posing as a converted sinner before an ecstatic group of revivalists, and, like Simon Suggs, he makes away with the collection plate by swearing to spread the gospel. But there is an important difference in point of view between *Simon Suggs* and *Huckleberry Finn*. Simon's society dissolves into his aphorism, "It's good to be shifty in a new country." Huck's society, though dissolute, is seen and apparently mastered by his incorruptibly innocent, Adamic eyes. Rebelling unconsciously against the confidence men and their mindless victims, rebelling in the sense that social ideals are of no help to him in the crisis, Huck feels his way through to the truth of rebellion: the just person may change the solitude of rebellion into an affirmation. As Camus observes, "The spirit of revolt can only exist in a society where a theoretic equality conceals great factual inequalities."[60] Precisely this spirit—inconceivable in a southern conservative such as Johnson Hooper—erupts in Mark Twain. His Huck Finn revolts against a society that threatens to disintegrate into picaresque chaos.

The trouble with Huck Finn's revolt is that it finally lacks intellectual seriousness in spite of the adventurous criticism that it is intended to release. By this conclusion I mean that an inquiring mind—Melville's, for example—does not stop at the point where knowledge becomes dangerous to accepted loyalties. Huck Finn escapes the dominion of death, and to this extent his rebellion is positive; but Huck goes too far, or rather, he has no place to go. His rebellion carries forward into an infatuation with vitalism and with the inchoate life. And therefore, because the unmasking of great factual inequalities is not only the rebel's but also the picaro's conventional activity, it may be well to ask: is Huck, for all his goodness, for all his opposition to the confidence men, something of a mythic picaro?

When the confidence men take over the raft, Huck reacts passively. For a long while he is unable to take action against them because—and the novel is clear about this—the con men symbolize a deformed part of Huck that is in conflict with his natural goodness. Not until or not unless this inner conflict is resolved will Huck be free to contend with his part-self, the Duke and King. A leading Twain authority expresses the theme of the conflict thus: "[Huck's] intuitive self, the spontaneous impulse from the deepest levels of personality, is placed in opposition to the acquired conscience, the overlayer of prejudice and false valuation imposed upon all members of society in the name of religion, morality, law, and culture."[61] Twain described *Huckleberry Finn* in later years as "a book of mine where a sound heart & a deformed conscience come into collision & conscience suffers defeat."[62] Rebellious goodness converts Huck's antisocial trickery into an affirmation; but, without such spontaneous loyalty to the good, Huck might well have found in the confidence men shades of his mature self.

Twain develops the idea of deformed conscience with a certain picaresque psychology. When we first encounter Huck, he is the slave of his environment, of those dead forms of convention and respectability that are soon to undergo the change through the river experience. "I don't take no stock in dead people" (*Huckleberry Finn*, p. 4), he comments on the story of Moses. Yet, ironically, he takes too much stock in the living dead, Miss Watson and Pap. It is one thing to reject Sunday school and the make-believe of Tom Sawyer; it is another to reject Miss Watson's decency or Pap's paternal claim. But he must reject them—and society—to find spiritual freedom, and thus, like the Spanish picaro, Huck turns lonesomely inward: "I felt so lonesome, I most wished I was dead. The stars was shining, and the leaves rustled in the woods ever so mournful; and I heard an owl, away off, who-whooing about somebody that was dead, and a whip-powill and a dog crying about somebody that was going to die" (p. 5). Out of the dying part of himself Huck builds what Henry Nash Smith, in an apt phrase, calls "the imagination of disaster."[63] At later times when Huck invents a pseudoautobiography to win the confidence of others, he dramatizes his own deep involvement with violent death or illness. It might be said, therefore, that Huck shares with Lazarillo a loneliness deriving from the morbid fear of death and from the shame that accompanies a despised social standing and that his creation of false personalities in resolution of his tension is in psychological motivation similar to the picaro's self-creation.

*Huckleberry Finn*, moreover, carries on the picaresque convention of parental humor. Huck's father Pap, the poor white town drunk, emerges from Huck's description as no less grotesque than the father of Don Pablos: "His hair was long and tangled and greasy, and hung down, and you could see his eyes shining through like he was behind vines. It was all black, no gray; so was his long, mixed-up whiskers. There warn't no color in his face, where his face showed; it was white; not like another man's white, but a white to make a body sick, a white to make a body's flesh crawl—a tree-toad white, a fish-belly white" (pp. 17–18). This is the father—family, society, civilization—and civilization is dead at the root, the haunted wilderness made flesh. Pap's whiteness is the oppressor race and the spectral land and the whiteness of flung settlements along the river and the whiteness of the fog in which Cairo, gateway to freedom, will be lost. The wilderness cries of death and the death is in the flesh, and the realm of death—which later has its King and Duke—claims goodness, innocence, all. Huck, trained by conscience to accept his legal tie to Pap, endures Pap's drunken frenzy until it is intolerable—when Pap ironically mistakes Huck for the Angel of Death. That terrifying scene in which Pap tries to murder Huck is plausible precisely because Huck does have death inside him, Pap's own legacy.

Huck, like the picaro, flees an intolerable psychic situation by taking to the road. But his road, apparently unlike the picaro's, is a river, natural and free. Therefore, before leaving Pap, Huck stages a symbolic death; and on the river he is reborn. "I warn't lonesome, now" (p. 36), he says matter-of-factly on discovering Jim at Jackson's Island: Jim is Huck's Leopold Bloom.

The breakaway from Pap establishes, however, that Huck is reluctant to save himself except under intolerable conditions. Chances arise, even on the river, for Huck to become a disintegrated confidence man. He persists in maintaining the rightness of "sivilization" and the wickedness of assisting an escaped slave. That persistence, moreover, becomes a central urgency in the novel: to Twain's postwar readers, Huck's seeming delinquency is clearly a correct compassion, and thus one is concerned for his, not Jim's, escape from mental enslavement. The appearance of the King and Duke—who, like Pap, will drive Huck to make a decision—is thus a narrative necessity.

Huck's spirit achieves form by being contrasted to the soulless world of the confidence men. In the Grangerford episode Huck never thinks of Jim, who has presumably been crushed by the steamboat. From this low point of heartlessness he works gradually up, at least until the evasion. First, instinctively, he tries to protect Jim from the Duke and King; then, as their swindles grow more exotic and sinister, Huck draws close to the refuge offered by Jim's humanity. The Pokeville camp meeting, the assassination of Boggs, and the Royal Nonesuch episodes build a marginal sympathy for the confidence men: Huck also despises the "greenhorns" and "flatheads" ashore. But at the same time the spectacle of man's inhumanity throws Jim's love into relief and prepares the way for Huck's acknowledgment of the slave's soul: "When I waked up, just at day-break, he was setting there with his head down betwixt his knees, moaning and mourning to himself. . . . I knowed what it was about. He was thinking about his wife and children, away up yonder, and he was low and homesick; because he hadn't ever been away from home before in his life; and I do believe he cared just as much for his people as white folks does for their'n. It don't seem natural, but I reckon it's so" (p. 131). By the time of the Wilks fraud Huck has sickened of the impostors' fake sentimentality, all "soul-butter and hogwash" (p. 138). This leads to his first big moral decision, when he steals money from the confidence men that belongs rightfully to Mary Jane Wilks. A second and greater decision is also induced by the confidence men. They have betrayed Jim; Huck, after struggling with his conscience, with that picaro part of himself, and deciding that to rescue Jim means social and, for all he knows, eternal damnation, concludes: "All right, then, I'll *go* to hell!" (p. 180). Huck's decision is a great moment in humorous literature, as W. H. Auden testifies: "When I first read *Huckleberry Finn* as a boy, I took Huck's decision as being a sudden realization, although he had grown up in a slave-owning community, that slavery was wrong. Therefore I completely failed to understand one of the most wonderful passages in the book, when Huck wrestles with his conscience. . . . What Huck does is a pure act of moral improvisation. What he decides tells him nothing about what he should do on other occasions, or what other people should do on other occasions."[64] Auden goes on to define the Americanness of moral improvisation, Americans being prone to value nonreadymade solutions and change for its own sake. Whatever its Americanness, Huck's decision is a remarkable contrivance, a moral improvisation. For not only does it have no profound basis in natural law—no doctrine of received truth about man as historical creature—but it is not even a free choice. I am not referring to the fact that, unknown to Huck, Jim has already been set free, but to the barrenness of Huck's commitment. Precisely at this moment of what seems positive virtue, Huck surrenders to conscience, to a morality and an idea, and loses forever the power to be Huck, a free human being capable of choice. In fact, what appears the culminating point in Huck's slow discovery of Jim's humanity is actually the resumption of status in Tom Sawyer's complacent world of moral sentiment. James M. Cox is right, I believe, to say that Huck's "central mode of being is that of escape and evasion."[65] In accordance with a quest not for freedom but for pleasure, Huck soon joins forces with Tom to torment poor Jim as if the slave's humanity had never existed. No longer an outcast, Huck has entered into debased civilization as surely as Lázaro de Tormes succeeds—at the price of his soul. By the end of *Huckleberry Finn*, Huck's future course is a Guzmán-like extension of an ascetic's despair. He's going to "light out for the Territory ahead of the rest, because Aunt Sally she's going to adopt me and sivilize me and I can't stand it" (p. 245), that is, have more Bad Boy adventures that, far from symbolizing his freedom from bondage to civilization, must, according to Twain's logic, confirm his petrifaction at the heart of convention.

Huck's apparent rejection of the confidence men has taken on symbolic significance of picaresque kind. Because a picaro takes his formal character from a hollow imitation of the corrupt society in which he struggles for existence, the picaro may symbolize that society. Just so, the King and Duke have come to symbolize society, conscience, civilization, and history. To reject such symbols is extreme; hence the solitary Adam, whom we hoped would prefigure Huck, may save himself only by absolute self-reliance. Does Huck succeed in rejecting the symbolic confidence men?

With all its apparent affirmation of rebellion, *Huckleberry Finn* is no less pessimistic than the Spanish picaresque novels—if we accept Twain's antihistorical valuations as pessimistic. Huck's "triumph" over a deformed conscience points to Twain's defeat by history, and in this connection can be seen Twain's concept of Adamic myth. According to Roger Salomon, Twain's idea of the Fall was that it resulted "less in making man forevermore innately sinful (i.e., *born with* an original sin) than in making him *after birth* vulnerable to training in sin because of his conscience." "In no way," Salomon continues, "could the Fall be considered 'fortunate' because Twain denied the redemptive agency of the conscience." Rather, conscience "was a mysterious instrument which rendered man helpless in the presence of corrupting institutions." Hence every man's life in society "was, at best, simply a long delaying action against corruption."[66] Huck Finn's redemptive love for Jim, if viewed against this background, becomes the kind of impractical absolutism or "good" imposture that had distressed Melville in *The Confidence-Man*: Huck and the messianic deaf-mute are both strangers to the historical community that ignores their messages of charity and heeds only the meaningless gospel of the symbolic confidence man.

Twain explicitly identifies the confidence men in *Huckleberry Finn* with civilization. Huck tells Jim that the King and Duke are no worse than historical reality: "All I say is, kings is kings, and you got to make allowances. Take them all around, they're a mighty ornery lot. It's the way they're raised" (p. 130). This, of course, is Twain, not the ignorant riverrat, talking. If we suspend disbelief, it sounds amusing enough. But if we recall that Twain once intended to write a novel about a boy who grows up, an unfortunate logic presents itself. Huck, to remain good and innocent, could never grow up. According to Twain's deterministic view of history, Huck's triumph over the picaro part of himself could not last: out there in the deadly Territory, Huck would become a picaro after all. His deformation is in progress already. When Huck reports the King's address to the mourners in the Wilks parlor, he is heeding the voice of conscience without questioning its moral authority.[67] It is a speech "full of tears and flapdoodle," it is "rot and slush," and it is "soul-butter and hogwash," but it has registered itself intimately in Huck's memory alongside other expressions of morality from Tom, Pap, and Miss Watson to Grangerford and Sherburn. All of society, in fact, is a kind of *picardía* symbolized by the confidence men and reflected by Huck.

## The Symbolic Confidence Man

Recognition of picaresque myth in *Huckleberry Finn* precludes the catharsis of roguery. Because readers enjoy clever tricks, guilt-free adventures, and the vigorous, instinctive life of a lovable rogue or Bad Boy, we can be deceived. We want to forget Tom Sawyer's evasion and to cherish memories of Huck and Jim on the raft, in the never-never world of the river. What we are loath to admit about Huck is his failed humanity, so we would like to believe that he escapes into freedom even at the sacrifice of love. The truth is that *Huckleberry Finn* has neither real freedom nor lasting love for our comfort. It is almost a nihilistic book. It is certainly a very sad book.

## *Dead Souls*: The Picaro as Artist

In the preceding paragraph and elsewhere in this study of the myth of the picaro, I must admit to several possible caveats. First, picaresque literature belongs, for the most part, to comedy. Appealing to a wide variety of senses, from a sense of the ludicrous and absurd, to a sense of liberation and celebration, to a sense of justice and equilibrium, picaresque literature is meant to be entertaining. Second, therefore, a critic of this literature needs to beware of exaggerating the manner in which some works mix the comic with the tragic. That certain comic novels possess a depth of import that diminishes the festive spirit is a matter of emphasis, not morbidity, and though descriptive terms such as alienation, disintegration, chaos, and identity failure, not to mention myth itself, may be necessitated, a critic who uses them should beware of cant that stifles humor with pious and portentous meaning. A similar caveat against symbol-hunting may be posted. The human imagination begets image upon image, before shaping these to meaning. For instance, Lewis Carroll's walruses and head-chopping queens may be subterraneous phantoms from Victorian England, but the critic who calls them symbols of oppressive society has parted company with childhood. In seeking to identify the symbolic form of picaresque narrative, I am attempting to construct a series of metaphors wherein the myth of the picaro continues its literary life. Melville's confidence man, behind his shifting masks, takes the form of all civilized endeavor. Twain's confidence men take the same form, representing all society throughout all history. Such metaphors extend to and join with ideas of hell, of death-in-life, and, as I now hope to explain, of art or imagination.

Nicolai Gogol's *Dead Souls* (1842) anticipates some of the symbolic suggestion of *The Confidence-Man* and *Huckleberry Finn* and Mann's *Felix Krull*. As in Melville's and Twain's works, the picaro in *Dead Souls* is associated with death, and the world of his confidence game is associated with hell. But Gogol's picaro begins to look rather like Mann's in that he is a kind of artist—a picaro-artist struggling with a hostile society yet yearning to belong to it. Like a confidence man, an artist in fiction tries to create illusions by talking of experiences he may not have had and of things that may not exist.

*Dead Souls* (Part I) tells the adventures of Chichikov, a disgraced civil servant, from his arrival in the provincial town of N. to his departure after a scheme for acquiring "dead souls" (deceased serfs still on censor rolls) is about to be exposed as a swindle. His plan is to pass himself off as a gentleman whose wealth and respectability are proved by the possession of "souls." It is a flimsy, typically picaresque plan, but it deceives the landowners of N., who are easily fooled by Chichikov's charm and address. Manilov, a sentimental ass, Sobakevich, a boorish materialist, Korobochka, a stingy widow, and the miser Plushkin are the dupes, each as soulless as the dead "souls" they possess. Yet Chichikov, like the picaro, is too transparent. He reveals his purpose to Nozdrev, a drunken gossip; then he inflames local jealousies by attempting to court the governor's daughter. In the reversal that follows, Chichikov becomes a subject of scandal, rumored to be a spy or a forger. Prudently, he steals away from N. in his wild, directionless troika.

Fragments of *Dead Souls* (Part II) show Chichikov pursuing his scheme in another part of Russia. Now, however, his proposed victims have human dimensions; for instance, Tientietnikov is an eccentric landowner suffering from the consciousness that he has failed himself and his country. A final fragment, evidently meant for a concluding place in the unfinished Part II, shows Chichikov in prison, suffering remorse of conscience and listening to an appeal to his better nature.

Not only does Chichikov share the picaro's lovelessness, selfishness, and yearning for respectability, but also he inhabits the "dead" society once portrayed in the Spanish picaresque novels.

Gogol was acquainted with Spanish literature, with *Don Quixote*, and possibly with picaresque novels. Pushkin had directed his attention to *Quixote* when giving him the subject of *Dead Souls*. The two works have most in common a freedom of design, allowing ample room for a satirical survey of manners and conditions, but Ludmilla Turkevich also sees in the characterization of Chichikov "an accurate inversion" of the character of Don Quixote.[68] Whereas the knight's ideal is to free society from injustice, Chichikov's ideal is to make the most of society's corruption. There is only slight internal evidence of Gogol's possible knowledge of the picaresque novels. Karl Selig notes some analogous episodes in *Dead Souls* and *Lazarillo*.[69] Chichikov's outwitting of the miser Plushkin corresponds broadly to Lazarillo's outwitting of the blind man; and in Part II the likable but vain landowner Tientietnikov—a man extremely sensitive about being addressed as "thou"—resembles the squire of *Lazarillo de Tormes* who left Old Castile because he was addressed familiarly. To such evidence of correspondence, I would add several details. The picaros in both works have accustomed themselves to the art of self-denial in order to maintain a marginal social standing; they both at some time hold positions in petty officialdom; they accept bribes, court women influential with their superiors, and generally keep up appearance by transparently exotic methods.

One of the interesting parallels between *Dead Souls* and the picaresque novels lies in Gogol's religious intention to present the picaro ultimately as a converted sinner.[70] Alemán attempted that theme in *Guzmán de Alfarache* and, like Gogol, failed to produce the necessary sequel. Does this mean that the picaresque representation of reality makes artistically implausible any structure of subjective belief that an author sincerely seeks to impose upon it? But, on the other hand, does not a special mood or tension within the objective real of the picaresque novel develop out of an author's subjectivity?

V. G. Belinsky wrote that there was in *Dead Souls* "a subjectivity that does not permit [Gogol] to pass by the world he depicts with apathetic indifference, but makes him pass the occurrences of the outer world through his living soul and in this way breathe a living soul into them."[71] Gogol's celebrated realism—the satirical panorama of Russian provincialism—is actually the picaresque world of dead appearances. The "real" to Gogol would exist on the subjective plane. Indeed, according to one of Gogol's letters, the first part of *Dead Souls* was merely "a pale introduction to the great epic poem which is taking shape in my mind"—a statement with an ominous addition: "and [which] will finally solve the riddle of my existence."[72]

Gogol's "epic poem" was to be a Russian commedia in prose. The picaresque introduction was to be hell, Part II, purgatory, Part III, paradise, or salvation. The fragmentary evidence of Part II lends weight to this argument because in those few chapters the characters begin to look human and spiritually tormented.

The riddle of Gogol's existence can never be known. Chichikov, too, is a riddle. Given his imaginative existence as a picaro, he could not have that other existence as a reformed sinner. His strange sin, after all, is to acquire what he once calls "unsubstantial things," and his symbolic activity is to give form to what exists unsubstantially in appearances. In real life this is a common mental process, not necessarily self-defeating; but in literature there is a felt difference between real life and mimesis; consequently, there must be a difference between the autonomous literary hero's mental activity and an author's subjective convictions. *Guzmán de Alfarache* is to the point. There the picaro's religious conversion could be seen as but the extension of his unredeemed self because it did not differ in kind from the earlier compulsive and solitary reforming of reality. In other words, if an author permits the conversion of a picaro, he tends to promote the idea that all forms, all faiths, are deceptive; he seems a confidence man himself, one who forms life out of death, meaning out of nihilism.

Perhaps Gogol's riddle is Chichikov's; at any rate both author and picaro have an ambiguous relationship to society.

Gogol wrote a number of stories about artists destroyed by reality. In *Nevsky Avenue* (1834) the artist Piscarov attempts to make reality conform to his dream and ends by cutting his throat. Meeting a prostitute on the avenue, he becomes infatuated by his image of her purity, seeks her out, proposes marriage, and is refused. Gogol moralizes: "It lies at all times, does Nevsky Avenue" (*Tales of Good and Evil*, p. 201). Nothing is what it seems; life is meaningless; art is meaning; and yet art's sudden involvement with life threatens the artist's creative existence. In a later story, *The Portrait* (1841–42), destruction is seen as the other aspect of creation. Chartkov, a talented young painter, has become fascinated by the gimlet eyes in an old portrait he has purchased. When the portrait frame yields a horde of gold, Chartkov sets up as a fashionable artist and grows rich, but his talent deteriorates. At last, maddened by failure to dedicate himself to art, Chartkov buys the best paintings on the market, removes them to his studio, and there destroys them. Again Gogol gives the moral: the devil's eyes had been represented in the old portrait. The artist, who is possessed by sheer, unilluminated reality, first deceives himself, then others. Thus Chartkov's first fashionable portrait, the life features of a silly girl superimposed upon an imaginative portrayal of Psyche, is a success because deception pleases his customer. The artist here fulfills the world's desire to be deceived; the more he does so, the more unreal he becomes.

This theme of the artist self-destroyed is implicit in *Dead Souls*. Chichikov, like Piscarov and Chartkov, is alienated from society because of his exceptional energy, intelligence, and charm, as well as his capacity to deny himself in pursuit of a dream. He is, of course, a parodistic version of the artist, being selfish and materialistic, and the disintegrated personality is viewed in comic rather than tragic terms. Like Piscarov and Chartkov he descends into reality, and its lack of real substance becomes the image of his own. Unlike them, he has no ideal conception; respectability is his goal. He cannot be destroyed because he is, already, a mythic symbol of a world of dead souls. Morally hollow, he is blown about like a Dantean sinner, the outcast of a dream world that is his true reality and out of which he is a nonentity.[73]

## The Apotheosis of the Confidence Man in Mann's *Felix Krull*

Thomas Mann's *Confessions of Felix Krull, Confidence Man* [*Bekenntnisse des Hochstaplers Felix Krull*] (1954) achieves what has rightly been called "the apotheosis of the literary confidence man."[74] *Felix Krull* sums up much of the four-hundred-year-old genre of the picaresque novel and at the same time transforms the anguish of the picaro into a feeling that looks like hope.

The Spanish picaro, coming to existence in a world from which God had withdrawn, took an enchanted voyage on the ship of picaresque life headed for a lonely shore where death promised *desengaño*. Mann's symbolic picaro, initially embarked on a similarly disillusioning journey, nonetheless gives a new moral sense to the enchantment by making dreams an essence of reality. This picaro possesses Keats's "negative capability" in that he finally submerges his ego in something larger than himself, in the archetypal feminine and whole theoretic structure of the universe. Perhaps, Mann seems to say, the will to illusion is good, after all. It places man where he ought to be, between nature and spirit, and that is good.

Mann's story of Felix Krull is the story of an artist as confidence man. "Felix Krull," he wrote of the original part of the novel published in 1911,

is in essence the story of an artist; in it the element of the unreal and illusional passes frankly over into the criminal. The idea of the book was suggested to me by the memoirs of a Rumanian adventurer named Manolescu. I was fascinated by the novel stylistic problem of direct autobiographical presentation on the model of my somewhat coarse-grained original; and still more by the grotesque idea of linking such a theme with another, traditional and beloved: *Dichtung und Wahrheit*, the aristocratic, confessional self-portrait of the artist. . . . In a sense [*Felix Krull*] may be the most personal [thing that I have done]; at least it expresses my personal attitude towards the traditional, which is both sympathetic and detached and which conditions my mission as an artist.

## The Symbolic Confidence Man

Indeed, the inward laws which are the basis of that "Bildungsroman" *The Magic Mountain* are the same in kind. [*Stories of Three Decades,* p. vii]

This fusion of rogue adventure (*Schelmenroman*), artist memoirs (*Dichtung und Wahrheit*), and spiritual history (*Bildungsroman*) keeps within the tradition of the picaresque novel but changes the context of the picaro's frustrated quest. Into the nonbeing of the picaro are taken attributes of the artist's being. Krull becomes a picaro endowed by the artistic nature of swindling with a potentially redemptive relationship to God and the world. As artist-picaro he inherits an explicit mythical role, that of Hermes, god of thieves and artists, the old trickster go-between of men and gods. Whether he uses his superhuman knowledge for good or ill, the artist-picaro is mankind's true representative because he sympathizes with the formative powers of the cosmos. Along with this missionary role goes a transformed relationship to the historic community. If the Spanish picaro is an outsider who may hope to find social identity only on the inside that denies him, the artist-picaro is an outsider with an identity that insiders desire and recognize: pretense serves mankind!

Mann's idea of the artist is therefore relevant to his idea of the confidence man. But it is useful to recall that Mann's idea of the artist changed between 1911 and the time when *Felix Krull* appeared as a novel in 1954. The early part of the story belongs to Mann's period of greatest concern with the artist's external/internal conflict with the "Bürgerlichkeit" and may be considered in relation to such works as *Tonio Kröger* (1903) and *Death in Venice* (1911).

The theme of *Tonio Kröger* is the artist's longing to resolve the tension between sensibility and responsibility, between artistic instincts and bourgeois morality. Kröger is well aware of the conflict that threatens to destroy him: "I stand between two worlds," he says, "at home in neither." His uneasy but artistically fruitful resolution of the conflict is to make art a responsible act: that is, the artist saves himself, even perhaps in the religious sense, by productivity. But in *Death in Venice* the artist Gustav von Aschenbach is destroyed by the inner conflict precisely because he has gone too far in worldly asceticism. Abnormal endeavors in the world of intellect have cut him off from his roots in life. Going to Venice to rest, he reacts violently as he is flooded by the beauty of life symbolized in the youth Tadzio. And as his unnatural longings become necessary to him, he permits his fancy to construct a set of circumstances that can lead only to death and, in the end, do.

The version of *Felix Krull* that appeared in 1911 parodies the conflict of artist and "Bürger." Krull seems to strike a balance in Kröger's manner because he uses his "art" to serve others; but in actuality his "art" is irresponsible, based upon a conditioned response to decadent middle-class desires, and selfish, directed to the attainment of a shallow respectability. There is an obsessional quality about Krull; his preoccupation with art makes him part of the twilight world of Aschenbach. Krull has reached a stage of spiritual exhaustion when he begins his parody memoirs in his fortieth year. Like Aschenbach, he has committed himself too intensively to the intellectual creation of forms only marginally related to society. But in the parody of the Aschenbach artist, Krull is committed to the art of self-creation, to the pathetic rather than the tragic sense of life. The bright comic action of *Felix Krull* is an ironic criticism of the dark and disintegrating world in which it occurs.

In 1943 Mann completed *Joseph* and, while hesitating to undertake *Doctor Faustus*, reread the *Krull* materials "with singular result," namely, "insight into the inner relation of the Faust-material with it (depending upon the solitariness-motif, here tragic-mystical, there humorous-criminal)."[75] He was interested now in writing from the point of view of unity. Here was a deeper sense of the correspondence of artist and picaro. The earlier theme had been primarily social: the artist's conflict with the "Bürgerlichkeit" seen as the picaro's conflict with decadent society. Now appeared a possible religious theme, the artist's and the picaro's solitary search for salvation by free, and therefore illicit, means. The Faust-soul could turn freedom into channels beneficial to society rather than against the social order as in the first Frankfurt *Faustbook* of 1587. In Mann's mature view the artist could help to recover an authentic spiritual order. By analogy, the picaro could be the negative counterpart of Faust, already allied to dubious powers but potentially free to use forbidden knowledge to restore goodness, reality, and trust. The artist-picaro emerged from the twilight world of 1911 with a new mission as mediator for man in the world of the spirit. The traditional picaresque creation of form out of appearances was now to be a metaphor for the human idea of God.

Krull's parody *Confessions*, like Lazarillo's parody of Augustine, began while he was ascetically withdrawn from the world. His memories are dead, and thus when he speaks of the past he gives it a goodly appearance it did not possess. With ironic reverence he accounts for his unstable and humiliating origins. His father, he says, manufactured Rhenish wine, and the public liked it because it was bottled handsomely with labels designed by his godfather Schimmelpreester (= the high priest of mold). The two men gave Felix his longing for the world and its people, and the child of darkness created his own twilight existence. Quite early he had taken refuge from a society despising his lack of respectability by means of "the independent and self-sufficient exercise of [his] imagination," and it was this sensibility that had given him a feeling of "secret superiority" (*Confessions of Felix Krull*, p. 11).

Krull's need for pretense is changed by Mann's context (the artist theme) into a strategy of the will. Krull decides "to study the human will and to practice on myself its mysterious, sometimes supernatural effects" (*Felix Krull*, p. 12). Where the Spanish picaro once practiced self-denial because survival depended upon it, Krull undertakes to deny himself as a prelude to dedicated assault on the social structure and in order to seize a worldly credit that gives life, he says, "meaning in your own eyes and lead[s] to your advancement" (p. 13). His first public exhibition of talent is a triumphant hoax. Appearing as a musical prodigy at Bad Langenschwalbach, he "plays" a violin with greased bow, converting sound into gesture and pure mimesis that earns him the approval of respectable families. After this success, Krull decides to exploit the difference between artist as *artist* and artist as *person* in accord with Schimmelpreester's complacent observation that "oddities are always associated with talent" (p. 20). Soon Krull is astonished by the "oddities" of the singer Müller-

Rose at a Wiesbaden theater. The beautiful actor and illusionist of the stage is in reality a disgusting boor: "This repulsive worm [reflects Krull] is the reality of the glorious butterfly in whom those deluded spectators believed they were beholding the realization of all their own secret dreams of beauty, grace, and perfection" (p. 28). From the experience, Krull draws the conclusion that there is "a general human need" to be deceived, a "mutual fulfillment" whereby the artist-picaro and the audience-dupes share a debased religious experience, literally *con-fide*. Thereafter, he dedicates himself to the creation of "a compelling and effective reality out of nothing, out of sheer inward knowledge and contemplation" (p. 34), and when he fulfills the needs of others for beauty, grace, and perfection, he brings it in his own flesh: beginning with the maid Genovefa, Krull "fulfills" one woman after another.

Following the suicide of the elder Krull the family moves to Frankfurt, where Mrs. Krull, like the mother of Lazarillo, takes in lodgers. Felix wanders the town at night exercising "the gift of perception" (p. 69) and seeking to find something in the world with which he may be united. On one occasion he is attracted to a brother and sister distantly glimpsed on their balcony. "I tried in imagination to force my way into their existence" (p. 69), he declares. Such double attractiveness represents to him "dreams of love, dreams of delight, and a longing for union," motivations that apply equally well to artist and to picaro. He finds his mission as a confidence man: "To throw such beautiful, airy bridges across all the chasms of strangeness that lie between man and man" (p. 73). Free rootless vision becomes the way to order. Krull now asserts that his real interest as author of the *Confessions* "lies not in language but rather in the extreme, silent, regions of human intercourse—that one, first of all, where strangeness and social rootlessness still create a free, primordial condition and glances meet and marry irresponsibly in dreamlike wantonness; but then, too, the other [that is, linguistic representation] in which the greatest possible closeness, intimacy, and commingling re-establish completely that wordless primordial condition" (p. 73). The world as will and idea, freedom and form: the artist-picaro contains the paradox in his own activity. And so Krull,

fully conscious of symbolic being, embraces the life of illusionism with professional pride rather than with a Lazarillo's anguish. The episode in which he fakes epilepsy in order to escape
military service teaches him that "to live symbolically, spells
true freedom" (p. 94).

When Krull goes to Paris to become a hotel liftboy, he is both
the disintegrated picaro and the artist in search of an integrating
vision of the whole.

The third part of the novel represents Krull's quasi-ritualistic
initiation into the mysteries of sentient being. Beginning with
inspiration and worship, continuing through a period of hesita-
tion followed by rededication and withdrawal from the world,
and issuing forth in a spiritual journey into cosmic theories of
nature and history and finally into the actuality of love, this part
of the novel shows the picaro mythically at home in a timeless,
placeless existence.

At the circus Krull is dazzled by Andromache the trapeze
artist, a creature of air like himself. Her death-defying art represents to him "what others devote to love" (p. 171), and he is
consequently inspired by a religion of art that is self-sufficient
but alienating from life and love. Thus the picaro, whose will to
illusion is both death-defying and loveless, would remain an
egocentrically omnipotent outcast in the all-renouncing flight
through nothingness. Immediately the dying of his humanity
seems probable: "The current of sympathy between me and the
world was losing vitality" (p. 182). When he refuses the advances
of Lord Strathbogie, he proudly rejects the temptation to stray
from his "true" vocation as illusionist. An immersion in nothingness has become, in the religious sense, a "calling." But then
Madame Houpflé arouses his male sexuality and transforms his
skills as a thief into a source of joy or benefit to humanity. Still a
hotel waiter by day, Krull masquerades by night as a gentleman,
thus burying his real self in his disguises: "I masqueraded in
both capacities and the undisguised reality behind the two appearances, the real I, could not be identified because it actually
did not exist" (p. 205). With this rebirth into symbolic existence
Krull may easily exchange his identity as Felix Krull the waiter
for a new identity as the Marquis de Venosta. Like a religious

convert, he gains a new name and title and obliterates "memories that belonged to my no longer valid past" (p. 231). Now neither himself nor the marquis, and yet both, a double identity, Krull sets out on a long journey during which he meets Professor Kuckuck, a sort of burlesque Teilhard de Chardin but also spokesman for Thomas Mann.[76] This talkative theorist maintains that the purely transitory possesses grandeur—a theory with instant appeal to a picaro: "Only the episodic, only what possessed a beginning and an end, was interesting and worthy of sympathy because transitoriness had given it a soul. But what was true of everything—the whole of cosmic Being had been given a soul by transitoriness, and the only thing that was eternal, soulless, and therefore unworthy of sympathy, was that Nothingness out of which it had been called forth to labour and to rejoice" (p. 248). From the picaro's point of view, this theory is a complete vindication: the symbolic confidence game enables the disintegrated man to acquire his own soul! Krull is elated, and soon, while observing reconstructed animals in Kuckuck's museum, he discovers "respectable" ancestry that picaros hitherto had lacked. Suddenly all being seems to Krull "preliminary moves in the direction of me—that is, of Man" (p. 271). The once-despised outcast, the picaro, is apotheosized as the end product of all natural history and the representative being in an episodic, picaresque cosmos. Amid apparent disintegration, Krull discovers primal indivisibility. But his integration is incomplete without the vital ingredient of love and human sympathy. Hence the novel ends with Krull's attachments to Zouzou and to her mother, Senhora Maria Pia Kuckuck, whom, at a bullfight, he is able to identify as goddess of fertility—and to whom submission in love is self-realization in universally oriented humanity.

As Donald F. Nelson has shown, Mann's use of myth and psychology in *Felix Krull* has decisive structural and thematic significance. Krull's "archetypal experiences . . . form a bridge of transition from the personal to the suprapersonal and universal, from a highly cultivated ego-consciousness to the realm of the collective unconscious." Prior to his encounter with Madame

Houpflé (Artemis-Hecate), Felix (Hermes) is narcissistically unable to love anything that does not pertain to self. Madame Houpflé's intervention creates his awareness of altruistic love. Thereafter, beneath the frivolous guise of his confidence game, Felix is engaged in an inner struggle to reconcile Eros with agape, conscious with unconscious forces. With Zouzou (Persephone) and, above all, Maria (Demeter), his human identity is resolved. Nelson sums up: "For Krull, the experience of the archetype is the force which draws him into the orbit of the unconscious, a realm where the mythical and the psychological merge. Without this connection with the subterranean springs of man's being, Krull's existence draws nourishment only from the one-sidedness of individual consciousness in which man is only a fragment of his original self. Thus, as Mann's novel assumes more and more a mythic dimension, the motif of the unconscious must correspondingly become more prominent, and the attempt to enter it and to recover a lost unity becomes the psychic motivating force behind Krull's actions."[77] I have cited these statements at length because they do more than describe Mann's novel: they concisely summarize a transcendence of the myth of the picaro by a myth of unity and love.

*Felix Krull* is half-picaresque. Haunted by the specter of death, Krull, like Lazarillo de Tormes, desperately wants to be loved. Lazarillo almost succeeds in establishing a brotherly relationship with the squire from Old Castile, but he fails and loses his humanity. On the other hand, Felix Krull is a lover of women, even a philosopher of love. He reveals his essentially loving nature when he tries to persuade the prickly Portuguese maiden named Zouzou to abandon her puritan aversion to sex; he tells her that the natural solitude of man is miraculously ended by love, "the digression on Nature's part that, to the astonishment of the universe, wipes out the division between one person and another, between the me and the you" (*Felix Krull*, p. 327). In both *Lazarillo* and *Krull* the picaro's anguished yearning for love, for beauty, grace, and perfection, for the great symbolical integration of his disintegrating world, is felt because the picaresque novel is always, at its best, the story of our human search for meaning. When Krull's desire to love and be loved is fulfilled by the numinous image of the Great Mother, he is no longer a picaro. He has crossed the boundaries from illusion to reality, from death to life, from matter to spirit, and from solitude to humanity.

# 5

# The Tragicomedy of Self-Creation

The picaresque novel is a genuine kind of literary art that originates in a myth about man's relation to himself, to society, and to God. It achieves form during the breakup of the medieval world, loses formal potency during the rise of rationalism, Protestantism, and capitalism, and then reappears in symbolic form in comparatively recent times as part of a reaction against aspects of those movements. The Spanish picaresque novelists, the author of *Lazarillo*, Alemán, and Quevedo are the writers to whose works we must turn for understanding of the central tradition. Later novelists who further this understanding are Melville, Gogol, Twain, and Mann. Related in revealing ways to the genre are Lesage, Defoe, Fielding, Smollett, Dickens, and Thackeray; these writers, too, assist in defining the picaresque idea. I have called that idea—that common denominator of a genre composed of separate works—disintegration and have attempted to show that the word reflects a concern of picaresque writers with problems of knowledge, morality, and religion.

If this major literary phenomenon cannot be satisfactorily explained as result of influences, it can be, I believe, by realization that it is a myth, the myth of the picaro. For myth, the child of creative impulse, continues to manifest itself as long as there remains a language of the human soul. That is, the picaresque myth, as any other myth recently dominating and expressing us, functions in our lives and describes realities that feeling immediately perceives. The emergence into literary art, the historical genesis of certain myths of which the picaresque is one, reveals images and symbols that organize, though they do not determine, significant life experience. Although the myth of the picaro enters the field of consciousness in sixteenth-century Spain, it is not thereby a specific manifestation of Spanish culture alone. What emerges from the first novels is indeed, more than four centuries later, a world of here and now, increasingly global, increasingly, as a story of cultural failure and of personal invisibility, picaresque.

Irresistibly, I am drawn to speculate about the spiritual ambience of the myth of the picaro. Certainly if my analysis of narrative structures is correct, I would conclude that the picaresque novels reveal a recurrent nudity of the self before time. That desperate movement of the modern mind, and to the mind, called Cartesianism after a seventeenth-century skeptical philosopher of science, represents a paring down of the real world to essentials. Similarly, the modern imagination since the sixteenth century often, as in picaresque fiction, reveals a movement of negation, of reduction to an individual consciousness preexisting culture itself, which it then may be preparing to recapitulate and recreate, in Yeats's words,

> down where all the ladders start,
> In the foul rag-and-bone shop of the heart.
> ["The Circus Animals' Desertion"]

The moral passion, the honesty of the authentic picaresque novels, strips from man his social masks until he is "nothing man" or "invisible man" confronting, with ancestral craftiness, the millennia of his solitude. Picaresque myth may be an ultimate kind of humanism whereby we are led to a tower or abyss from which to contemplate and accept life as it is with all its folly. Essentially a con artist, potentially a poetmaker of new social identities and new cultures, the picaro presents a masquerade of episodic adventures that are inevitably "to be continued" as long as experience remains open and mankind sane and human, this side of Orwellian 1984. The informing idea of the myth of the picaro is that it has the power to identify and to reverse modern man's alienation from himself, from humanity, and from the universe. His negatives are necessary to express the light.

Autobiographical form allows picaresque myth its fullest

dimension of meaning as a literature of loneliness. And that personal world of the "I," of being that precedes becoming, originates in an Eros that has lost cultural visibility and despairs of its fulfillment in harmony with agape: to "love one's neighbor *as* oneself" is a spiritual task of such profound magnitude that any failure to accomplish it, be the fault individual or social, may polarize the self in a self-loving psychic condition divided from, even against, the self-sacrificing one. Whether it is a question of picaro or confidence man, we have followed a story of spiritual quest for community, for what Jean-Paul Sartre terms the Other, for what I throughout this study have been naming love. The phenomenon of first-person narration of the most revealing picaresque novels brings to light how polarized the individual consciousness must have already become by the early sixteenth century. And indeed the myths of love that emerged in the troubadour legends of the twelfth century attest to a new historical problem of the person juxtaposed against authoritarian civilization. The birth of the modern novel, I submit, occurred when the soul of Western man, increasingly aware of death in itself and in the heart of dominant culture, had been struggling to find its way back to humanity out of the labyrinth of loneliness.

The "I" dissolving into the "we" creates the literature of love. I am not referring here to a Manichean opposition of good and evil, two preexisting principles, nor do I think a critic should avail himself of moral judgments that make a picaro "bad" and a saint "good," though, to be sure, novelists such as Alemán and Quevedo show picaros as evil insofar as they close into themselves and cannot love. What I have in mind is a bipolarity, a tension between the literature of loneliness and the literature of love out of which the modern novel (and much else besides) has come into being. From *Lazarillo de Tormes* to James Joyce's *Ulysses* and William Faulkner's *Absalom, Absalom!* the light of love has been defined by and won from the darkness of not-love. A transfiguring death-to-oneself proceeding from the natural self has been linked to the dialectic of sin and grace, for he who has not love is nothing, in spiritual truth.

He is Picaro.

Given such serious purport, picaresque novels might seem to belong entirely to tragic literature. Why, one may well ask, are they ostensibly formed as comedy?

According to P. E. Russell, Spanish authors of the Golden Age "believed that laughter and the ridiculous were provoked by some form of ugliness, of *turpitudo*, symbolized by the distorting mask worn by the players in ancient comedy." At the root of the ridiculous was a "deviation from the natural order of things," a deviation "that could not easily be eliminated though also, if it was to be laughable, it must be incapable of causing serious harm."[1] Moreover, Golden-Age writers expected the audience for comedy to feel no commiseration toward the characters whose folly was exposed to laughter. Thus our own postromantic compulsion to participate emotionally in comedy, with pity and sympathetic understanding extended to the picaro (in complimentary guise as rogue, antihero, delinquent, or underdog), may lead us to forget that Lazarillo, Guzmán, and Pablos were meant to be funny, at least up to the point when their follies become criminal. What, then, is the exhibition of their folly wherein they deviate from the natural order? The answer, I believe, is to be found in the picaro's pretensions to freedom and to self-creation. From the moment Lazarillo has his head bashed against the stone bull, he is alone and belongs to himself—so he himself declares at the point in time when he rationalizes his loss of identity as a social success. Similarly, other picaros come to be endowed with no-self, deprived of being human, and converted or conditioned into the apathetic confidence man with his bogus game of integration. The comedy of self-creation envisions tragic disintegration precisely because human freedom without *pietas* and outside the cosmic hierarchy irradiated by love is—for Renaissance man—ridiculous.

Our contemporary view of self-creation differs dramatically from that of the Renaissance. We have inherited a cult and ideology of, as well as a passion for, individual freedom that makes self-creation the noble basis for man's dreams, for his art and religion, for all that would give vital meaning to his survival as human. Without the passion for self-creation, Erich Fromm warns, modern man will lose to forms of exploitative control the conditions for mobilizing the love of life: "The human passions transform man from a mere thing into a hero, into a being that in spite of tremendous handicaps tries to make sense of life. He wants to be his own creator, to transform his state of being unfinished into one with some goal and some purpose, allowing him to achieve some degree of integration."[2] Fromm affirms our strivings to be free and to love, and he sees these as counters to a worldwide increase of necrophilia, or the attraction to what is dead, decaying, lifeless, and purely mechanical. It would not be too farfetched to recognize in the myth of the picaro some similar, though imaginative, not psychoanalytical, explanation of decadence as, paradoxically, life turning against itself in the striving to make sense of it. That is, to the Spanish picaresque novelists, creation of self outside orthodox theological patterns is folly, the way of spiritual death; and though contemporary man, by contrast, sees his salvation in self-creation, there remains the possibility of frustration and failure, of escape from freedom, and of conditioning into spiritual death. Here, at the psychic root, is a continuity of picaresque myth, for what it comes down to is not just the way of life of vagabonds and juvenile delinquents but *any way of life that seems to lead away and down from meaning and full humanity.* Such a contingency surely shapes a great deal of twentieth-century fiction and philosophy: modern man struggles to find identity in a less than meaningful world.

Since the appearance of the first modern novels, the picaresque novels, thinkers have been aware of cultural failure. The whole edifice of meaning that we know as Christianity, the multifaceted myth that gave, and still gives to some, an idea of order with respect to personal conduct, social organization, and spiritual history, has, for many, fallen apart. The magic of the Word has dissolved into thin air. The symbolism of the language by which we knew ourselves and our destiny seems weak, no longer touching us where we live. Men of prophetic soul such as Herman Melville despaired to see the gods going home, yet knew in their hearts they would have to find another Holy Land. Melville found his in the myths of Asia and Oceania, back where all the myths, including Christianity, started. Unlike Melville, humanists such as Wallace Stevens rejoiced that man is free of the gods at last. And some writers stayed within the Christian tradition: T. S. Eliot embraced orthodoxy, and William Faulkner and D. H. Lawrence reworked Christian symbolism, placing particular emotional emphasis upon pity, compassion, and sacrifice and upon the theme of resurrection. Whatever ground has been lost and found, the task of the writer in modern times has become immensely difficult. He can no longer rely upon a community of meaning. The stories and poems that he makes have to generate their own meaning. Surely in all the literary epochs there has been no time when a writer's quest for knowledge has assumed such importance, yet at the same time been so beleaguered by chaotic appearances, theories, and ideologies, as ours. Yet our psychic survival could partly depend upon this quest.

In their efforts to describe and evaluate modern literature, critics and writers seem to agree upon a number of related observations. The first observation is that, since the later Middle Ages, there has been an accelerating decline in what is called the "other-worldly point of view." Thus a writer is virtually denied the old belief systems and their social expression as, to quote Joseph Conrad, "a fixed standard of conduct." Hence many modern writers express in their works a sense of loss, especially of relationship between man and man. Outraged by the complexity, incoherence, and violence of modern times, they may look back to a time of social order when life-significant symbols were shared. A second observation of critics is that the literary generations of the twentieth century are best distinguished in their manner of responding to the fact of death—that is, in their manner of somehow getting beyond it. As R. W. B. Lewis has written, "The first fact of modern historical life is the death that presses in on it from all sides: death in battle, death in prison, death in the pit of the soul and the very heart of culture. . . . Yet," Lewis continues, "the true artist is constantly seeking ways to confound death."[3] In other words, the typical narrative pattern in modern literature is a quest—an imaginary picaresque voyage into the world, into the bad jungle of ourselves, until we see, together, where we are. It is a journey toward some affirmation of life, and it belongs to comedy because it would be a celebration of joy with freedom authenticated in the aesthetic, not the ideological sense.

And with respect to freedom, the artist differs from the revolutionist. Whereas a revolutionist, according to Eric Hoffer in *The True Believer*, seeks to inspire mass movements and expresses a pity for the downtrodden and injured that has been hatched out of his hatred for the powers that be, an artist has that kind of love toward mankind at large that makes him able to endure the general condition of evil and suffering, regardless of any relations these may have to his own life. Whereas an artist reveals, often at great personal cost, a profound skepticism of collective human efforts, a revolutionist preaches and glorifies such efforts, often at his own great peril, for in discrediting a specific ruling order for specific grievances, he may give rise to far greater tyrannies. A revolutionist, though he speaks of freedom, is committed to a cause; an artist, like the true scholar, may be said to adopt the Socratic ideal of detachment before possible worlds of the truth. An artist resists the call to identify completely with the everyday social process and thereby to confront all that is wrong in our midst. His call is the call of life, as it is for Joyce's Stephen Dedalus. An artist's freedom is to be free of falsity of all kinds, to be free to affirm authentic experience. Nothing kills that freedom so much as the Calypso-Circe promise of a Brave New World or a 1984, where few would dare to question, even if blessed with a sense of the past, the meaning of life.

The modern artist is closer to a picaro than to a revolutionist. Not only does the artist recognize that he is both isolated and imprisoned within society, he also understands and accepts the conditions of survival. And he accepts them because in his search for forms, he discerns that everything is created, everything made—selfhood is made, society is made, love is made—and that the good, the true, and the beautiful are forever destroyed, forever reborn. This positive ongoing creation, this view of time as eternal revolution, is latently prefigured in the myth of the picaro, a story of the casting out of the free individual, of his essential aloneness, and of the disintegration of received values and reality. In its original, Spanish form, the myth was profoundly pessimistic because man's real nature as free could not be celebrated by the closed systems of prevailing belief. In later, modified form, the myth lingered in a kind of individualism that persists in a "naturally" loveless state outside society. In more recent times, outsidedness has become descriptive of the human condition and the artist has been elevated to the role of representative man, the myth of the picaro is a universal story, the picaro now neither outcast nor sinner but the trickster of eternity and master forger, through imagination, of reality. At the same time, the symbolic picaro has power to transform outsidedness into insidedness: insidedness is his freedom, the disaster and the glory of being alive. He is free to choose love and to transcend the destructive element of self through faith in a God of perpetual creation. When every day is a new creation, the old narrative of personal center is preferred to historical chronicle. Something of the intimacy with which *Lazarillo de Tormes* may have been felt is restored. The tragedy of lonely bondage to freedom is returned to consciousness in forms akin to the first modern novels of four hundred years ago. But now self-creation is winning through to the other side of ambiguity; it is comedy, the celebration of life.

Two contemporary novels are flavored with picarism, Ralph Ellison's *Invisible Man* (1952) and Joyce Cary's *The Horse's Mouth* (1944). Cary's work is not a picaresque novel; Ellison's is close enough to the central tradition to qualify as a masterpiece of the genre. Both these novels nevertheless help to illustrate continuity and transformation of the myth of the picaro.

*Invisible Man* seems to conform closely to picaresque tradition.[4] Mock-autobiographical in form, it is the episodic story of an innocent social outcast, who for most of his life has masqueraded in identities given him by others and whose own will to illusion has maintained these masks at the cost of achieved identity, reality, and humanity. The nameless narrator of the title is acutely conscious, at last, of the transparency of any selfhood superimposed by society, yet, since he is literally living underground in a state of total isolation from others, he seems to resemble the loveless picaro reduced to a mechanical personification of the negative, rather than a person preparing to surface to a new life of responsibility. Distinctions between right and wrong have been exposed as ambiguous, another picaresque motif. Even at the end, Invisible Man still embraces trickery, enjoying, like B'rer Rabbit, the joke of making society bear the expense of its failure to penetrate his confidence man's disguise.

But if Invisible Man enjoys his joke—in a novel that is over-burdened with jokes, including the sociological joke (= black Americans are highly visible) of the title—he knows, unlike the picaro, that his life is far from hollow. In fact, after all his violent experiences as a victim of racial stereotyping, he has achieved, not lost, his form and brought his soul boldly into the light. As he declares in the prologue, "Without light I am not only invisible, but formless as well; and to be unaware of one's form is to live a death. I myself, after existing some twenty years, did not become alive until I discovered my invisibility" (p. 6). Thus the actual form of Ellison's novel is an antipicaresque journey toward personal freedom and toward the eventual recovery of a soul left uncontaminated by society. Midway through the novel, Invisible Man discovers his ability to speak for humanity, and his thoughts take the form of a meditation upon the ending of Joyce's *Portrait of the Artist as a Young Man*: "Stephen's problem, like ours, was not actually one of creating the uncreated con-science of his race, but of creating the *uncreated features of his face*. Our task is that of making ourselves individuals. The conscience of a race is the gift of its individuals who see, evaluate, record. . . . We create the race by creating ourselves and then to our great astonishment we will have created something far more important: We will have created a culture" (p. 268). Like Huckle-berry Finn, with whom Invisible Man also identifies himself, the archetypal American struggles against patterns of conformity, for these are inimical to democracy and personal passion. Iden-tity is won when the individual self is freed from the definitions of others. Thereafter, real life begins as a personal world "of infinite possibilities," as Ellison has his hero observe in the epi-logue. Invisible Man's refusal to accept limits means he is no longer either an outcast or a tragic victim. His self-creation is salvation from disintegration. His role-playing, like the picaro's, enables him to survive by manipulating the illusions of society, but he himself—that is, as an essential person celebrating himself in Whitmanesque fashion—has an uncompromising sense of who he is and where he has been.

The varieties of disorder in modern life account for literature that continues the myth of the picaro. But it is obvious that the myth is transformed as soon as the picaro is free to create his own reality, reconstituting, out of experience, a common and responsible humanity.

*The Horse's Mouth* is the third part of *First Trilogy*, a comic epic worthy to stand beside *Don Quixote* and *Tom Jones* and probably the only significant development in the writing of fiction since *Ulysses*. Cary's tripartite novel dramatizes the feelings and perceptions of three characters in turn, a cook, a lawyer, and an artist; by juxtaposing their autobiographies he achieves the inclusiveness of epic, and by depicting how each character moves from illusion to reality and to acceptance of life as it is, he unfolds a comic vision. As the artist Gulley Jimson says, "To forgive is wisdom, to forget is genius. And easier. Because it's true. It's a new world every heart beat. The sun rises seventy-five times a minute. After all, what is a people? It doesn't exist. Only individuals exist—lying low in their own rat-holes. As far apart as free drinks" (p. 227). The remark captures the essence of Cary's comic vision that celebrates man in a state of freedom, even though man's solitude is a tragedy circumscribed, not by the ritualized world of the tribe (be it a primitive tribe or totalitarian state), but by the synthesizing power of imagination and by common emotion. Man, in his developing freedom, is always threatened by others exercising their freedom, so man and society live in a constant state of tension. As observed earlier in this study, such a view of eternal flux, a view going back at least to Heraclitus, becoming a medieval commonplace in Petrarch and a major premise of Hobbes's *Leviathan*, anticipates and parallels the picaresque myth of disintegration. But Cary is no peddler of darkness, a fact that sets him apart from the Aldous Huxleys and the Ernest Hemingways and the common run of modern pretenders to extreme, easy truth. Although Cary depicts the worlds of individuals who incessantly strive toward a personal achievement and who thereby run headfirst into one another, this activity would be incomplete without certain constants of human nature manifesting themselves in an infinite variety of particular variation. Constants such as love and symbolmaking unify a world split up into complete individuals. Accordingly, the function of art is to uncover for our contemplation the beauty and order that are potential in the universe. Art, as Cary sees it, liberates us from the multiplicity of life. In the eloquent conclusion of *Art and Reality*, Cary pays tribute to this power of great art: "It is only in great art and the logic of the subconscious where judgment has become part of the individual emotional character that we move freely in a world which is at once concept and feeling, rational order and common emotion, in a dream which is truer than actual life and a reality which is only there made actual, complete and purposeful to our experience" (pp. 174–75). In sum, Cary's vision is of a world in flux, out of which man creates order, meaning, and personal identity and achieves an ecstatic joy equivalent to divine grace.

A number of critics have placed *The Horse's Mouth* within picaresque tradition. Robert Alter, for example, declares that the work "embodies the distinctive heroism and hedonism of the picaresque anti-heroic attitude" and finds the artist-trickster, Gulley Jimson, "an eternal adolescent" possessed of "the remarkable picaresque faculty of regarding life as a game."[5] Robert Bloom discovers in this novel "a decidedly picaresque use of space" and obscurely concludes that "the picaro in Gulley overmasters the representative symbolic artist."[6] Criticism of this kind tells us more about confusion in literary vocabulary than about the art of Joyce Cary. *The Horse's Mouth*, it is true, exhibits certain affinities to the episodic fictions of Defoe, Fielding, or Dickens, and the character of Gulley is flavored with delightful roguery as well as with aspirations to convert patterns of social failure into triumphs of honored acceptance. These affinities and ingredients, however, do not make *The Horse's Mouth* a picaresque novel nor its hero a picaro.

Cary's use of mock-autobiography in this novel does not in itself indicate picaresque tradition, but it does help to explain what is happening to the myth of the picaro in contemporary literature.

Old Gulley Jimson dictates his memoirs of events that have led to a stroke ending his not undistinguished career as painter. Art is everything, his religion, his morality, his world of everyday people, be they millionaires or barmaids. Like William Blake, whose poetry guides this pilgrim to beatific visions, Gulley perceives eternity in the overlooked and commonplace, even in the elbows and feet of his acquaintances. But since imagination is everything, Gulley tries to extract necessities of his life work from a society unable to comprehend him and consequently spends most of his time using that imaginative force in schemes to get money. When he gets money, he squanders it generously. If he is impractical, he is also destructive. Although his friends would like to protect him from himself—Nosy, the boy who clings to him as the Fool to Lear, Sara, his former common-law wife and model, Professor Alabaster, an art critic who recognizes Gulley's genius—their unsolicited loyalties and disinterested affections are not enough to prevent the destructiveness that is the natural concomitant of his creativity. He threatens and swindles the rich and invades the world of "Boorjoy" respectability, to little or no avail. His frustrated rage either lands him in prison or makes him a fugitive from the law. And, significantly, his greatest vision, "The Creation," is painted on the wall of a derelict chapel that officialdom demolishes before his very eyes. His and society's destructive element notwithstanding, Gulley grows spiritually. Recognizing both the folly of giving in to hatreds and grievances and the fact that he needs the world, he is moved to tears of compassion when he learns of the deaths of Sara and of his old patron and enemy, Hickson. Gulley accepts the destruction of his paintings because, as he knows, his interest in them has been consumed in the free exercise of creating them, in giving form to the divine messages received from "the horse's mouth." By the end of his life as an artist, Gulley is able to live by William Blake's dictum, "Go love without the help of anything on earth" (p. 30). Like King Lear, Gulley has his egocentricity purged away and replaced by compassion and by the wisdom that ripeness is all. On the eve of World War II, which looms as a symbol of a world of violent change, Gulley is looking beyond an outsider's despair to the special grace of laughter.

Even such a brief summary reveals *The Horse's Mouth* as a saint's confessions. The literary ancestry of this novel may be older than the picaresque, which first emerged as, in part, a parody of a soul's journey to God. "I am no saint," declares the first picaro, Lazarillo de Tormes. Gulley Jimson, on the other hand, moves progressively, through paintings of "The Fall," "The Raising of Lazarus," and "The Creation," to apocalyptic vision of the wonders of love. At the climax of *The Horse's Mouth*, moments before his stroke, Gulley sees his painting of Creation move, that is, symbolic art attains the dimension of marvelous life! Ecstatic, he says, "I saw through the cloud about ten thousand angels in caps, helmets, bowlers and even one top hat, sitting on walls, dustbins, gutters, roofs, window sills and other people's cabbages, laughing. That's funny, I thought, they've all seen the same joke. God bless them. It must be a work of eternity, a chestnut, a horse-laugh" (p. 308–9). Even though the painting moves because the wall is being demolished and the people laugh at Gulley, not with him, the ironies are gentle: Saint Gulley has received the benediction of reality.

It is now clear that the "dehumanization of art" observed by Ortega y Gasset in 1925 did not mean that artists intended to abnegate art's old cultural responsibilities. Modern art no longer accepts values derived from the past, but, as Joseph Frank points out, "art undertook the unprecedented task of *creating by itself* the cultural, religious, or metaphysical content from which art had always hitherto drawn its aims and inspiration." Values are derived, not from the "gods" of the artist's culture, but—and this is crucial—from his activity as artist, from "his religious devotion to the function of art itself as the *source* of a new realm of 'the sacred'."[7] The artist's new relation to his work is, then, in a religious sense mystical, and his efforts to express the essence of reality invest him with the kind of authority hitherto associated with prophets and saints, as long as we accept his premises and pretenses.

To accept them is not easy. Our frequent incomprehension of creative acts does indeed induce a kind of dehumanization of art.

This is the juncture where skepticism conceives of the artist as picaro: both would create reality out of nothing. Yet this fusion of roles altogether transforms the structure of the picaro's existence, opens it so that disintegration is preliminary to the recovery of the highest spiritual values.

The autobiographical novels by any definition—including the loose one about rogues and tricksters who have adventures on the road—would lend themselves to a new, intimately human mythos of conversion. At least since Apuleius, whose wandering hero is initiated into the cult of Isis, narratives of picaresque kind (again, loosely) have been adaptable to the pressures of religious feeling, and the potentiality of the self's reconstitution after spiritual death is exactly what animates the irony of *Lazarillo de Tormes* with its parody of the Lazarus archetype. Thus if the modern novelist adopts, however unconsciously, the picaresque form, he does so because the form is well suited to his task, the artist's task of creating cultural, religious, or metaphysical content. The appearances he invades by means of his surrogate or projected self, the personal center, must precipitate some essence at last, however private and mystical the formulation. The only certainty of this narrative of self-creation is freedom. And freedom is now, historically considered, empowered to convert chaos into order, loneliness into love.

The situation is new and important. The modified picaresque form of eighteenth-century fiction celebrated the picaro's freedom, but social myth controlled it. Twentieth-century literary art eliminates this control and makes the artist's relation to his work the paradigm of the human condition, that is, Everyman's quest for a personal mythology, Everyman's self-creation. When the quest fails, identity fails, and it is as if the individual were being deformed and dehumanized by a worldwide *picardía*. Then the myth of the picaro dominates and expresses us. But when the quest succeeds—not an ironic Lazarillo-like social success but a spiritual penetration to essences—the myth of the picaro has lost its four-hundred-year-old hold on human imagination, and a new and hopeful myth, as yet unnamed but powerfully felt, is becoming the shaping force in civilization.

## The Tragicomedy of Self-Creation

Perhaps it is not the novel that is dying but the picaresque novel. Perhaps the long-anticipated death of the literary genre has been announced prematurely, obvious as it is that serious fiction has largely been abandoned by commercial publishers. The loss of readership led Ortega y Gasset to prophesy in *Notes on the Novel* that the genre would die from a fundamental cause, the depletion of possible subjects. Yet, I think, the relation of literature to culture is a good deal more organic, as well as more democratic, than Ortega would allow half a century ago. How can there be a loss of subject matter when, more then ever before in history, we are beginning to be thrilled to our very depths by the essentiality of human freedom? Since the novel is that literary genre closer to historical actuality, its hesitations and heartbeats, than any other, including history itself, are we to assume that novelists will abandon a medium of communication that has been a kind of cultural proving ground of the life of the individual soul? The genre of the novel has new work to do. We have labored long with and wearied of the picaresque myth from which the first modern novels emerged. We have troubled our spirit, and rightly so, with images of man's loneliness, his alienation from society and from himself, and we have witnessed the global suffering consequent to man's thrust to become his own god. But, after all, we have been telling ourselves a myth. We have been letting our fear of love gnaw at the roots of sleep. There is possible a new dawn of human consciousness rising from the wasteland of worn-out absolutes. In this new world of potentiality man may not find justice, but he may find himself and a home for his restless spirit. He will then no longer be picaro. He will tell another story about himself.

For a while, the comedy of self-creation may continue to express the picaresque idea of disintegration and so become tragicomedy. Human destructiveness, intertwined with creativeness, will confine us to certain tragic facts. Our literature will have more to say about forms of decadence and death. But whatever the rhetoric about necrophilia, apathy, alienation, brain-conditioning, childhood traumata, materialism, and social-political-economic determinisms of all kinds—all prophetically summed up when a blind man hit Lazarillo's head against a stone—the picaresque novel's sustained inquiry into civilization and its discontents has gone all the way to chaos and back.

Now the new potentialities of human freedom declare an old imperative. As Gulley Jimson says, quoting Blake, "Go love."

# Notes

### 1: Introduction

1. Francis Fergusson, "'Myth' and the Literary Scruple," p. 140.

2. G. S. Kirk, *Myth*, p. 8.

3. Ibid., p. 41.

4. Cited in Joseph Campbell, "Bios and Mythos," p. 21.

5. John B. Vickery, ed., *Myth and Literature*, p. ix.

6. See Charles Moorman, "Myth and Medieval Literature," pp. 171–86.

7. Claudio Guillén, *Literature as System*, p. 71. Essay 3, "Toward a Definition of the Picaresque," was read in Utrecht on 21–26 August 1961 and first published in the *Proceedings of the IIId Congress of the International Comparative Literature Association*, edited by W. A. P. Smit, The Hague, 1962. At the time when I was first formulating my own thesis about picaresque myth, I was not acquainted with this important essay, although I was familiar with Guillén's earlier criticism.

8. Joseph Campbell, *The Masks of God*, 4:3–4.

9. Ibid., p. 4.

10. Stephen Gilman, *The Spain of Fernando de Rojas*.

11. Gilman's *converso* thesis is that of his mentor, Américo Castro, whose approach to Spanish history and literature has sometimes been attacked as racial but is usually accepted as nonracial (Spanish New Christians were not Jews) and as a necessary investigation of backgrounds to modern fiction. Among recent studies to argue the pertinence to the picaresque novel of the *converso* situation are: Carroll B. Johnson, "*El Buscón*"; Bruno M. Damiani, *Francisco Delicado*; Donald McGrady, "Social Irony in *Lazarillo de Tormes* and Its Implications for Authorship" and *Mateo Alemán*; and Guillén, *Literature as System*, pp. 101–2. Alexander A. Parker's cautious approach to the problem should be noted in *Literature and the Delinquent*, pp. 13–14.

12. Everett Stonequist, *The Marginal Man*, cited in Gilman, *Spain of Fernando de Rojas*, p. 136.

13. Gilman, *Spain of Fernando de Rojas*, pp. 104, 85.

14. Ibid., pp. 20, 23.

15. Ibid., pp. 76–77, 106, 144–53.

16. Karl Kerényi, "The Trickster in Relation to Greek Mythology," p. 185.

17. Guillén, *Literature as System*, p. 106.

18. Although the critical consensus has long been that a picaro seldom has a villainous or viciously wicked nature, the Vice of medieval morality plays is an amoral elemental force closely resembling the trickster archetype and thus a sort of first cousin to the picaro. When, it seems to me, a picaro's relationship to his

crimes and to his victims is not moral but artistic, the picaro's kinship to the Vice may be closer than that of cousin. Quevedo's Pablos may not be an artist-criminal of the dimensions of Shakespeare's Iago, but he can be equally obnoxious. In Chapter 4, I hazard the guess that Shakespearean and Miltonic villains constituted an important influence on Melville in his creation of the confidence man, a figure who may well fuse picaro and Vice in his allegorical makeup. On the tradition of the Vice, see Bernard Spivak, *Shakespeare and the Allegory of Evil*.

19. For an authoritative account of the period see Fernand Braudel, *The Mediterranean and the Mediterranean World in the Age of Philip II*.

20. José Ortega y Gasset, *Man and Crisis*, p. 186.

21. Carl Friedrich, *The Age of the Baroque, 1610–1660*, p. 53.

22. I discovered this emblem from the first edition of *La pícara Justina* in the British Museum and first reproduced it in 1963 as the frontispiece of my doctoral dissertation at the University of Cambridge. Alexander A. Parker subsequently reproduced the emblem as frontispiece to his *Literature and the Delinquent*, 1967. Parker has been praised for the discovery of the emblem by Fernando Lázaro Carreter, "Glosas Críticas a *Los Pícaros en la Literatura* de Alexander A. Parker." Parker's contention that *Lazarillo de Tormes* is not the first picaresque novel is refuted by this very emblem, which shows Lazarillo taking in tow the Ship of Picaresque Life.

23. Braudel, *Mediterranean*, 2:832.

24. Cited in R. W. B. Lewis, *The Picaresque Saint*, p. 26.

25. Guillén, *Literature as System*, p. 80, introduces "half-outsider," a term of greater critical value than Chandler's popular term, "anti-hero." "For the 'unfortunate traveller' soon learns that there is no material survival outside of society, and no real refuge—no pastoral paradise—beyond it. Social role-playing is as ludicrous as it is indispensable. This is where the solution of 'roguish' behavior is preferred. Now a *pícaro*, the hero chooses to compromise and live on the razor's edge between vagabondage and delinquency. He can, in short, *neither join nor actually reject his fellow men*. He becomes what I would like to call a 'half-outsider'."

26. René Wellek and Austin Warren, *Theory of Literature*, p. 245.

27. Claudio Guillén, "The Anatomies of Roguery," p. 48.

28. On satiric elements in picaresque narrative see Ronald Paulson, *The Fictions of Satire*, pp. 58–73, and *Satire and the Novel in Eighteenth-Century England*, pp. 24–29. Paulson's emphasis upon realism and upon the servant-master relationship does not invalidate his discussion of satire, though it is misleading to consider picaresque novels as realistic or the servant-master relationship as a defining characteristic of them.

29. Parker, *Literature and the Delinquent*, p. 4.

30. On the distinction between antihero and literary hero see Pedro Salinas, "El *Héroe* literario y la novela picaresca española." Summaries of etymological studies of *pícaro* are to be found in Michael Robert Ramon, "Nueva interpretación del pícaro y de la novela picaresca española hecha a base de un estudio de las tres obras maestras del género"; Alberto del Monte, *Itinerario del romanzo picaresco spagnola*, pp. 3–6; and Juan Luis Alborg, *Historia de la literatura española Edad Media a y Renacimiento*, pp. 765–66. Of unusual interest because it links *picaro* to religious heterodoxy is T. E. May, " 'Pícaro'."

31. On the stasis of society in the *Satyricon* see Erich Auerbach, *Mimesis*, pp. 26f.

32. See Peter N. Dunn, "El individuo y la sociedad en *La Vida del Buscón*."

33. Parker, *Literature and the Delinquent*, pp. 25–27, stresses realism in the picaresque genre as a whole. This view has been repudiated by, among others, Fernando Lázaro Carreter, *Lazarillo de Tormes en la picaresca*, pp. 50–57, who suggests the possibility of picaresque myth in which a picaresque novel is "un proceso dinámico, con su dialéctica propia, en el que cada obra supuso una toma de posición distinta ante una misma poética" (pp. 198–99).

34. Américo Castro, Introduction to *La vida de Lazarillo de Tormes*, p. xii.

35. Stuart Miller, *The Picaresque Novel*, pp. 133–34.

### 2: The Soul's Dark Journey

1. The standard survey of the *Lazarillo*'s literary antecedents has long been Frank W. Chandler's *Romances of Roguery*. Recent concise investigations concerning *Lazarillo* are Francisco Rico, *La novela picaresca española*, and Fernando Lázaro Carreter, *Lazarillo de Tormes en la picaresca*. Alexander Scobie, *Aspects of the Ancient Romance and Its Heritage*, documents the possibility of Apuleian influence on Spanish fiction. A recent commentary on the erudition of the novel's author is in Donald McGrady, "Social Irony in *Lazarillo de Tormes* and Its Implications for Authorship." Because of its date of publication, 1528, Francisco Delicado's *Retrato de la Lozana andaluza* might be considered either as the first picaresque novel or as an important precursor of *Lazarillo*; Bruno M. Damiani, *Francisco Delicado*, leans to the latter view. I believe *Lozana* also lacks the illusionism essential to picaresque myth: see my review of Damiani's book in *Modern Language Review* 60 (1976): 79.

2. Marcel Bataillon, Introduction to *La vie de Lazarillo de Tormes*, pp. 9, 13, 36, cited in Howard Mancing, "The Deceptiveness of *Lazarillo de Tormes*," p. 426.

3. Scobie, *Aspects*, p. 93n., reports that the translation of *Metamorphoses* ascribel to Diego López de Cotegana may date not from 1513 but from ca. 1525.

4. Hans Meyerhoff, *Time in Literature*, pp. 1–2.

5. On the text see Rico, *La novela picaresca española*, pp. ix–x. McGrady, "Social Irony," p. 567n., speculates upon the oddity of three separate editions, attributing it to the death of the author, who would have prohibited his novel's publication or reproduction in MS form during his lifetime.

6. See Albert A. Sicroff, "Sobre el estilo de *Lazarillo de Tormes*."

7. Since F. Courtney Tarr's study, "Literary and Artistic Unity in the *Lazarillo de Tormes*," there have been many defenses of the novel's integrity. See Claudio Guillén, "La disposición temporal del *Lazarillo de Tormes*"; Raymond S. Willis, "Lazarillo and the Pardoner"; Louis C. Pérez, "On Laughter in the *Lazarillo de Tormes*"; Stephen Gilman, "The Death of Lazarillo de Tormes"; Rico, *La novela picaresca española*; Douglas M. Carey, "Asides and Interiority in *Lazarillo de Tormes*"; and Mancing, "Deceptiveness."

8. For a summary of the problems of authorship and composition date, see Alberto del Monte, *Itinerario del romanzo picaresco spagnolo*, pp. 12–15, and Juan Luis Alborg, *Historia de la literatura española Edad Media y Renacimiento*, pp. 772–77. Mendoza, satirist, poet, historian, and humanist, has long seemed the most likely candidate for author of *Lazarillo*; the Valdés attribution, based on the supposed Erasmian quality of the anticlericalism, is disputed by Marcel Bataillon in his introduction to *Lazarillo*; but see Manuel J. Asensio, "La intención religiosa del *Lazarillo de Tormes* y Juan de Valdés" and "Más sobre el *Lazarillo de Tormes*," for reconsideration of the Valdés possibility. Américo Castro interprets word usage in the novel as indicating *converso* authorship, *The Structure of Spanish History*, pp.

557–58, but this view is no longer in favor according to McGrady, "Social Irony." Rico, *La novela picaresca española* argues for a late date of composition.

9. On the influence of Erasmus in Spain, I have consulted Marcel Bataillon, *Erasme et l'Espagne*, and the translation in which he made changes, *Erasmo y España*. On the conflict of Erasmists with the Inquisition see John E. Longhurst, *Erasmus and the Spanish Inquisition*, pp. 70–77. The condemnation of Erasmus posed a problem for the Inquisition because Erasmus had repudiated Luther in 1521 and could count on a considerable following at Charles's court. But the Inquisition, by treating Erasmism as the same kind of heresy as Lutheranism, gradually tightened its control. Juan de Valdés fled to Italy shortly after the appearance of his *Diálogo de doctrina cristiana* in 1529.

10. The historical background to picaresque literature is indirectly illuminated by Fernand Braudel, *The Mediterranean and the Mediterranean World in the Age of Philip II*, 2:740–56. Also informative are Roger B. Merriman, *The Rise of the Spanish Empire in the Old World and the New*, and R. Trevor Davies, *The Golden Century of Spain, 1501–1621*.

11. See Gilman, "Death of Lazarillo de Tormes."

12. The point is made by Francisco Márquez Villanueva, *Espiritualidad y literatura en el siglo XVI*, p. 95, cited in Mancing, "Deceptiveness," p. 431.

13. *La vida de Lazarillo de Tormes y de sus fortunas y adversidades*, edited by Julio Cejador y Frauca, Clásicos Castellanos, has been the most readily available edition and has been used for this reason. Hispanists now favor the editions by Rico, *La novela picaresca española*, and by Royston O. Jones.

14. According to Charles Philip Wagner, Introduction to *The Life of Lazarillo de Tormes*, p. xx, the forms *invicto* and *invictísimo* were honorifics regularly applied to Charles V, but the form *victorioso* is more specific. In 1538 Charles suffered a defeat, but Pavia was the "greatest victory of the age" (Davies, *Golden Century*, p. 89).

15. See Del Monte, *Itinerario*, p. 10.

16. See Royston O. Jones's edition of *Lazarillo*, p. xv, for a discussion of the problem.

17. This critical approach, put forward by Guillén, "La disposición temporal," has proved a turning point in modern *Lazarillo* studies.

18. Formal aspects of autobiography are examined in Roy Pascal, *Design and Truth in Autobiography*, pp. 1–11. Pascal stresses the "interplay" of past and present in autobiography and finds the significance of the form "more the revelation of the present situation than the uncovering of the past."

19. On self-assertiveness as overcompensation for feelings of shame and inferiority in the picaro of later novels see Alexander A. Parker, "The Psychology of the 'Pícaro' in *El Buscón*," and Sherman Eoff, "The Picaresque Psychology of Guzmán de Alfarache."

20. Compare Francisco Maldonado de Guevara, *Interpretación del Lazarillo de Tormes*.

21. See Henry Thomas, *Spanish and Portuguese Romances of Chivalry*. Claudio Guillén, *Literature as System*, pp. 135–58, shows how the picaresque had become, by the time of Cervantes, an identifiable literary kind juxtaposed to heroic literature. The idea of a "dialogue" or dialectic, the picaresque forming one polarity, is a theoretical basis for my discussion of eighteenth-century novels, Chapter 3.

22. Maldonado, *Interpretación*, p. 36.

23. Sicroff, "Sobre el estilo," pp. 160–63, discusses these biblical parodies as helping to delineate the character.

24. For the evidence that the scene is based upon a traditional story see Raymond Foulché-Delbosc, "Remarques sur *Lazarillo de Tormes*." In general, a folkloristic aspect of *Lazarillo* points up its lack of realism and its potential as myth. See the important work by Lázaro Carreter, *Lazarillo de Tormes en la picaresca*.

25. In the chapel of S. Maria del Carmine in Florence is a fresco by Masaccio (1401–28) of Saints Peter and John healing the cripple. A nearby fresco of Saints Peter and John healing the sick with their shadows depicts, with astonishing power, the face of a Lazarillo-like beggar boy who looks as if he has lost faith in miracles. Such pictorial irony provides a context for later picaresque literature.

26. One critic remarks upon the appropriateness of the bull as a symbol of masculine maturity in Lazarillo's initiation rite: see Dale B. J. Randall, *The Golden Tapestry*, p. 63n.

27. Chandler, *Romances of Roguery*, p. 46: "The anti-hero is everything and nothing: everything in what he does, nothing in character. Yet weak and heartless though he be, his wit secures him immunity from contempt or condemnation. He has mirth and spontaneity, if he lack pity for the crippled, or if his sympathies respond only to exaggerated Castilian pride. . . . For the Spaniard acts, but rarely feels; he passes and repasses upon the scene, but scarcely wills. There is in him still a good deal of the marionette operated upon a single automatic principle. And this principle is always avarice."

28. On the psychology of self-assertion see, for example, Rollo May, *Power and Innocence*. After discussing Melville's *Billy Budd*, May distinguishes innocence and spirituality, the latter of which "tempers the self, deepens consciousness and awareness, purges and sharpens our sight . . . whereas innocence acts as a blinder and tends to keep us from growing, from new awareness, from identifying with the sufferings of mankind as well as its joys (both being foreign to the innocent person)" (p. 210). This insight may also apply to the character of Lazarillo: he is still innocent when he strikes the blind man, but he has already begun to be deformed in spirit.

29. Anson C. Piper, "The 'Breadly Paradise' of Lazarillo de Tormes," p. 269.

30. McGrady, "Social Irony," pp. 558, 564.

31. The jest, which also appears in the *Liber facetiarum et similitudinum* (ca. 1550), may derive ultimately from a passage in the Book of Job that is spoken in the Office of the Dead: see Angel González Palencia, *Del "Lazarillo" a Quevedo*, pp. 3–39.

32. See Gilman, "Death of Lazarillo de Tormes."

33. Chandler, *Romances of Roguery*, p. 46.

34. Douglas N. Carey notes how interior light ceases to act as a guide for Lázaro in "Asides and Interiority in *Lazarillo de Tormes*."

35. Gilman, "Death of Lazarillo de Tormes," pp. 153–54.

36. In an interesting article, "The Function of the Norm in *Don Quixote*," Oscar Mandel discusses four types of comic fiction: (1) the good deviant from a reprehensible society (for example, *Joseph Andrews*); (2) the reprehensible deviant from a good society (for example, *Pride and Prejudice*); (3) the good deviant from a good society (rare, possibly *Tristram Shandy*); and (4) the reprehensible deviant from a reprehensible society. I have put forward *Lazarillo* as an example of the

fourth type. Anagnorisis is common to (2) and (4) but, since the error-stricken individual in the latter is treated ironically, there is no relief.

37. Compare a similar interpretation in Piper, " 'Breadly Paradise'."

38. Since the strategy of the Inquisition courts of the early 1520s was to brand Erasmism as "illuminism" and Lutheranism as virtually the same kind of heresy (see Longhurst, *Erasmus and the Spanish Inquisition*), it is tempting to see the author's attitude toward his protagonist in a historical context.

39. See n. 7.

40. Mancing, "Deceptiveness," p. 429.

41. See Howard R. Patch, *The Goddess Fortuna in Medieval Literature*, p. 31.

42. Mancing, "Deceptiveness," pp. 427, 430–31.

43. Sicroff, "Sobre el estilo," pp. 159–60.

44. The term for the theme appears in Guillén, "La disposición temporal," p. 279, where he declares that "la disolución del concepto del tiempo" is "la desintegración del individuo."

45. Cited in Pascal, *Design and Truth*, p. 18.

46. Erich Auerbach, *Mimesis*, p. 53.

47. It is, of course, difficult to judge whether the "illumination" of Lazarillo is a deliberate reference to certain reformers of the early 1520s who were known as *iluministas* or *alumbrados*. They taught that the will must be surrendered to the divine in a state of mystic exaltation. The illuminists were more heterodox than the Erasmists and were, consequently, very vulnerable to the Inquisition. With the prosecution of Alcarez in 1524, illuminism as a force in the general movement of reform was virtually destroyed. The doctrine—if it was a doctrine, and we only have the prosecution's word for it—that man must see his own worthlessness before he receives the grace of God declares, in effect, that man lacks free will. In my opinion, the author of *Lazarillo* urges no such condition of moral irresponsibility, but rather the contrary, for the "illuminations" of Lázaro are always false, hence rationalizations of moral desuetude. On the *iluministas* see Longhurst, *Erasmus and the Spanish Inquisition*, pp. 16–19.

48. T. E. May, "Good and Evil in the *Buscón*," p. 327.

49. Benedetto Croce, "Studi su poesie antiche e moderne."

50. See Peter N. Dunn, "El individuo y la sociedad en *La Vida del Buscón*."

51. On the idea of usurpation in Renaissance literature see Rebecca West, *The Court and the Castle*, pp. 57–58.

52. Pessimism is a strong link between *Lazarillo* and *Celestina*. A. D. Deyermond has shown in *The Petrarchan Sources of the "Celestina"* that Rojas was influenced by the pessimistic doctrine of Petrarch in *De Remediis Utriusque Fortunae*. Stephen Gilman discusses the matter further in *The Spain of Fernando de Rojas*.

53. José Ortega y Gasset, *Man and Crisis*, p. 186.

54. See R. H. Tawney, *Religion and the Rise of Capitalism*, and Max Weber, *The Protestant Ethic and the Spirit of Capitalism*.

55. Johan Huizinga, *The Waning of the Middle Ages*, p. 147.

56. Erich Fromm, *The Fear of Freedom*, pp. 15, 18.

57. W. B. Stanford, *The Ulysses Theme*, pp. 13, 7.

58. One picaresque novelist regarded Odysseus as the perfect trickster: see Edward Glaser, "Quevedo versus Pérez de Montalván."

59. Guillén, *Literature as System*, p. 106.

60. Cited in P. E. Russell, "English Seventeenth-Century Interpretations of Spanish Literature," p. 70.

61. Cited in Randall, *Golden Tapestry*, p. 59.

62. William Dean Howells, *My Literary Passions*, p. 143.

63. On the picaro and existentialism see Rafael Benítez Claros, *Existencialismo y picaresca*; D. Alvarez, "La picaresca española y la literatura existencialista"; and Guillén, *Literature as System*, pp. 104–6, who notes that "in the midst of bankrupt revolutions and the orthodoxy of disbelief, Camus' *homme revolté* is no more a hero of our time than the powerless antihero."

64. See Raymond Foulché-Delbosc, "Bibliographie de Mateo Alemán—1598–1615." On the subtitle see Alice H. Bushee, "Atalaya de la vida humana." This subtitle was apparently Alemán's final choice. The word "Pícaro" occurs in the censor's *aprobación*, where the title is given as *Primera Parte del Pícaro Guzmán de Alfarache*, and also in the dedication in which Alemán himself speaks of the "desechado Pícaro" (rejected picaro). The three 1599 editions insert pícaro on the title page, much to the later regret of the author. But Donald McGrady concludes in *Mateo Alemán*, pp. 66–67, that Alemán originally was responsible for both titles, *Pícaro* for Part I, *Watchtower on Human Life* for Part II, in accord with a basic duality of a novel in which adventures and moralizing are emphasized in turn.

65. On the popularity of *Guzmán* see James Fitzmaurice-Kelly, Introduction to *The Rogue*, Vol. 1.

66. See Irving A. Leonard, "*Guzmán de Alfarache* in the Lima Book Trade, 1613."

67. See Fitzmaurice-Kelly, Introduction to *The Rogue*, and Manuel García Blanco, *Mateo Alemán y la novela picaresca alemana*. Randall, *Golden Tapestry*, gives ample evidence of the popularity in England of *Lazarillo*, *Guzmán*, and *Buscón*.

68. Alain-René Lesage, *Oeuvres*, 5:4.

69. Gerald Brenan, *The Literature of the Spanish People from Roman Times to the Present Day*, p. 172.

70. Lesage, *Oeuvres*, 5:2, 4.

71. George Ticknor, *History of Spanish Literature*, 3:59–60.

72. Chandler, *Romances of Roguery*, p. 64.

73. George Tyler Northup, *An introduction to Spanish Literature*, p. 181. The statement is unrevised from the 1925 edition.

74. On Alemán biography see Francisco Rodríguez Marín, *Discursos leídos ante la Real Academia Española*; Urban Cronan, "Mateo Alemán and Miguel de Cervantes Saavedra"; Francisco A. de Icaza, *Sucesos Reales que parecen imaginados de Gutierre de Cetina, Juan de la Cueva y Mateo Alemán*, pp. 161–206, 253–63; J. A. Van Praag, "Sobre el sentido del *Guzmán de Alfarache*"; Germán Bleiberg, "Mateo Alemán y los galeotes" and "Nuevos datos biográficos de Mateo Alemán"; McGrady, *Mateo Alemán*; and especially Rico, *La novela picaresca española*, pp. 80–108, 148–49.

75. McGrady, *Mateo Alemán*, pp. 20, 70.

76. Fonger De Haan, *An Outline of the History of the Novela Picaresca in Spain*, p. 19.

77. Miguel Herrero García, "Nueva interpretación de la novela picaresca."

78. Enrique Moreno Báez, *Lección y sentido del Guzmán de Alfarache*.

79. Ibid., p. 85. See also Moreno Báez, "¿Hay una tesis en el *Guzmán de Alfarache*?"

80. Brenan, *Literature of the Spanish People*, pp. 171–73.

81. McGrady, *Mateo Alemán*, p. 56.

82. Samuel Gili y Gaya, ed., Introduction to *Guzmán de Alfarache*, 1:12.

83. Américo Castro, "Perspectiva de la novela picaresca."

84. See Van Praag, "Sobre el sentido," and Del Monte, *Itinerario*.

85. See Russell, "English Seventeenth-Century Interpretations."

86. William Chillingworth, *The Religion of Protestants a Safe Way to Salvation*, p. 110.

87. See Francisco Sánchez y Escribano, "La fórmula del Barroco literario presentida en un incidente del *Guzmán de Alfarache*." For general orientation see Helmut Hatzfeld, "A Clarification of the Baroque Problem in the Romance Literatures."

88. I have consulted Marvin T. Herrick, "The Fusion of Horatian and Aristotelian Literary Criticism, 1531–1555," and René Bray, *La formation de la doctrine classique en France*. I am also indebted to George Haley, *Vicente Espinel and Marcos de Obregón*, pp. 69–86; Haley shows how relevant is the problem of history and poetry to a study of an early seventeenth-century Spanish novelist.

89. Herrick, "Fusion," p. 3.

90. As with *Lazarillo*, I have used a readily available edition of *Guzmán de Alfarache*, edited by Samuel Gili y Gaya, Clásicos Castellanos. Hispanists recommend the edition by Rico in *La novela picaresca española*.

91. I assume that "aumento" is an error for "argumento."

92. Jean Chappelain, "Au Lecteur."

93. These English verses by "I. F." are in Mateo Alemán, *The Rogue*, 1:30.

94. I use the distinction made famous by E. M. Forster in *Aspects of the Novel*.

95. Ian Watt, *The Rise of the Novel*, p. 24.

96. See M. I. Gray, *An Index to "Guzmán de Alfarache."*

97. J. A. Jones reaches a somewhat parallel conclusion in "The Duality and Complexity of *Guzmán de Alfarache*": "His conversion may well be a final realization of his evil ways after having approached the edge of an abyss of nothingness. But we cannot help feelng that Guzmán is also being moved by his instinct for self-preservation. His change of heart is stimulated by the most basic and selfish motive of fear, and although this may furnish a fully acceptable theological starting-point for the life of grace, it can equally fill us with doubt concerning Guzmán's sincerity, especially as he has already at another point in his life been prepared to prostitute the religious life for physical comfort and material sufficiency. Guzmán undergoes the conversion under pressure. Reform offers the only path out and he accepts it. His change of heart and soul can thus appear to be no more than another piece of opportunistic conformism in order to secure selfish ends. The conversion can be regarded in a more cynical and skeptical light, and the novel can be seen to end on a more ambiguous note than has hitherto been conceded. If we grant this measure of ambiguity, then we are perhaps half-way towards explaining the dualistic structure which has provoked so much criticism and debate" (p. 42). Further on the subject of *Guzmán*'s structure, see the full-length study by Angel San Miguel, *Sentido y estructura del "Guzmán de Alfarache" de Mateo Alemán*: he argues for a symmetrical structure in a story intended to teach virtue through vice. My own view is that *Guzmán* is a unified narrative as a novel only if we set aside the author's ambiguous intention.

98. Carlos Blanco Aguinaga, "Cervantes y la picaresca," p. 313. On Cervantes's unwarranted reputation as a picaresque novelist, see Esther J. Crooks, *The Influence of Cervantes in France in the Seventeenth Century*; George Hainsworth, *Les*

*"Novelas Exemplares" de Cervantes en France au XVIIe siècle*; and Edward M. Wilson, "Cervantes and English Literature of the Seventeenth Century."

99. Mabbe's translation of "agregados" as "grafted" sets up, for the student of literature, a whole complex of ideas about hybrids, as in *The Inferno*, where Dante sees them as unnatural and contrary to God's plan. Alemán's younger contemporary, Shakespeare, symbolically presents bastards as "unnatural" (for example, Edmund in *King Lear*).

100. McGrady, *Mateo Alemán*, p. 176n., traces the device of the spider and the snake to Pliny's *Natural History*, 10:95. The idea of cosmic strife, going back to Heraclitus (d. about 480 B.C.), is a commonplace in seventeenth- and eighteenth-century English literature and can be associated there with picaresque myth.

101. Eoff, "Picaresque Psychology," p. 112.

102. Ibid., pp. 114, 119.

103. On asceticism emptied of its meaning see José F. Montesinos, "Gracián o la picaresca pura."

104. The significance of this passage for *Guzmán* is noted by R. A. Del Piero, "The Picaresque Philosphy in *Guzmán de Alfarache*."

105. See Alexander A. Parker, "The Spanish Drama of the Golden Age."

106. Alemán conceived of the death of Sayavedra as a witty thrust at the plagiarist, Luján, who had published a spurious sequel to *Guzmán*.

107. On this point see Roland Grass, "Morality in the Picaresque Novel."

108. Other comparisons of *Guzmán* with *Lazarillo* may be consulted in Lázaro Carreter, *Lazarillo de Tormes en la picaresca*, pp. 195–229; McGrady, *Mateo Alemán*, pp. 60–66; Del Monte, *Itinerario*; and Gonzalo Sobejano, "De la intención y valor del *Guzmán de Alfarache*."

109. Cited in Brenan, *Literature of the Spanish People*, p. 259.

110. James Fitzmaurice-Kelly, "*La vida del Buscón*," p. 7.

111. Randall, *Golden Tapestry*, p. 210.

112. Henry Ettinghausen, *Francisco de Quevedo and the Neostoic Movement*, pp. 15, 16, 19, 30. See also pp. 37, 77.

113. Ibid., p. 127.

114. Francisco de Quevedo y Villegas, *Historia de la vida del Buscón, llamado Don Pablos*, edited by Américo Castro, Clásicos Castellanos, is used here, but the reader may be referred to the new edition of Fernando Lázaro Carreter (Barcelona, 1968).

115. Dale B. J. Randall, "The Classical Ending of Quevedo's *Buscón*," p. 108.

116. Alexander A. Parker, *Literature and the Delinquent*, p. 62. Parker's argument is indebted to T. E. May, "Good and Evil in the *Buscón*."

117. Ibid., p. 60.

118. Carroll B. Johnson, "*El Buscón*."

119. Francisco Ayala, *Experiencia e invención*, pp. 161–62.

120. Parker, *Literature and the Delinquent*, pp. 58, 72.

121. Ayala, *Experiencia*, pp. 162, 163.

122. Parker, *Literature and the Delinquent*, p. 71.

123. Fernando Lázaro Carreter, "Glosas críticas a *Los Pícaros en la Literatura* de Alexander A. Parker."

124. C. B. Morris, *The Unity and Structure of Quevedo's Buscón*, p. 6.

### 3: The Conversion of the Natural Man

1. Stephen Gilman, *The Spain of Fernando de Rojas*, p. 177.

2. Henry James, *The Art of the Novel*, p. 30.

3. Maximillian E. Novak, "Freedom, Libertinism, and the Picaresque," pp. 43, 36.

4. John J. Richetti, *Popular Fiction before Richardson*, p. 11. The chapter "Rogues and Whores: Heroes and Anti-Heroes," pp. 23–59, shows how ideology or social myth affects the structure of picaresque narratives.

5. Ibid., p. 35.

6. Ronald Paulson, *Satire and the Novel in Eighteenth-Century England*, p. 43. "The irony of the Spanish picaresque is based on the amorality of the pilgrimage (or quest), which points up the secularized quality of the world through which the protagonist passes. In England, the Protestant strain of Christianity taught that every man, even the least, lives a life full of symbolic significance; thus the biography is the basic literary unit, not the episode as in the works of the classical writers (the whole life, not the Aristotelian action). The emphasis is on the individual whose life is followed; the life is no longer merely a pretext which accommodates or interacts with a picture of society. A man goes on the journey or the voyage of his life (a common metaphor in such works) and his encounters with people are conflicts, like the picaresque servant-master struggles, but these conflicts serve to define the traveler and not the people encountered; in fact they are usually his battering attempts to win through to his true destiny. His encounters become stages in his development toward good or evil, failure or completeness. His progression is a series of choices between good and bad alternatives of action. The ending, whether of a saint's life or a criminal's biography, is his conversion." Paulson's studies, including *The Fictions of Satire*, treat the picaresque as a mode of satire with emphasis upon realism, the servant-master relationship, and adventures on the road. Yet he describes works of Defoe as "a nonsatiric branch of the picaresque novel" (*Satire and the Novel*, p. 41), which seems to be a distinction without a difference. It is my view that satire is eclipsed by picaresque myth; when the myth of the picaro is most evident in a novel, the author's vision cuts beneath the levels of satire. Defoe is probably the English author who comes closer than any other to expressing picaresque myth.

7. Bernard Spivak, *Shakespeare and the Allegory of Evil*, pp. 195, 46–47, 45.

8. Novak, "Freedom," distinguishes "a closed world of social forms" (novel of manners) from "open form" (picaresque novel), and on the basis of this distinction accepts Lesage, Defoe, and Smollett as picaresque novelists. Whereas the distinction is, I think, inapplicable to the triad of Spanish picaresque novels, it is valid for eighteenth-century novels in which picarism is unconventional or anticonventional. Even then, a Lesage, Defoe, or Smollett can express partial or full liberation from middle- and upper-class social and political conventions yet remain more or less unconsciously devoted to integrative social myth. The importance of a theme of freedom is not in dispute, as I emphasize in Chapter 5 of this study, but freedom of self-creation is ironically treated by the Spanish picaresque novelists.

9. Maurice Bardon, ed., *Histoire de Gil Blas de Santillane*, 1:viii. See also Marguerite Iknayan, "The Fortunes of *Gil Blas* during the Romantic Period."

10. James Fitzmaurice-Kelly, "The Picaresque Novel." The entry in the fifteenth edition of *Encyclopaedia Britannica*, 1977, continues the same superficial description.

11. On Lesage and his sources see Charles Dédéyan, *A.-R. Lesage*; Leo Clarétie, *Lesage romancier*; and Eugene Lintilhac, *Lesage*.

12. George Ticknor, *History of Spanish Literature*, 3:51–69.

13. "Le tableau le plus ressemblant de la nature humaine, telle qu'elle est au XVIIIe en France, est encore le vieux *Gil Blas* de Lesage" (Marie Henri Beyle, *Correspondance de Stendhal*, 1:217). Lesage's influence on Stendhal as picaresque is traced by S. de Sacy, "Le miroir sur la grande route."

14. Hervey Allen, *Anthony Adverse*, 1:xii. Allen's historical romance suffered critically from the "picaresque" tag, used pejoratively by reviewers.

15. See Arnold Kettle, *An Introduction to the English Novel*, 1:55–62; Bruce McCullough, *Representative English Novelists*; Novak, "Freedom"; Alexander A. Parker, *Literature and the Delinquent*; Robert Alter, *Rogue's Progress*; and Christine J. Whitbourn, ed., *Knaves and Swindlers*.

16. See Thomas Nashe, *The Works of Thomas Nashe*, 5:23, and G. R. Hibbard, *Thomas Nashe*.

17. Frank W. Chandler, *The Literature of Roguery*, 1:225. For hesitating support of Chandler see James B. Wharey, "Bunyan's Mr. Badman and the Picaresque Novel." But see Henri Talon, *John Bunyan*, pp. 225–39, showing that *Mr. Badman* is unnovelistic in technique and psychology.

18. J. A. Mitchie, "The Unity of *Moll Flanders*," pp. 88–89.

19. On similarities between *Roderick Random* and *Gil Blas* see Alexandre Lawrence, "L'influence de Lesage sur Smollett."

20. Chandler, *Literature of Roguery*, 2:314.

21. Chandler's views of Dickens as picaresque (*Literature of Roguery*, 2:411–27) have been vigorously refuted by Sherman Eoff, "*Oliver Twist* and the Spanish Picaresque Novel" and *The Modern Spanish Novel*, pp. 27–36.

22. Chandler, *Literature of Roguery*, 2:462. Chandler's opinion is unsupported by Geoffrey Tillotson, *Thackeray the Novelist*, or by Gordon N. Ray, *Thackeray*, pp. 339f.

23. The late E. M. W. Tillyard found the "inner spirit" of *Vanity Fair* "picaresque" in *The Epic Strain in the English Novel*. "One form the picaresque narrative keeps on taking," Tillyard declares, "has to do with the underdog, the little man, the fellow a bit worse off than the average, who has his adventures and troubles and somehow just survives. . . . A second and more important form of the picaresque is the story of a resourceful rogue who prospers for a long spell and is then found out, or who finds himself out and repents" (p. 14). "The picaresque story . . . is a genuine literary kind because it is based on a permanent proclivity of human nature; the proclivity to sympathize with anti-social behavior while knowing that it cannot go on for ever. Falstaff and his rejection are its most famous expression in English. The careers of Rawdon Crawley and Becky Sharp in Thackeray's *Vanity Fair* furnish a superb example of it. We want Becky to win her gambles, until Rawdon develops a human affection and the beginning of a moral sense. Then we waver, and Rawdon becomes the successful agent of a transfer of feelings. *Vanity Fair*, by these terms, is not an epic but a first-rate picaresque romance" (p. 119). Tillyard's terms represent, I think, an indistinct analysis. While it may be true that antisocial behavior engages the reader's sympathy, the critical question is, what does "antisocial" mean? Does it mean, as Tillyard, to judge by his examples of Falstaff and Becky Sharp, seems to say, reprehensible behavior of an individual that is measured by established social norms? If so, it is antisocial in the antithetical sense but not in the sense of the picaresque. The picaro's reprehensible behavior occurs at times when established norms have disintegrated, leaving society as morally reprehensible as the deviant individual.

Both Falstaff and Becky Sharp are antagonists as well as protagonists; the social vision of *Henry IV* or *Vanity Fair* is far from desperate; and it is therefore my opinion that Falstaff and Becky are not picaros in the critical sense.

24. I have not included discussion of two European novelists sometimes considered as picaresque writers, Grimmelshausen and Diderot. For recent evaluations, see J. M. Ritchie, "Grimmelshausen's *Simplicissimus* and *The Runagate Courage*," and A. R. Strugnell, "Diderot's *Neveu de Rameau*."

25. Secondary sources on the intellectual background of this period are: Geoffrey Atkinson, *Le sentiment de la Nature et le Retour à la vie simple (1690–1740)*; A. J. Ayer, *The Problem of Knowledge*; René Bray, *La Formation de la doctrine classique en France*; J. B. Bury, *The Idea of Progress*; R. S. Crane, "Suggestions toward a Genealogy of the *Man of Feeling*"; Bonamy Dobrée, *English Literature in the Early Eighteenth Century, 1700–1740*; C. H. Driver, "John Locke"; Hoxie Neale Fairchild, *Religious Trends in English Poetry*; Bernard Groethuysen, *Philosophie de la révolution française*; Paul Hazard, *European Thought in the Eighteenth Century*; R. H. Tawney, *Religion and the Rise of Capitalism*; Arthur Tilley, *The Decline of the Age of Louis XIV*; Ernst Troeltsch, *The Social Teaching of the Christian Churches*; Ernest Tuveson, "The Importance of Shaftesbury"; Max Weber, *The Protestant Ethic and the Spirit of Capitalism*; Basil Willey, *The Eighteenth Century Background* and *The Seventeenth Century Background*.

26. John Locke, *An Essay Concerning Human Understanding*, bk. IV, Chapter 19, sec. 4, cited by Willey, *Eighteenth Century Background*, p. 7.

27. The influence of Descartes and Locke but not of Hobbes on the novel is discussed by Ian Watt, *The Rise of the Novel*, pp. 9–34.

28. See Crane, "Suggestions toward a Genealogy."

29. Cited from the rare first "imperfect" edition of the *Inquiry Concerning Virtue* in Tuveson, "Importance of Shaftesbury," p. 275.

30. Cited in this context by Erich Auerbach, *Mimesis*, p. 366.

31. A character in Lesage's *Le Diable Boîteux* (1707).

32. See Tilley, *Decline*.

33. Revolutionary aspects of Lesage's works are briefly discussed by Groethuysen, *Philosophie*, p. 91.

34. See Pierra Gaxotte, *La France de Louis XIV*, and André Levêque, " 'L'Honnête Homme' et 'l'Homme de Bien' au XVIIe siècle." Quevedo's character Pablos also is scorned for not knowing his place and keeping it, but *Buscón* is a world of evil and unreality with no internal standard by which to judge character and incident. For Molière and Lesage, the standard is everything and it shows.

35. From "Déclaration de l'auteur" in the 1747 edition of *Gil Blas*.

36. Georg Lukács, *The Historical Novel*, pp. 19–20.

37. Thomas Holcroft, Preface to *Alwyn* (1780), cited in Miriam Allott, *Novelists on the Novel*, p. 13.

38. See Arthur W. Secord, "Studies in the Narrative Method of Defoe."

39. Valuable Defoe studies include: Hans H. Andersen, "The Paradox of Trade and Morality in Defoe"; Jonathan Bishop, "Knowledge, Action, and Interpretation in Defoe's Novels"; Dobrée, *English Literature in the Early Eighteenth Century*; Fairchild, *Religious Trends*, pp. 67–77; Brian Fitzgerald, *Daniel Defoe*; Maximillian E. Novak, "The Problem of Necessity in Defoe's Fiction" and "Robinson Crusoe's Fear and the Search for the Natural Man"; Watt, *Rise of the Novel*; Richetti, *Popular Fiction*; and Mitchie, "Unity of *Moll Flanders*." Pertinent

but not consulted when this essay was concluded is George A. Starr, *Defoe and Spiritual Autobiography.*

40. Defoe quotes these lines in *Serious Reflections during the Life and Surprising Adventures of Robinson Crusoe,* p. 106.

41. Fairchild, *Religious Trends,* p. 68.

42. Dobrée, *English Literature in the Early Eighteenth Century,* p. 48.

43. Kettle, *Introduction to the English Novel,* 1:55.

44. Novak, "The Problem of Necessity."

45. Critiques of *Jonathan Wild* appear in William R. Irwin, *The Making of Jonathan Wild,* and Frederick Homes Dudden, *Henry Fielding,* 1:449–501. Richetti, *Popular Fiction,* p. 57, remarks that Fielding's *Wild* is "an enemy of the spirit" who cooperates "with the actual machinery of society" and is thus outside the operation of ideology or social myth. Had Fielding written an ironic autobiography in the manner of the classic Spanish authors of the picaresque, his *Jonathan Wild* would have come close to central picaresque tradition. Significantly, Fielding creates not a picaro but a monster.

46. Cited in Dudden, *Henry Fielding,* 1:333. *Jonathan Wild* was probably composed in large part before *Joseph Andrews.*

47. The possible influence of *Buscón* on Fielding has not previously been noted. The British Museum lists the following English and French translations of *Buscón* to 1745: *The Life and adventures of Buscón the witty Spaniard,* Put into English by a Person of Honour . . . (London, 1652); J[ohn] D[avies], trans., *The Life and adventures of Buscón the witty Spaniard* . . . (London, 1657; 2d ed. 1670); W. B., trans., *The Famous History of Auristella . . . Together with the pleasant history of Paul of Segovia* [abridgement] (London, 1683); (Sir) Roger L'Estrange, trans., *The Spanish Decameron, or Ten Novels made English* (London, 1687); (Capt.) J. Stevens, trans. [?], *Quevedo's Comical Works* [includes *The Life of Paul the Spanish Sharper*] (London, 1707, 2d ed., 1709; another ed., 1742); Mr. Pinneda, trans., *The Works of . . . Quevedo* [includes *The Life of Paul, The Spanish Sharper*] (London, 1745); Sieur de la Geneste, trans., *L'Avantureur Buscon, histoire facecieuse* (Paris, 1635; another ed., Rouen, 1641; another ed., Troyes, 1705), and *Les Oeuvres de . . . Quevedo* [includes *Buscón, histoire facecieuse*] (Rouen, 1645); Sr. Raclots, trans., *Les Oeuvres de . . . Quevedo* [includes *L'Avanturier Buscón*] (Brussels, 1699; another ed., Cologne, 1711). That Don Diego is not Pablos's moral superior has been discussed in the previous chapter. However, Quevedo's anti-Semitism, in depiction of Don Diego, was probably lost on English readers, who would be inclined to consider this character a true aristocrat. Possibly Fielding so considered him, as well as Smollett in *Ferdinand Count Fathom.*

48. Watt, *Rise of the Novel,* p. 94.

49. Cited from *Omoo* (1847) in Fred W. Boege, *Smollett's Reputation as a Novelist,* p. 129.

50. Walter Scott, *Lives of the Novelists,* pp. 69–70.

51. Spivak, *Shakespeare,* p. 45.

52. According to the summary of *Der Landstörzerin Courasche* (1670) in Kenneth C. Hayens, *Grimmelshausen,* pp. 156–87, Courage, an illegitimate child, is reared in a small Bohemian town; when the imperial commander, Count Bucquoy, storms the town in 1620, her nurse dresses her, then thirteen, in boy's clothes; she is seized by troopers, however, soon becoming a heavy drinker, savage fighter, and an expert in collecting booty; her sex discovered, she becomes

mistress to a captain, marrying him on his deathbed; she then moves to Vienna, becomes a prostitute, is forced to flee to Prague; from then on her adventures include five more marriages, the last to a dissolute musketeer with whom she hawks tobacco and brandy, but he, like the other husbands, is killed; "Mother" Courage survives to join a gypsy band, among whom she gains a reputation for witchcraft. A number of details in Smollett's portrait of Fathom's mother suggest Grimmelshausen's story as a source. Fathom's mother is a winesalesman and whore, five times widowed in one campaign; she consorts with a German trooper named Fadom whom, after the Treaty of Utrecht, she follows to Bohemia and Prague; later, after Fadom's death, she is reputed to have supernatural powers; but she is killed collecting booty from the Turks. Of this, Smollett, possibly punning, says, "Thus ended the mortal pilgrimage of this modern amazon; who, in point of courage, was not inferior to . . . any heroine of ancient times" (*Ferdinand Count Fathom*, Chapter 4).

53. See F. McCombie, "*Count Fathom* and *El Buscón*."

54. Compare philosophical implications of the romantic Satan in Albert Camus, *The Rebel*.

55. Lewis M. Knapp, *Tobias Smollett*, p. 303.

56. Identification of Fathom with Satan is particularly pointed in the Wilhelmina episode, Chapters 13–14.

57. See Ronald Paulson, "Satire in the Early Novels of Smollett."

58. M. A. Goldberg believes that Smollett was a disciple of the Scottish "Common Sense" School; see *Smollett and the Scottish School*.

59. See J. H. Stonehouse, ed., *Catalog of the Library of Charles Dickens*. Listed are *Adventures of Lazarillo de Tormes*, 1821; T. Roscoe's *Spanish, Italian, and German Novelists*, 11 vols., 1826–36; and *Spanish Decameron, or Ten Novels*, made English by R[oger] L['Estrange], 1687. Roscoe's *Spanish Novelists* has translations of *Lazarillo*, *Guzmán*, *Buscón*, and *Rinconete y Cortadillo*.

60. Eoff, "*Oliver Twist*." I am indebted to Eoff's detailed discussion of picaresque and antipicaresque elements in *Oliver Twist*.

61. Cited in John Foster, *The Life of Charles Dickens*, pp. 26, 28.

62. For the relevance of the passage to Thackeray's thought, see Tillotson, *Thackeray*, pp. 133f.

63. Cited in ibid., p. 206. This passage appears in the original novel printed in *Fraser's Magazine*, Jan.–Dec. 1844, as *The Luck of Barry Lyndon*. When the novel was reprinted in 1856 as *The Memoirs of Barry Lyndon, Esq.*, several passages, including this one, were omitted.

64. Chandler, *Literature of Roguery*, 2:462.

### 4: The Symbolic Confidence Man

1. Charles Feidelson, Jr., *Symbolism and American Literature*, p. 174.

2. Henry James, letter to H. G. Wells, 10 July 1915, in *The Letters of Henry James*, 2:490.

3. Lionel Trilling, *The Liberal Imagination*, p. 206.

4. Nicolai Gogol, letter to Pogodin, 28 November 1836, cited in David Magarshack, *Gogol*, p. 155.

5. Thomas Mann, *Essays of Three Decades*, p. 422.

6. Ibid., p. 438.

7. Walter Blair, *Native American Humor*, pp. 86–87, discusses the possibility of European influence on Johnson Hooper's *Simon Suggs* (1845) and concludes: "It

is possible to perceive that with nothing except a knowledge of life on the frontier and acquaintance with Southwestern humor, Hooper could have learned to draw Simon Suggs." This contention is upheld by Frank Tryon Meriwether, "The Rogue in the Life and Humor of the Old Southwest," who concludes: "The frontier rogue is a spontaneous development, reflecting the life of the Old Southwest" (p. vi). But the question of Spanish influence remains open. Such works as Stanley T. Williams's *The Spanish Background of American Literature* and Jay B. Hubbell's *The South in American Literature, 1607–1900* give a clearer conception of influences on American culture than has been available in the past. But much remains to be done to relate the works of specific American authors to specific European influences. In this respect there have been a number of useful studies of Cervantes: M. F. Heiser, "Cervantes in the United States," Olin Harris Moore, "Mark Twain and Don Quixote," and Harry Levin, "*Don Quixote* and *Moby-Dick*." Spanish novelists other than Cervantes have received little attention apart from Williams's graceful but too-general study. It would seem safe to assume that the Spanish picaresque novels—that is, novels such as *Lazarillo, Guzmán*, and *Buscón*—influenced the American picaresque very indirectly by filtering through the works of Cervantes, Lesage, Fielding, or Smollett, among possible others. These novelists were well established in the United States before 1789, according to Alexander Cowie, *The Rise of the American Novel*. Hubbell shows that interest in the "frontier" French and English novelists was widespread in the nineteenth century.

Melville and Howells are the major American novelists of the nineteenth century for whom there is evidence that they had a knowledge of the Spanish picaresque novels. Melville bought *Guzmán* in 1849 and borrowed *Lazarillo* in 1850. Howells read *Lazarillo* in 1855 and counted this work among his "literary passions." It is a plausible theory that Howells, Mark Twain's literary cohort, introduced him to the Spanish novels.

When we consider the problem of the Spanish influence on American fiction generally, it is useful to keep in mind the fact that George Ticknor's *History of Spanish Literature* opened for most Americans a new literary frontier. Spanish literature was little read, *Don Quixote* occasionally excepted. The important creations of such writers as Thomas Chandler Haliburton and Hooper were presumably little influenced by Spanish literature, if at all.

How much Cervantes himself influenced the American picaresque is a difficult question to decide. Perhaps *Don Quixote* was uncritically read as a picaresque novel; perhaps American writers inverted the character of the knight in order to portray an American rogue. Something may be said for both arguments. Esther J. Crooks, *The Influence of Cervantes in France in the Seventeenth Century*, and Edward M. Wilson, "Cervantes and English Literature of the Seventeenth Century," have shown that Cervantes was admired outside of Spain as a writer of farce and burlesque. Quixote was an "extravagant" and Sancho an "antihero." Late eighteenth-century imitations of Cervantes tend to follow this pattern. In England there were *The Female Quixote* (1752) by Charlotte Lennox and *The Spiritual Quixote* (1773) by Richard Graves; in the United States there were *Female Quixotism* (1801) by Tabitha Tenney and *Modern Chivalry* (1792–1815) by Hugh Henry Brackenridge. *Modern Chivalry* is a case in point. Brackenridge, a conservative Pennsylvanian of Scottish birth, imitated *Don Quixote* first because its rambling structure provided scope for the survey of manners and customs, second because it suggested a contrast between the gentleman and the rogue that could lead to a satire on democratic equalitarianism. Brackenridge's Quixote is Captain Farrago, a typical gentleman and rationalist; his Sancho is Teague O'Regan, an Irish bogtrotter with aspirations to become a legislator in the new country. Thus Brackenridge reverses the roles: the master represents common sense and the servant is extravagant. And thus the antiheroic Sancho, O'Regan, truly begins to resemble a picaro, at least in the fact of being a pariah. It is, perhaps, no accident that later American humorists such as Johnson Hooper—who almost certainly knew *Don Quixote*—present a similar contrast of gentleman (Sanchoesque Quixote) and rogue (Quixotic Sancho), as suggested by W. Stanley Hoole, *Alias Simon Suggs*, p. 197n.

The possibility of a deliberate inversion of the character of Don Quixote presents itself in Melville's *Confidence-Man*. Melville purchased the Jarvis translation of *Quixote* in September 1855. In "The Piazza," composed about February 1856, the impact of discovery (or rediscovery) is recorded: Melville there refers to Quixote as "That sagest sage that ever lived." In *The Confidence-Man*—which he was writing in 1855–56—Melville names Quixote as one of the "original" characters in literature. In his penciled annotations to the Jarvis edition, Melville approves of a sentence in Louis Viardot's introductory memoir: "Don Quixote is but the case of a man of diseased brain; his monomania is that of a good man who revolts at injustice, and who would exalt virtue" (see Levin, "*Don Quixote* and *Moby-Dick*," pp. 217–26). Since Melville in the *Confidence-Man* exalts indirectly the virtues of charity and brotherhood, it is easy to recognize the appeal *Don Quixote* may have had for him. Also in the Jarvis text Melville underscores Quixote's defense of courtly love, then annotates the passage: [*Don Quixote*:] "I have already often said it, and now repeat it, that a knight-errant without a mistress is like a tree without leaves, a building without cement, a shadow without a body that causes it." [Melville's note:] "—or, as Confucious said, 'a dog without a master,' or to drop Cervantes & Confucious parables—a god-like mind without a God."

For Melville, Dulcinea is Christian faith: her/its loss would result in a meaningless world lacking charity and brotherhood. *The Confidence-Man* presents such a world without Dulcinea. Thus it is possible to argue that the confidence man is an inverted Quixote, shorn of faith and fixed identity, seeing man not as better, but as worse than he is. Daniel G. Hoffman so argues in *Form and Fable in American Fiction*, p. 287.

8. On the general background of the trickster in American folklore see Richard M. Dorson, *American Folklore*; on indigenous trickster tales see Stith Thompson, *Motif-Index of Folk Literature*, 1:120; and on the recurrence of trickster motifs in American humor see James H. Penrod, "The Folk Hero as Prankster in the Old Southwestern Yarns."

9. See Blair, *Native American Humor*; Constance Rourke, *American Humor*, pp. 3–76; and V. L. O. Chittick, *Thomas Chandler Haliburton*, pp. 179–384. Chittick's research on the creator of Sam Slick is particularly valuable.

10. See Hoffman, *Form and Fable*, and Kenneth S. Lynn, *Mark Twain and Southwestern Humor*.

11. See R. W. B. Lewis, *The American Adam*. Other stimulating treatments of the theme are Henry Nash Smith, *Virgin Land*, and W. H. Auden, "Henry James."

12. Herman Melville, "Hawthorne and His *Mosses*," p. 192. Melville refers to the "Calvinistic sense of Innate Depravity" he discerns in Hawthorne's stories.

13. Marius Bewley, *The Eccentric Design*, p. 19.

14. Thomas P. Abernethy, *From Frontier to Plantation in Tennessee*, p. 359.

15. On Melville as critic of nineteenth-century beliefs see Ralph Henry Gabriel, *The Course of American Democratic Thought*, pp. 67–77.

16. Rourke, *American Humor*, p. 31.

17. Cited in Chittick, *Haliburton*, p. 362.

18. Cited in ibid., pp. 327–28.

19. Cited in Richardson Wright, *Hawkers & Walkers in Early America*, p. 28.

20. Chittick, *Haliburton*, pp. 179–235.

21. The *Spirit of the Times*, edited by William T. Porter, appeared from 1831 to 1860. It began as a sporting paper, and the stories of backwoods life tended to grow organically out of factual sporting narratives. See Norris W. Yates, *William T. Porter and the "Spirit of the Times."*

22. For the pattern of thought and occasional wording of this paragraph I am indebted to Lynn, *Mark Twain and Southwestern Humor*, pp. 46–99. Lynn stresses the influence of *The Spectator* on the structural technique of southwestern stories. An earlier American political contrast of gentleman and rogue—one influenced by Cervantes—is evident in Brackenridge's *Modern Chivalry* (1792–1815).

23. See Hoole, *Alias Simon Suggs*.

24. This and the two preceding quotations are also stressed by Lynn, *Mark Twain and Southwestern Humor*, pp. 78f.

25. Hooper inscribed his copy of *Quixote* for his sister-in-law, date uncertain; see Hoole, *Alias Simon Suggs*, p. 197n.

26. See John W. Nichol, "Melville and the Midwest." There would appear to be no direct reference by Melville to the western experience at the time he was there. But Yates, *William T. Porter*, p. 110, notes a letter in *Spirit of the Times*, 11 (1841): 67, from "H. M." whom he describes as "a sporting man who was apparently an easterner making a long stay in Illinois." Initials, date, and description may point to Melville as the writer. If Melville did write such a letter, it would establish his early interest in native American humor publications. Certainly such native humor was soon to play its part in *Typee*, *Omoo*, and *Moby-Dick*.

27. See William H. Gilman, *Melville's Early Life and Redburn*.

28. D. H. Lawrence, *Studies in Classic American Literature*, pp. 142–74. For Lawrence, Ahab impotently assaults Moby-Dick, "the last phallic being of the white man." By implication, Ahab is an expression of Melville's own unconscious urges.

29. See William Ellery Sedgwick, *Herman Melville*.

30. Studies of *The Confidence-Man* are too numerous to be listed here, but among them are: Watson G. Branch, "The Genesis, Composition, and Structure of *The Confidence-Man*"; A. Carl Bredahl, Jr., *Melville's Angles of Vision*; Frank Jaster, "Melville's Cosmopolitan"; Alan Lebowitz, *Progress into Silence*; Joseph Baim, "The Confidence-Man as 'Trickster'"; Edgar A. Dryden, *Melville's Thematics of Form*, esp. Chapter 5, "The Novelist as Impostor: Subversive Form in *The Confidence-Man*," pp. 149–95; Edward Mitchell, "From Action to Essence"; Leon F. Seltzer, "Camus's Absurd and the World of Melville's *Confidence-Man*"; H. Bruce Franklin, *The Wake of the Gods*, esp. Chapter 6, "*The Confidence-Man*: The Destroyer's Eastern Masquerade," pp. 153–87; the indispensable Introduction by Elizabeth S. Foster to *The Confidence-Man*; Hoffman, *Form and Fable*, pp. 279–313; Milton R. Stern, *The Fine Hammered Steel of Herman Melville*; Merlin Bowen, *The Long Encounter*; Edward H. Rosenberry, *Melville and the Comic*

*Spirit*; Lawrance Thompson, *Melville's Quarrel with God*; Egbert S. Oliver, "Melville's Picture of Emerson and Thoreau in *The Confidence-Man*"; Richard Chase, "Melville's Confidence Man"; John W. Shroeder, "Sources and Symbols for Melville's *Confidence-Man*"; Roy Harvey Pierce, "Melville's Indian-Hater"; Nathalia Wright, "The Confidence Men of Melville and Cooper"; William Van O'Connor, "Melville on the Nature of Hope"; John G. Cawelti, "Some Notes on the Structure of *The Confidence-Man*"; Harrison Hayford, "Poe in *The Confidence-Man*"; James E. Miller, Jr., "*The Confidence-Man*"; John J. Gross, "Melville's *The Confidence-Man*"; Edward H. Rosenberry, "Melville's Ship of Fools"; and Walter Dubler, "Theme and Structure in Melville's *The Confidence Man*."

On Melville's reading, see Merton M. Sealts, Jr., "Melville's Reading." An unidentified edition of *Lazarillo de Tormes* was borrowed from Evert Duyckinck in 1850. The previous year Melville bought "Guzman 3 vol." in London, also an unidentified volume. The British Museum Catalogue lists two three-volume English translations before 1849: *Pleasant Adventures of Guzman* [*sic*] *of Alfarache* . . . Translated from Lesage by A. O'Connor. 3 vols. (London, 1812; 2d ed., 3 vols., 1817); *The Life and Adventures of Guzman d'Alfarache; or, The Spanish Rogue*. Translated from the . . . French edition of Mon. Le Sage. By John Henry Brady. 2d ed., 3 vols. (London, 1823). Melville's spelling might indicate the Brady version; but both English versions derive from Lesage's spurious translation.

31. The full context suggests irony: "And as, in real life, the proprieties will not allow people to act out themselves with that unreserve permitted to the stage; so, in books of fiction, they look not only for more entertainment, but, at bottom, even for more reality, than real life itself can show. Thus, though they want novelty, they want nature, too, but nature unfettered, exhilarated, in effect transformed." See Dryden, *Thematics of Form*, for extended analysis.

32. Compare *Moby-Dick*, p. 486: "There is no steady unretracing progress in this life; we do not advance through fixed gradations, and at the last one pause:—through infancy's unconscious spell, boyhood's thoughtless faith, adolescence's doubt (the common doom), then scepticism, then disbelief, resting at last in manhood's pondering repose of If." In *Pierre*, the thematic "Chronologicals and Horologicals" lecture is entitled "EI"—the Greek word for "If."

33. Franklin, *Wake of the Gods*, p. 154.

34. On novels with mythological motif, see John J. White, *Mythology in the Modern Novel*.

35. Frank Kermode, *The Sense of an Ending*, p. 39. Kermode's distinction would presumably not apply to "creative mythology" in Joseph Campbell's sense, as discussed in Chapter 1 of this study.

36. In modern fiction generally, but notably in that of James, Conrad, and Faulkner, not only is a process of vision dramatized but also the reader is led to "see."

37. Herman Melville, *The Confidence-Man*, pp. 379–80: "Glad & content the sacred river glides on. But at St. Louis the course of this dream is run. Down on it like a Pawnee from ambush foams the yellow-jacket Missouri."

38. Foster, Introduction to *The Confidence-Man*, pp. lv–lvii.

39. Compare *Moby-Dick*, Chapter 115.

40. See Oliver, "Melville's Picture."

41. Melville's concept of the balanced head and heart is studied in Bowen, *Long Encounter*.

42. Jaster, "Melville's Cosmopolitan," p. 205.

43. *Confidence-Man*, p. 274. The cosmopolitan is speaking: "I have confidence in man. But what was told me not a half-hour since? I was told that I would find it written—'Believe not his many words—an enemy speaketh sweetly with his lips'—and also I was told that I would find a good deal more to the same effect, and all in this book. I could not think it; and, coming here to look for myself, what do I read? Not only just what was quoted, but also, as was engaged, more to the same purpose, such as this: 'With much communication he will tempt thee; he will smile upon thee, and speak thee fair, and say What wantest thou? If thou be for his profit he will use thee; he will make thee bear, and will not be sorry for it. Observe and take good heed. When thou hearest these things, awake in thy sleep.' " "Who's that describing the confidence-man?" [is then asked by someone hidden behind one of the curtained berths.].

44. Franklin, *Wake of the Gods*, p. 157.

45. Branch, "The Genesis," discusses a four-part structure of encounters, colloquies, frame, and insertions.

46. On the possibility that Melville planned a sequel see Howard C. Horsford, "Evidence of Melville's Plans for a Sequel to *The Confidence-Man*." Foster sees the novel complete as it is. Hoffman, *Form and Fable*, pp. 309–10, suggests the Judgment Day interpretation.

47. This sinister habit is frequently credited to the fever-ridden poor whites in southwestern humor: see James H. Penrod, "Folk Motifs in Old Southwestern Humor."

48. On Moredock's flawed humanity see Pierce, "Melville's Indian-Hater."

49. Daniel G. Hoffman, "Melville's 'Story of China Aster'," sees the Prometheanism of *Moby-Dick* checked here by satanism. The ultimate confidence man is death, when the Promethean spirit is perverted to private ends at the expense of mankind.

50. Thompson's argument in *Melville's Quarrel*, pp. 297–328, is that Melville himself saw evil as part of the divine nature. I suggest that Melville was less cynical than this and that he was not a thinker to hide some absolute heresy behind his drama of ambiguity.

51. Branch, "The Genesis," sees a probable source of Melville's novel in an Albany newspaper article, dated 28 April 1855, announcing that the "Original Confidence Man," famous for his swindles in New York City in 1849, had reappeared in Albany.

52. Thompson, *Melville's Quarrel*, pp. 298–99, refers Melville's pun to Carlyle's *Heroes and Hero-Worship*. Carlyle declares that a "Great Man" is "an *original* man . . . Poet, Prophet, God . . . the primal reality of things." Melville partly imitates Carlyle's inflated style in *Moby-Dick*; it would, however, seem probable that he pricked Carlyle's inflated ideas in *The Confidence-Man*.

53. See Lionel Trilling, *Sincerity and Authenticity*. Particularly illuminating is Trilling's discussion, p. 137, of J. H. Plumb's *The Death of the Past*, which expresses the view that the past is on the point of being extirpated from the consciousness of modern man.

54. Martin Hume, *Spanish Influence on English Literature*, p. 183.

55. Frank W. Chandler, *The Literature of Roguery*, 2:489.

56. On *Huckleberry Finn*, but not specifically related to the picaresque idea, are the following studies: Arthur G. Pettit, *Mark Twain & the South*; James M. Cox, *Mark Twain*; Henry Nash Smith, "A Sound Heart and a Deformed Conscience"

and Introduction to *Adventures of Huckleberry Finn*; Albert E. Stone, Jr., *The Innocent Eye*; Roger B. Salomon, *Twain and the Image of History*; Walter Blair, *Mark Twain & Huck Finn*; Donna Gerstenberger, "Huckleberry Finn and the World's Illusions"; Kenneth S. Lynn, "Huck and Jim"; Edward Wasiolek, "The Structure of Make-Believe"; Frances V. Brownell, "The Role of Jim in *Huckleberry Finn*"; Frank Baldanza, "The Structure of *Huckleberry Finn*"; Trilling, *Liberal Imagination*, pp. 104–17; Edgar M. Branch, "The Two Providences"; and James G. Harrison, "A Note on the Duke in *Huck Finn*."

57. Samuel L. Clemens, letter to William Dean Howells, 5 July 1875, Samuel Langhorn Clemens, *Mark Twain—Howells Letters*, 1:91–92. Howells used the word "picaresque" admiringly in praising *The Prince and the Pauper* in a letter to Twain, 13 December 1880 (*Letters*, 1:338), and was fond of recommending "picaresque" works as models for American naturalists. In the *Atlantic Monthly*, 26 (1870): 759, he wrote that "the truly American novel, when it comes to be written, will be a story of personal adventure after the fashion of *Gil Blas*, and many earlier English fictions." *Don Quixote* and *Lazarillo de Tormes* were lifelong favorites, and Howells once attempted to translate *Lazarillo* in 1855. In *My Literary Passions* Howells devoted a chapter to *Lazarillo* and concluded, "I am sure that the intending author of American fiction would do well to study the Spanish picaresque novels, for in their simplicity of design he will find one of the best forms for an American story." One would like to know how influential such opinions were on Twain. Williams, *Spanish Background*, 1:234, surmises that Howells and Twain often discussed their mutual interest in Spanish literature. I find no concrete evidence that Twain knew the Spanish picaresque novels. Cervantes is a different matter: see Moore, "Mark Twain and Don Quixote."

58. Blair, *Mark Twain & Huck Finn*.

59. Ibid., pp. 243, 253, 270, 284.

60. Albert Camus, *The Rebel*, p. 26.

61. Smith, Introduction to *Adventures of Huckleberry Finn*, p. xvi.

62. Cited in ibid., p. xvi n., from Notebook 28a[I], TS, p. 35 (1895), Mark Twain Papers, University of California Library, Berkeley.

63. Ibid., p. xix.

64. W. H. Auden, "Huck and Oliver," pp. 113–14.

65. Cox, *Mark Twain*, p. 173. Cox's Freudian interpretation of Twain's "conscience" as "repression," with the "pleasure principle" opposed to these, does much to elucidate the ending of *Huckleberry Finn* as "frustration."

66. Salomon, *Twain and the Image of History*, pp. 142, 146.

67. I am indebted for this observation to Smith, "A Sound Heart," p. 91. The King's remarks, originally in direct discourse, were, on revision, put into indirect discourse, thus becoming fused as an element of Huck's consciousness.

68. Ludmilla Buketoff Turkevich, *Cervantes in Russia*, p. 50.

69. Karl Ludwig Selig, "Concerning Gogol's *Dead Souls* and *Lazarillo de Tormes*."

70. On the religious intention, see Nikolai Andreyev, Introduction to *Dead Souls*, p. vi.

71. Cited in Magarshack, *Gogol*, p. 214.

72. Nicolai Gogol, letter to Danilevsky, 21 May 1842 (O.S.), cited in ibid., p. 210.

73. For a lively discussion of Gogol's unreality of characterization see T. E. Little, "Dead Souls."

74. Alastair Fowler, "The Confidence Man," p. 784. By far the best work in English on *Felix Krull* is Donald F. Nelson, *Portrait of the Artist as Hermes*. On Mann's general themes I have consulted Fritz Kaufmann, *Thomas Mann*, and J. M. Lindsay, *Thomas Mann*. A stimulating essay (with which I partially disagree) is Robert B. Heilman, "Variations on Picaresque (*Felix Krull*)." I have also consulted the following articles: Erich Heller, "Parody, Tragic and Comic"; Oskar Seidlin, "Picaresque Elements in Thomas Mann's Work"; and Werner Hollmann, "Thomas Mann's *Felix Krull* and *Lazarillo*."

75. From *Die Entstehung des Doktor Faustus*, cited in Heilman, "Variations," p. 557.

76. Ignace Feuerlicht, *Thomas Mann*, notes that, in Mann's view, life on earth is only an ephemeral episode. Teilhard de Chardin, celebrated Jesuit and paleontologist, presents theories of cosmic evolution in *The Phenomenon of Man* (1959) and earlier books.

77. Nelson, *Portrait*, pp. 65–66.

### 5: The Tragicomedy of Self-Creation

1. P. E. Russell, "*Don Quixote* as a Funny Book," pp. 320–21.

2. Erich Fromm, *The Anatomy of Human Destructiveness*, pp. 8–9.

3. R. W. B. Lewis, *The Picaresque Saint*, p. 19.

4. Interesting though brief discussions of *Invisible Man* as picaresque are found in John M. Reilly, ed., *Twentieth Century Interpretations of Invisible Man*, pp. 22–31, and in Stuart Miller, *The Picaresque Novel*, pp. 134–35.

5. Robert Alter, *Rogue's Progress*, pp. 130–32.

6. Robert Bloom, *The Indeterminate World*, pp. 46, 103. Recently, critics have dropped the picaresque attribution to Cary's work: see R. W. Noble, *Joyce Cary*, and Jack Wolkenfeld, *Joyce Cary*.

7. Joseph Frank, *The Widening Gyre*, p. 175.

# Bibliography

## Primary Sources

Alemán, Mateo. *Guzmán de Alfarache*. Edited by Samuel Gili y Gaya. Clásicos Castellanos. 5 vols. Madrid, 1926.

———. *The Rogue, or the Life of Guzmán de Alfarache*. Edited with an introduction by James Fitzmaurice-Kelly. Translated by James Mabbe. 4 vols. London, 1924.

Allen, Hervey. *Anthony Adverse*. Limited ed. 3 vols. Mount Vernon, N.Y., 1937.

Apuleius, Lucius. *The Transformations of Lucius, Otherwise Known as The Golden Ass*. Translated by Robert Graves. Penguin Books. Harmondsworth, 1950.

Aristotle. *The Poetics*. Translated by Preston H. Epps. Chapel Hill, N.C., 1942.

Augustine. *The Confessions of Saint Augustine*. Translated by Edward B. Pusey. Modern Library. New York, 1949.

Baldwin, Joseph G. *The Flush Times of Alabama and Mississippi*. American Century Series. New York, 1957.

Beyle, Marie Henri [Stendhal]. *Correspondance de Stendhal*. Edited by Ad. Paupe and P. A. Cheramy. 3 vols. Paris, 1908.

Bunyan, John. *Life and Death of Mr. Badman, and, the Holy War*. Edited by John Brown. Cambridge, 1905.

Cary, Joyce. *Art and Reality*. Cambridge, 1958.

———. *The Horse's Mouth*. New York, 1944.

Cervantes Saavedra, Miguel de. *Don Quixote*. Translated by J. M. Cohen. Penguin Books. Harmondsworth, 1950.

———. *Three Exemplary Novels*. Translated by Samuel Putnam. London, 1952.

Chillingworth, William. *The Religion of Protestants a Safe Way to Salvation*. Bohn edition. London, 1846.

# Bibliography

Clemens, Samuel Langhorne [Mark Twain]. *Adventures of Huckleberry Finn.* Edited with an introduction by Henry Nash Smith. Riverside editions. Boston, 1958.

———. *Mark Twain–Howells Letters: The Correspondence of Samuel L. Clemens and William D. Howells, 1872–1910.* Edited by Henry Nash Smith and William M. Gibson. 2 vols. Cambridge, Mass., 1960.

Cooper, Anthony Ashley (Third Earl of Shaftesbury). *Characteristics of Men, Manners, Opinions, Times.* Edited by John M. Robertson. 2 vols. London, 1900.

Defoe, Daniel. *The History and Remarkable Life of the Truly Honourable Col. Jacque . . .* Printed from the 1st ed. London, 1923.

———. *Novels and Selected Writings.* Shakespeare Head edition. 14 vols. Oxford, 1927–28.

———. *Serious Reflections during the Life and Surprising Adventures of Robinson Crusoe.* Edited by George A. Aitken. London, 1895.

Descartes, René. *Descartes' Philosophical Writings.* Translated by Norman K. Smith. London, 1952.

Dickens, Charles. *Complete Works.* Edited by F. G. Kitton. 15 vols. London, 1903–8.

———. *Oliver Twist.* 3d ed. London, 1841.

Eachard, John. *Mr. Hobbs's State of Nature Consider'd.* Edited by Peter Ure. English Reprints Series. Liverpool, 1958.

Ellison, Ralph. *Invisible Man.* New York, 1952.

Fielding, Henry. *Miscellanies.* 3 vols. Vol. 1, *The Life of Mr. Jonathan Wild the Great.* London, 1743.

———. *Novels.* Shakespeare Head edition. Oxford, 1926.

Gogol, Nikolai. *Dead Souls.* Everyman's Library. London, 1960.

———. *Tales of Good and Evil.* Translated by David Magarshack. New York, 1957.

Grass, Günter. *The Tin Drum.* Penguin Books. Harmondsworth, 1965.

Grimmelshausen, Hans Jacob Christoffel von. *Simplicissimus the Vagabond.* Translated by A. T. S. Goodrick. London, 1924.

Hawthorne, Nathaniel. *The English Notebooks.* Edited by Randall Stewart. New York, 1941.

Hobbes, Thomas. *Leviathan, or the Matter, Forme and Power of a Commonwealth Ecclesiasticall and Civil.* Edited by Michael Oakeshott. Oxford, 1960.

Hooper, Johnson Jones. *Adventures of Captain Simon Suggs.* Philadelphia, 1851.

James, Henry. *The Letters of Henry James*. Edited by Percy Lubbock. 2 vols. New York, 1920.

La Bruyère, Jean de. *Les Caractères de La Bruyère*. 2 vols. Paris, 1873.

*La vida de Lazarillo de Tormes y de sus fortunas y adversidades*. Edited by Julio Cejador y Frauca. Clásicos Castellanos. 3d ed. Madrid, 1934.

Lesage, Alain-René. *The Adventures of Gil Blas of Santillane*. Translated by Tobias Smollett. London, 1881.

_____. *Asmodeus, or The Devil on Two Sticks [Le diable boîteux]*. Translated by J. Thomas. London, 1924.

_____. *Histoire de Gil Blas de Santillane*. Edited by Maurice Bardon. 2 vols. Paris, 1955.

_____. *Oeuvres*. Vol. 5, *Guzmán d'Alfarache*. Paris, 1821.

_____. *Théâtre: Turcaret, Crispin rival de son maître, La Tontine*. Edited by Maurice Bardon. Paris, 1948.

Mann, Thomas. *Confessions of Felix Krull, Confidence Man*. Translated by Denver Lindley. Penguin Books. Harmondsworth, 1958.

_____. *Essays of Three Decades*. Translated by H. T. Lowe-Porter. London, 1947.

_____. *Stories of Three Decades*. London, 1946.

Melville, Herman. *The Complete Stories*. Edited by J. Leyda. London, 1951.

_____. *The Confidence-Man: His Masquerade*. Edited with an introduction by Elizabeth S. Foster. New York, 1954.

_____. "Hawthorne and His *Mosses*." In *The Shock of Recognition*, edited by Edmund Wilson. London, 1956.

_____. *The Letters of Herman Melville*. Edited by Merrill R. Davis and William H. Gilman. New Haven, 1960.

_____. *Moby-Dick; or, The Whale*. Edited by Luther S. Mansfield and Howard P. Vincent. New York, 1952.

_____. *Pierre, or, The Ambiguities*. Edited with an introduction by Henry A. Murray. New York, 1949.

_____. *Works*. 12 vols. London, 1922–23.

Nashe, Thomas. *The Works of Thomas Nashe*. Edited by Ronald B. McKerrow. 5 vols. Oxford, 1958.

Pascal, Blaise. *The Pensées*. Translated by J. M. Cohen. Penguin Books. Harmondsworth, 1961.

Petronius Arbiter. *The Satyricon*. Translated by P. Dinnage. London, 1953.

# Bibliography

Quevedo y Villegas, Francisco de. *Historia de la vida del Buscón, llamado Don Pablos.* Edited by Américo Castro. Clásicos Castellanos. Madrid, 1927.

―――――. *La vida del Buscón llamado Don Pablos.* Edited by Fernando Lázaro Carreter. Barcelona, 1968.

Rojas, Fernando de. *Celestina. A Play in Twenty-one Acts.* Translated by Mack Hendricks Singleton. Madison, Wis., 1958.

Smollett, Tobias. *The Adventures of Ferdinand Count Fathom.* 2 vols. London, 1753.

―――――. *Novels.* Shakespeare Head edition. 11 vols. Oxford, 1925–26.

―――――. *Roderick Random.* 2d ed. 2 vols. London, 1748.

Thackeray, William Makepeace. *Barry Lyndon.* The Oxford Thackeray. Oxford, 1909.

Wilmot, John, earl of Rochester. *Poems.* Edited by Vivian de Sola Pinto. London, 1953.


## Secondary Sources

Abernethy, Thomas P. *From Frontier to Plantation in Tennessee: A Study in Frontier Democracy.* Chapel Hill, N.C., 1932.

Adams, Richard P. "The Unity and Coherence of *Huckleberry Finn*." *Tulane Studies in English* 6 (1956): 87–103.

Alborg, Juan Luis. *Historia de la literatura española Edad Media y Renacimiento.* 2d ed. Madrid, 1972.

Allen, H. Warner. "The Picaresque Novel: An Essay in Comparative Literature." In *Celestina, or The Tragi-Comedy of Calisto and Melibea,* by Fernando de Rojas. London, 1908.

Allen, Walter. *The English Novel.* London, 1954.

Allott, Miriam. *Novelists on the Novel.* London, 1959.

Alter, Robert. *Rogue's Progress: Studies in the Picaresque Novel.* Cambridge, Mass., 1965.

Alvarez, D. "La picaresca española y la literatura existencialista." *Humanidades* 10 (1958): 207–12.

Anderson, Hans H. "The Paradox of Trade and Morality in Defoe." *Modern Philology* 39 (1941): 23–46.

Andreyev, Nikolai. Introduction to *Dead Souls,* by Nikolai Gogol. Everyman's Library. London, 1960.

Arvin, Newton. *Herman Melville.* New York, 1950.

Asensio, Manuel J. "La intención religiosa del *Lazarillo de Tormes* y Juan de Valdés." *Hispanic Review* 27 (1959): 78–102.

———. "Más sobre el *Lazarillo de Tormes*." *Hispanic Review* 28 (1960): 245–50.

Atkinson, Geoffrey. *Le sentiment de la Nature et le Retour à la vie simple (1690–1740)*. Paris, 1960.

Atkinson, William C. "Studies in Literary Decadence: The Picaresque Novel." *Bulletin of Spanish Studies* 4 (1927): 19–27.

Auden, W. H. "Balaam and the Ass: The Master-Servant Relationship in Literature." *Thought* 29 (1954): 237–70.

———. "Henry James: The American Scene." In *American Critical Essays: Twentieth Century*, edited by Harold Beaver. The World's Classics. London, 1959.

———. "Huck and Oliver." In *Mark Twain: A Collection of Critical Essays*, edited by Henry Nash Smith. Englewood Cliffs, N.J., 1963.

Auerbach, Erich. *Mimesis: The Representation of Reality in Western Literature*. Translated by Willard Trask. Princeton, 1953.

Ayala, Francisco. *Experiencia e invención: Ensayos sobre el escritor y su mundo*. Madrid, 1960.

Aydelotte, Frank. *Elizabethan Rogues and Vagabonds*. Oxford, 1913.

Ayer, A. J. *The Problem of Knowledge*. Harmondsworth, 1956.

Baim, Joseph. "The Confidence-Man as 'Trickster'." *American Transcendental Quarterly* 1 (1969): 81–83.

Baker, Ernest A. *The History of the English Novel*. Vol. 2, *The Elizabethan Age and After*. Vol. 3, *The Later Romances and the Establishment of Realism*. London, 1929.

Baldanza, Frank. "The Structure of *Huckleberry Finn*." *American Literature* 27 (1955): 347–55.

Bardon, Maurice. *Don Quichotte en France au XVIIe et XVIIIe siècles, 1605–1815*. Paris, 1931.

———. Preface to *Histoire de Gil Blas de Santillane*, by Alain-René Lesage, Vol. 1. Paris, 1955.

Barker, John William. "Notas sobre la influencia de Quevedo en la literatura inglesa." *Boletín de la Biblioteca de Menéndez Pelayo* 21 (1945): 429–35.

Bataillon, Marcel. *El sentido del Lazarillo de Tormes*. Paris, 1954.

———. *Erasme et l'Espagne*. Paris, 1937.

———. *Erasmo y España: Estudios sobre la historia espiritual del siglo XVI*. Translated by Antonio Alatorre. 2d rev. ed. Mexico City, 1966.

———. Introduction to *La vie de Lazarillo de Tormes*. Paris, 1958.

# Bibliography

————. *Le roman picaresque*. Paris, 1931.

————. *Pícaros y Picaresca. La Pícara Justina*. Madrid, 1969.

Battestin, Martin C. *The Moral Basis of Fielding's Art: A Study of "Joseph Andrews."* Middletown, Conn., 1959.

Beberfall, Lester. "The *Pícaro* in Context." *Hispania* 37 (1954): 288–92.

Bell, Aubrey F. G. *Cervantes*. Norman, Okla., 1947.

Benítez Claros, Rafael. *Existencialismo y picaresca*. Madrid, 1958.

Bewley, Marius. *The Eccentric Design: Form in the Classic American Novel*. London, 1959.

Bishop, Jonathan. "Knowledge, Action, and Interpretation in Defoe's Novels." *Journal of the History of Ideas* 13 (1952): 3–16.

Blair, Walter. *Mark Twain & Huck Finn*. Berkeley, 1960.

————. *Native American Humor (1800–1900)*. New York, 1937.

Blanco Aguinaga, Carlos. "Cervantes y la picaresca: Notas sobre dos tipos de realismo." *Nueva Revista de Filología Hispánica* 11 (1957): 313–42.

————. "Guzmán de Alfarache y el pecado original." *Buenos Aires Literaria* 8 (1953): 7–13.

Bleiberg, Germán. "Mateo Alemán y los galeotes (En torno a documentos inéditos del siglo XVI)." *Revista de Occidente* 13 (1966): 330–73.

————. "Nuevos datos biográficos de Mateo Alemán." In *Actas del segunde Congreso Internacional de Hispanistas*, edited by J. Sánchez Romeraldo and Norbert Poulussen. Nijmegen, 1967.

Bloom, Robert. *The Indeterminate World: A Study in the Novels of Joyce Cary*. Philadelphia, 1962.

Boege, Fred W. *Smollett's Reputation as a Novelist*. Princeton, 1947.

Booth, Wayne C. *The Rhetoric of Fiction*. Chicago and London, 1961.

Borgers, Oscar. "Le roman picaresque: Réalisme et fiction." *Les Lettres Romanes* 14 (1960): 295–305.

Bowen, Merlin. *The Long Encounter: Self and Experience in the Writings of Herman Melville*. Chicago, 1960.

Branch, Edgar M. "The Two Providences: Thematic Form in *Huckleberry Finn*." *College English* 11 (1950): 188–95.

Branch, Watson G. "The Genesis, Composition, and Structure of *The Confidence-Man*." *Nineteenth-Century Fiction* 27 (1973): 424–48.

Braswell, William. *Melville's Religious Thought: An Essay in Interpretation*. Durham, N.C., 1943.

Braudel, Fernand. *The Mediterranean and the Mediterranean World in the Age of Philip II*. Translated by Siân Reynolds. 2 vols. New York, Evanston, San Francisco, and London, 1972.

Bray, René. *La formation de la doctrine classique en France*. Paris, 1927.

Bredahl, A. Carl, Jr. *Melville's Angles of Vision*. Gainesville, Fla., 1972.

Brenan, Gerald. *The Literature of the Spanish People from Roman Times to the Present Day*. 2d rev. ed. Cambridge, 1953.

Brownell, Frances V. "The Role of Jim in *Huckleberry Finn*." *Boston University Studies in English* 1 (1955): 74–83.

Bury, J. B. *The Idea of Progress*. London, 1932.

Bushee, Alice H. "Atalaya de la vida humana." *Modern Language Notes* 29 (1914): 197–98.

Cameron, Wallace J. "The Theme of Hunger in the Spanish Picaresque Novel." Ph.D. dissertation, State University of Iowa, 1956.

Campbell, Joseph. "Bios and Mythos: Prolegomena to a Science of Mythology." In *Myth and Literature: Contemporary Theory and Practice*, edited by John B. Vickery. Lincoln, Neb., 1966.

––––––. *The Masks of God*. 4 vols. Vol. 4, *Creative Mythology*. London, 1968.

Camus, Albert. *The Rebel*. Translated by Anthony Bower. Harmondsworth, 1962.

Caneva, Rafael. "Picaresca: Anticaballería y realismo." *Universidad de Antioquia* 109 (1952): 67–87, 110 (1953): 373–89.

Carey, Douglas M. "Asides and Interiority in *Lazarillo de Tormes*: A Study in Psychological Realism." *Studies in Philology* 66 (1969): 119–34.

Carilla, Emilio. *Quevedo (Entre dos centenarios)*. Tucumán, 1949.

Castro, Américo. Introduction to *La vida de Lazarillo de Tormes*, edited by E. W. Hesse and H. F. Williams. Madison, Wis., 1948.

––––––. "Lo picaresco." In *El Pensamiento de Cervantes*, by Américo Castro. Madrid, 1925.

––––––. "Perspectiva de la novela picaresca." *Revista de la Biblioteca Archivo y Museo del Ayuntamiento de Madrid* 12 (1935): 123–38.

———. *The Structure of Spanish History*. Translated by Edmund L. King. Princeton, 1954.

Cawelti, John G. "Some Notes on the Structure of *The Confidence-Man*." *American Literature* 29 (1957): 278–88.

Cejador y Frauca, Julio. Introduction to *La vida de Lazarillo de Tormes y sus fortunas y adversidades*, edited by Julio Cejador y Frauca. Clásicos Castellanos. 3d ed. Madrid, 1934.

Chandler, Frank Wadleigh. *The Literature of Roguery*. 2 vols. Boston and New York, 1907.

———. *Romances of Roguery*. Part I: *The Picaresque Novel in Spain*. New York, 1899.

Chappelain, Jean. "Au Lecteur." In *Le Gueux, ou la vie de Guzmán d'Alfarache*, translated by Jean Chappelain. Paris, 1638.

Chase, Richard. *The American Novel and Its Tradition*. London, 1958.

———. "Melville's Confidence-Man." *Kenyon Review* 11 (1949): 122–40.

Chittick, V. L. O. *Thomas Chandler Haliburton*. New York, 1924.

Claretie, Leó. *Lesage romancier: D'après des nouveaux documents*. Paris, 1890.

Cordier, Henri. *Essai bibliographique sur les oeuvres d'Alain-René Lesage*. Paris, 1910.

Cossio, José María de. "Las continuaciones del *Lazarillo de Tormes*." *Revista de Filología Española* 25 (1941): 514–23.

Cowie, Alexander. *The Rise of the American Novel*. New York, 1948.

Cox, James M. *Mark Twain: The Fate of Humor*. Princeton, 1966.

———. "Remarks on the Sad Initiation of Huckleberry Finn." *Sewanee Review* 62 (1954): 389–405.

Crane, R. S. "Suggestions toward a Genealogy of the *Man of Feeling*." *ELH* 1 (1934): 205–30.

Croce, Benedetto. "Studi su poesie antiche e moderne: *Lazarillo de Tormes*. La storia dell'escudero." *La Critica* 37 (1939): 91–97.

Crocker, Lester G. "*Hamlet, Don Quijote, La Vida es Sueño*: The Quest for Values." *PMLA* 69 (1954): 278–313.

Crockett, Harold Kelly. "The Picaresque Tradition in English Fiction to 1770: A Study of Popular Backgrounds, with Particular Attention to Fielding and Smollett." Ph.D. dissertation, University of Illinois, 1955.

Cronan, Urban. "Mateo Alemán and Miguel de Cervantes Saavedra." *Revue Hispanique* 25 (1911): 468–75.

# Bibliography

Crooks, Esther J. *The Influence of Cervantes in France in the Seventeenth Century*. Baltimore, 1931.

Cross, Wilbur L. *The Development of the English Novel*. New York, 1922.

Curtius, Ernst Robert. *European Literature and the Latin Middle Ages*. Translated by Willard Trask. London, 1953.

Damiani, Bruno M. *Francisco Delicado*. New York, 1974.

D'Arcy, M. C. *The Mind and Heart of Love: Lion and Unicorn: A Study in Eros and Agape*. New York, 1956.

Davies, R. Trevor. *The Golden Century of Spain, 1501–1621*. London, 1937.

Davis, Merrell R. *Melville's Mardi: A Chartless Voyage*. New Haven, 1952.

Davis, Robert Gorham. "The Sense of the Real in English Fiction." *Comparative Literature* 3 (1951): 200–217.

Dédéyan, Charles. *A.-R. Lesage: Gil Blas*. Paris, 1956.

De Haan, Fonger. *An Outline of the History of the Novela Picaresca in Spain*. New York and The Hague, 1903.

Del Monte, Alberto. *Itinerario del romanzo picaresco spagnolo*. Florence, 1957–58.

Del Piero, R. A. "The Picaresque Philosophy in *Guzmán de Alfarache*." *Modern Language Forum* 42 (1958): 152–56.

DeRougemont, Denis. *Love Declared: Essays on the Myths of Love*. Translated by Richard Howard. Boston, 1964.

DeVoto, Bernard. *Mark Twain's America*. Cambridge, Mass., 1932.

Deyermond, A. D. *The Petrarchan Sources of the "Celestina."* Oxford, 1960.

Digeon, Aurelien. *The Novels of Fielding*. London, 1925.

Dobrée, Bonamy. *English Literature in the Early Eighteenth Century, 1700–1740*. Oxford, 1959.

Dooley, D. J. "Some Uses and Mutations of the Picaresque." *Dalhousie Review* 37 (1957–58): 363–77.

Dorson, Richard M. *American Folklore*. Chicago, 1959.

Driver, C. H. "John Locke." In *The Social and Political Ideas of Some English Thinkers of the Augustan Age A.D. 1650–1750*, edited by F. J. C. Hearnshaw. London, 1928.

Dryden, Edgar A. *Melville's Thematics of Form*. Baltimore, 1968.

Dubler, Walter. "Theme and Structure in Melville's *The Confidence-Man*." *American Literature* 33 (1961): 307–19.

Dudden, Frederick Homes. *Henry Fielding, His Life, Works, and Times*. 2 vols. Oxford, 1952.

# Bibliography

Dunn, Peter N. *Castillo Solórzano and the Decline of the Spanish Novel*. Oxford, 1952.

―――. "El individuo y la sociedad en *La vida del Buscón*." *Bulletin Hispanique* 52 (1950): 375–96.

Elliott, Robert C. *The Power of Satire: Magic, Ritual, Art*. Princeton, 1960.

Ellman, Richard, and Feidelson, Charles, Jr., eds. *The Modern Tradition: Backgrounds of Modern Literature*. New York, 1965.

Empson, William. *Some Versions of Pastoral*. London, 1935.

Ennis, Lambert. *Thackeray: The Sentimental Cynic*. Evanston, Ill., 1950.

Eoff, Sherman. *The Modern Spanish Novel*. London, 1962.

―――. "*Oliver Twist* and the Spanish Picaresque Novel." *Studies in Philology* 54 (1957): 440–47.

―――. "The Picaresque Psychology of Guzmán de Alfarache." *Hispanic Review* 21 (1953): 107–19.

―――. "Tragedy of the Unwanted Person, in Three Versions: Pablos de Segovia, Pito Pérez, Pascual Duarte." *Hispania* 39 (1956): 190–96.

Ettinghausen, Henry. *Francisco de Quevedo and the Neostoic Movement*. London, 1972.

Fairchild, Hoxie Neale. *Religious Trends in English Poetry*. Vol. 1, *1700–1740*. New York, 1939.

Fergusson, Francis. "'Myth' and the Literary Scruple." In *Myth and Literature: Contemporary Theory and Practice*, edited by John B. Vickery. Lincoln, Neb., 1966.

Fernández, Sergio. "El *Guzmán de Alfarache* de Mateo Alemán." *Hispania* 35 (1952): 422–24.

Feuerlicht, Ignace. *Thomas Mann*. New York, 1968.

Feidelson, Charles, Jr. *Symbolism and American Literature*. Chicago, 1953.

Fitzgerald, Brian. *Daniel Defoe: A Study in Conflict*. London, 1954.

Fitzmaurice-Kelly, James. Introduction to *The Rogue, or the Life of Guzmán de Alfarache*, by Mateo Alemán. Translated by James Mabbe. Vol. 1. London and New York, 1924.

―――. "The Picaresque Novel." In *Encyclopedia Britannica* 17 (1958): 907.

―――. "*La vida del Buscón*." *Revue Hispanique* 43 (1918): 1–9.

Forster, E. M. *Aspects of the Novel*. New York, 1954.

Foster, Elizabeth S. Introduction to *The Confidence-Man: His Masquerade*, by Herman Melville. New York, 1954.

Foster, John. *The Life of Charles Dickens*. Edited by J. W. T. Ley. London, 1928.

Foulché-Delbosc, Raymond. "Bibliographie de Mateo Alemán —1598–1615." *Revue Hispanique* 42 (1918): 481–556.

———. "Remarques sur *Lazarillo de Tormes*." *Revue Hispanique* 7 (1900): 81–97.

Fowler, Alastair. "The Confidence Man." *Listener*, May 4, 1961, p. 781.

Frank, Joseph. *The Widening Gyre*. New Brunswick, N.J., 1963.

Franklin, H. Bruce. *The Wake of the Gods: Melville's Mythology*. Stanford, 1963.

Friedrich, Carl. *The Age of the Baroque, 1610–1660*. New York, 1952.

Fromm, Erich. *The Anatomy of Human Destructiveness*. London, 1974.

———. *The Fear of Freedom*. London, 1942.

Fullerton, William M. "Gil Blas." *Quarterly Review* 215 (1911): 335–51.

Gabriel, Ralph Henry. *The Course of American Democratic Thought*. New York, 1940.

García Blanco, Manuel. *Mateo Alemán y la novela picaresca alemana*. Madrid, 1928.

Gaxotte, Pierre. *La France de Louis XIV*. Paris, 1946.

Gerstenberger, Donna. "Huckleberry Finn and the World's Illusions." *Western Humanities Review* 104 (1960): 401–6.

Gili y Gaya, Samuel. Introduction to *Guzmán de Alfarache*, by Mateo Alemán. Clásicos Castellanos. Vol. 1. Madrid, 1926.

Gillet, Joseph E. "A Note on the *Lazarillo de Tormes*." *Modern Language Notes* 55 (1940): 130–34.

Gilman, Stephen. *The Art of the "Celestina."* Madison, Wis., 1956.

———. "The Death of Lazarillo de Tormes." *PMLA* 81 (1966): 149–66.

———. *The Spain of Fernando de Rojas: The Intellectual and Social Landscape of "La Celestina."* Princeton, 1972.

Gilman, William H. *Melville's Early Life and Redburn*. New York, 1951.

Glaser, Edward. "Quevedo versus Pérez de Montalván: The *Auto del Polifemo* and the Odyssean Tradition in Golden Age Spain." *Hispanic Review* 28 (1960): 103–20.

Goldberg, M. A. *Smollett and the Scottish School: Studies in Eighteenth-Century Thought*. Albuquerque, N.M., 1959.

Gómez de las Cortinas, J. Frutos. "El antihéroe y su actitud vital (Sentido de la novela picaresca)." *Cuadernos de Literatura* 7 (1950): 98–139.

González Palencia, Angel. *Del "Lazarillo" a Quevedo: Estudios históricos-literarios.* Madrid, 1946.

Granges de Surgères, Marquis de. "Les traductions françaises du *Guzman d'Alfarache.*" *Bulletin du Bibliophile* 1885, pp. 289–314.

Grass, Roland. "Morality in the Picaresque Novel." *Hispania* 42 (1959): 192–98.

Gray, M. I. *An Index to "Guzmán de Alfarache."* New Brunswick, N.J., 1949.

Green, F. *La peinture des moeurs de la bonne société dans le roman française de 1715 à 1761.* Paris, 1924.

Groethuysen, Bernard. *Philosophie de la révolution française.* 2d ed. Paris, 1956–57.

Gross, John J. "Melville's *The Confidence-Man*: The Problem of Source and Meaning." *Neuphilologische Mitteilungen* 60 (1959): 299–310.

Guillén, Claudio. "The Anatomies of Roguery: A Comparative Study in the Origins and the Nature of Picaresque Literature." Ph.D. dissertation, Harvard University, 1953.

————. "La disposición temporal del *Lazarillo de Tormes.*" *Hispanic Review* 25 (1957): 264–79.

————. *Literature as System.* Princeton, 1971.

Hainsworth, George. *Les "Novelas Exemplares" de Cervantes en France au XVIIe siècle.* Paris, 1922.

Haley, George. *Vicente Espinel and Marcos de Obregón: A Life and Its Literary Representation.* Providence, R.I., 1959.

Harrison, James G. "A Note on the Duke in *Huck Finn*: The Journeyman Printer as a Picaro." *Mark Twain Quarterly* 8 (1947): 1–2.

Hatzfeld, Helmut. "A Clarification of the Baroque Problem in the Romance Literatures." *Comparative Literature* 1 (1949): 113–39.

Haydn, Hiram. *The Counter-Renaissance.* New York, 1950.

Hayens, Kenneth C. *Grimmelshausen.* London, 1932.

Hayford, Harrison. "Poe in *The Confidence-Man.*" *Nineteenth-Century Fiction* 14 (1959): 207–18.

Hazard, Paul. *European Thought in the Eighteenth Century: From Montesquieu to Lessing.* Translated by J. L. May. London, 1954.

Heilman, Robert B. "Variations on Picaresque (*Felix Krull*)."

*Sewanee Review* 66 (1958): 547–77.

Heiser, M. F. "Cervantes in the United States." *Hispanic Review* 15 (1947): 409–35.

Heller, Erich. "Parody, Tragic and Comic: Mann's *Doctor Faustus* and *Felix Krull*." *Sewanee Review* 67 (1958): 519–46.

Herrero García, Miguel. "Nueva interpretación de la novela picaresca." *Revista de Filología Española* 24 (1937): 343–62.

Herrick, Marvin T. "The Fusion of Horatian and Aristotelian Literary Criticism, 1531–1555." *Illinois Studies in Language and Literature* 32 (1946): 1–117.

Hespelt, E. Herman. "The First German Translation of *Lazarillo de Tormes*." *Hispanic Review* 4 (1936): 170–75.

Hibbard, G. R. *Thomas Nashe: A Critical Introduction*. London, 1962.

Hoffer, Eric. *The True Believer: Thoughts on the Nature of Mass Movements*. New York, 1951.

Hoffman, Daniel G. *Form and Fable in American Fiction*. New York, 1961.

――――. "Melville's 'Story of China Aster'." *American Literature* 22 (1950): 137–49.

Hoffman, Frederick J. *The Mortal No: Death and the Modern Imagination*. Princeton, 1964.

Hollmann, Werner. "Thomas Mann's *Felix Krull* and *Lazarillo*." *Modern Language Notes* 66 (1951): 445–51.

Honig, Edwin. *Dark Conceit: The Making of Allegory*. Evanston, Ill., 1959.

Hoole, W. Stanley. *Alias Simon Suggs: The Life and Times of Johnson Jones Hooper*. University, Ala., 1952.

Horsford, Howard C. "Evidence of Melville's Plans for a Sequel to *The Confidence-Man*." *American Literature* 24 (1952): 85–89.

Howard, Leon. *Herman Melville*. Berkeley, 1951.

Howells, William Dean. "Lazarillo de Tormes." In *My Literary Passions*, by William Dean Howells. New York, 1895.

Hubbell, Jay B. *The South in American Literature, 1607–1900*. Durham, N.C., 1954.

Huizinga, Johan. *Erasmus and the Age of Reformation*. Translated by Charles F. Hopman. New York, 1957.

――――. *Men and Ideas: Essays*. Translated by James S. Holmes and Hans van Marle. Meridian Books. New York, 1959.

――――. *The Waning of the Middle Ages*. Translated by Charles F. Hopman. New York, 1956.

# Bibliography

Hume, Martin. *Spanish Influence on English Literature.* London, 1905.

Icaza, Francisco A. de. *Sucesos reales que parecen imaginados de Gutierre de Cetina, Juan de la Cueva y Mateo Alemán.* Madrid, 1919.

Iknayan, Marguerite. "The Fortunes of *Gil Blas* during the Romantic Period." *French Review* 30 (1958): 370–77.

Irwin, William R. *The Making of Jonathan Wild.* New York, 1941.

James, Henry. *The Art of the Novel: Critical Prefaces.* New York, 1934.

Janss, Hans Robert. "Ursprung und Bedeutung der Ich-Form im *Lazarillo de Tormes.*" *Romanistisches Jahrbuch* 8 (1957): 290–311.

Jaster, Frank. "Melville's Cosmopolitan: The Experience of Life in *The Confidence-Man: His Masquerade.*" *Southern Quarterly* 8 (1970): 201–10.

Johnson, Carroll B. "*El Buscón*: D. Pablos, D. Diego y D. Francisco." *Hispanófila* 51 (1974): 1–26.

Jones, J. A. "The Duality and Complexity of *Guzmán de Alfarache*: Some Thoughts on the Structure and Interpretation of Alemán's Novel." In *Knaves and Swindlers: Essays on the Picaresque Novel in Europe*, edited by Christine J. Whitbourn. London, 1974.

Jones, Royston O., ed. *La vida de Lazarillo y de sus fortunas y adversidades.* Manchester, England, 1963.

Jusserand, J. J. *The English Novel in the Time of Shakespeare.* Translated by Elizabeth Lee. Rev. ed. London, 1899.

Kahrl, George M. *Tobias Smollett, Traveller-Novelist.* Chicago, 1945.

Kaufmann, Fritz. *Thomas Mann: The World as Will and Representation.* Boston, 1957.

Keller, Donald S. "*Lazarillo de Tormes*, 1554–1954: An Analytical Bibliography of Twelve Recent Studies." *Hispania* 37 (1954): 453–56.

Kerényi, Karl. "The Trickster in Relation to Greek Mythology." In *The Trickster: A Study in American Indian Mythology*, by Paul Radin. London, 1956.

Kermode, Frank. *The Sense of an Ending: Studies in the Theory of Fiction.* London, 1966.

Kettle, Arnold. *An Introduction to the English Novel.* 2 vols. London, 1951.

Kirk, G. S. *Myth: Its Meaning and Functions in Ancient and Other*

# Bibliography

*Cultures*. London, Berkeley, and Los Angeles, 1970.

Knapp, Lewis Mansfield. *Tobias Smollett: Doctor of Men and Manners*. Princeton, 1949.

Kuhlmann, Susan. *Knave, Fool, and Genius: The Confidence Man as He Appears in Nineteenth-Century American Fiction*. Chapel Hill, N.C., 1973.

Laurenti, Joseph L. *Bibliografía de la literatura picaresca*. New York, 1973.

Lawrence, Alexandre. "L'influence de Lesage sur Smollett." *Revue de Litérature Comparée* 12 (1932): 533–45.

Lawrence, D. H. *Studies in Classic American Literature*. New York, 1923.

Lázaro Carreter, Fernando. "Glosas críticas a *Los Pícaros en la Literatura* de Alexander A. Parker." *Hispanic Review* 41 (1973): 469–97.

————. *Lazarillo de Tormes en la picaresca*. Barcelona, 1972.

Leavis, F. R. *The Great Tradition: George Eliot, Henry James, Joseph Conrad*. Peregrine Books. Harmondsworth, 1962.

Lebowitz, Alan. *Progress into Silence: A Study of Melville's Heroes*. Bloomington and London, 1970.

Leonard, Irving A. "*Guzmán de Alfarache* in the Lima Book Trade, 1613." *Hispanic Review* 11 (1943): 210–20.

Levêque, André. "'L'Honnête Homme' et 'l'Homme de Bien' au XVIIe siècle." *PMLA* 72 (1957): 620–32.

Levin, Harry. "*Don Quixote* and *Moby-Dick*." In *Cervantes Across the Centuries*, edited by Angel Flores and M. J. Benardete. New York, 1947.

————. *The Power of Blackness: Hawthorne, Poe, Melville*. London, 1958.

Lewis, R. W. B. *The American Adam: Innocence, Tragedy and Tradition in the Nineteenth Century*. Chicago, 1955.

————. *The Picaresque Saint: Representative Figures in Contemporary Fiction*. Philadelphia and New York, 1959.

Lindsay, J. M. *Thomas Mann*. Oxford, 1954.

Lintilhac, Eugène. *Lesage*. Paris, 1893.

Lira Urquieta, Pedro. *Sobre Quevedo y otros clásicos*. Madrid, 1958.

Little, T. E. "Dead Souls." In *Knaves and Swindlers: Essays on the Picaresque Novel in Europe*, edited by Christine J. Whitbourn. London, 1974.

Longhurst, John E. *Erasmus and the Spanish Inquisition: The Case of Juan de Valdés*. Albuquerque, N.M., 1950.

# Bibliography

Lukács, Georg. *The Historical Novel.* Translated by Hannah and Stanley Mitchell. London, 1962.

Lynn, Kenneth S. "Huck and Jim." *Yale Review* 47 (1958): 421–31.

———. *Mark Twain and Southwestern Humor.* London, 1959.

Macaya Lahman, Enrique. *Bibliografía del Lazarillo de Tormes.* San José, Costa Rica, 1935.

McCombie, F. "*Count Fathom* and *El Buscón.*" *Notes and Queries* 7 (1960): 297–99.

McCormick, John. *Catastrophe and Imagination: An Interpretation of the Recent English and American Novel.* London, 1957.

McCullough, Bruce. *Representative English Novelists: Defoe to Conrad.* New York, 1946.

McGrady, Donald. *Mateo Alemán.* New York, 1968.

———. "Social Irony in *Lazarillo de Tormes* and Its Implications for Authorship." *Romance Philology* 23 (1970): 557–67.

McKillop, Alan Dugald. *The Early Masters of English Fiction.* Lawrence, Kan., 1956.

McLuhan, Marshall. *The Gutenberg Galaxy: The Making of Typographic Man.* Toronto, 1962.

Madariaga, Salvador de. *Don Quixote: An Introductory Essay in Psychology.* Rev. ed. London, 1961.

Magarshack, David. *Gogol: A Life.* London, 1957.

Maldonado de Guevara, Francisco. *Interpretación del Lazarillo de Tormes.* Madrid, 1957.

Mancing, Howard. "The Deceptiveness of *Lazarillo de Tormes.*" *PMLA* 90 (1975): 426–32.

Mandel, Oscar. "The Function of the Norm in *Don Quixote.*" *Modern Philology* 55 (1957): 154–63.

May, Rollo. *Power and Innocence: A Search for the Sources of Violence.* New York, 1972.

May, T. E. "Good and Evil in the *Buscón*: A Survey." *Modern Language Review* 45 (1950): 319–35.

———. "Pícaro: A Suggestion." *Romanic Review* 43 (1952): 27–33.

Menéndez Pidal, Ramón. *The Spaniards in Their History.* Translated by Walter Starkie. London, 1950.

Mérimée, Ernest. *A History of Spanish Literature.* Rev. ed. Translated by S. Griswold Morley. London, 1931.

Meriwether, Frank Tryon. "The Rogue in the Life and Humor of the Old Southwest." Ph.D. dissertation, Louisiana State University, 1952.

# Bibliography

Merriman, Roger B. *The Rise of the Spanish Empire in the Old World and the New.* 4 vols. New York, 1918–34.

Meyerhoff, Hans. *Time in Literature.* Berkeley, 1955.

Miller, James E., Jr. "*The Confidence-Man:* His Guises." *PMLA* 74 (1959): 102–11.

Miller, Stuart. *The Picaresque Novel.* Cleveland, 1967.

Mitchell, Edward. "From Action to Essence: Some Notes on the Structure of Melville's *The Confidence-Man.*" *American Literature* 40 (1968): 27–37.

Mitchie, J. A. "The Unity of *Moll Flanders.*" In *Knaves and Swindlers: Essays on the Picaresque Novel in Europe,* edited by Christine J. Whitbourn. London, 1974.

Monteser, Frederick. *The Picaresque Element in Western Literature.* University, Ala., 1975.

Montesinos, José F. "Gracián o la picaresca pura." *Cruz y Raya* 1 (1933): 37–63.

Moore, Olin Harris. "Mark Twain and Don Quixote." *PMLA* 37 (1922): 324–46.

Moorman, Charles. "Myth and Medieval Literature: *Sir Gawain and the Green Knight.*" In *Myth and Literature: Contemporary Theory and Practice,* edited by John B. Vickery. Lincoln, Neb., 1966.

Moreno Báez, Enrique. "¿Hay una tesis en el *Guzmán de Alfarache?*" *Revista de Universidad de Buenos Aires* 3 (1945): 269–91.

————. *Lección y sentido del Guzmán de Alfarache.* Madrid, 1948.

Morreale, Margarita. "Reflejos de la vida española en el *Lazarillo.*" *Clavileño* 5 (1954): 28–31.

Morris, C. B. *The Unity and Structure of Quevedo's Buscón: Desgracias encadenadas.* Hull, 1965.

Murray, Henry A. Introduction to *Pierre, or, The Ambiguities,* by Herman Melville. New York, 1949.

Nelson, Donald F. *Portrait of the Artist as Hermes: A Study of Myth and Psychology in Thomas Mann's "Felix Krull."* Chapel Hill, N.C., 1971.

Nichol, John W. "Melville and the Midwest." *PMLA* 66 (1951): 613–25.

Noble, R. W. *Joyce Cary.* Edinburgh, 1973.

Northup, George Tyler. *An Introduction to Spanish Literature.* 3d rev. ed. Chicago, 1960.

Novak, Maximillian E. "Freedom, Libertinism, and the Picaresque." In *Racism in the Eighteenth Century.* Studies in Eighteenth-Century Culture, 3. Edited by Harold E. Pagliaro. Cleveland and London, 1973.

―――. "The Problem of Necessity in Defoe's Fiction." *Philological Quarterly* 40 (1961): 513–24.

―――. "Robinson Crusoe's Fear and the Search for Natural Man." *Modern Philology* 58 (1961): 238–45.

Nykl, A. R. "Pícaro." *Revue Hispanique* 77 (1929): 172–86.

Oakeshott, Michael. Introduction to *Leviathan*, by Thomas Hobbes. Oxford, 1960.

O'Connor, William Van. "Melville on the Nature of Hope." *University of Kansas City Review* 22 (1955): 123–30.

Oliver, Egbert S. "Melville's Picture of Emerson and Thoreau in *The Confidence-Man*." *College English* 8 (1946): 61–72.

Ornstein, Robert. "The Ending of *Huckleberry Finn*." *Modern Language Notes* 74 (1959): 698–702.

Ortega y Gasset, José. *The Dehumanization of Art and Other Essays on Art, Culture, and Literature*. Princeton, 1968.

―――. *Man and Crisis*. Translated by Mildred Adams. London, 1959.

Pane, Remigio Ugo. *English Translations from the Spanish, 1484–1943: A Bibliography*. New Brunswick, N.J., 1944.

Papell, Antonio. *Quevedo, su tiempo, su vida, su obra*. Barcelona, 1947.

Parker, Alexander A. *Literature and the Delinquent: The Picaresque Novel in Spain and Europe, 1599–1753*. Edinburgh, 1967.

―――. "The Psychology of the 'Pícaro' in *El Buscón*." *Modern Language Review* 42 (1947): 58–69.

―――. "The Spanish Drama of the Golden Age: A Method of Analysis and Interpretation." In *The Great Playwrights*, edited by Eric Bentley. Vol. 1. Garden City, N.Y., 1970.

Pascal, Roy. *Design and Truth in Autobiography*. London, 1960.

Patch, Howard R. *The Goddess Fortuna in Medieval Literature*. Cambridge, Mass., 1927.

Paulson, Ronald. *The Fictions of Satire*. Baltimore, 1967.

―――. *Satire and the Novel in Eighteenth-Century England*. New Haven and London, 1967.

―――. "Satire in the Early Novels of Smollett." *Journal of English and Germanic Philology* 59 (1960): 381–402.

Penrod, James H. "The Folk Hero as Prankster in the Old Southwestern Yarns." *Kentucky Folklore Record* 2 (1956): 5–12.

——. "Folk Motifs in Old Southwestern Humor." *Southern Folklore Quarterly* 19 (1955): 117–24.

Pereda Valdés, J. *La novela picaresca y el pícaro en España y América.* Montevideo, 1950.

Pérez, Louis C. "On Laughter in the *Lazarillo de Tormes.*" *Hispania* 43 (1960): 529–33.

Peseux-Richard, H. "A propos du mot *pícaro.*" *Revue Hispanique* 81 (1933): 247–49.

Pettit, Arthur G. *Mark Twain & the South.* Lexington, Ky., 1974.

Pierce, Roy Harvey. "Melville's Indian-Hater: A Note on a Meaning of *The Confidence-Man.*" *PMLA* 67 (1952): 942–48.

Piper, Anson C. "The 'Breadly Paradise' of Lazarillo de Tormes." *Hispania* 44 (1961): 269–71.

Putnam, Samuel. Introduction to *The Ingenious Gentleman Don Quixote de la Mancha,* by Cervantes. Vol. 1. London, 1953.

Radin, Paul. *The Trickster: A Study in American Indian Mythology.* With commentaries by Karl Kerényi and C. G. Jung. London, 1956.

Ramon, Michel Robert. "Nueva interpretación del pícaro y de la novela picaresca hecha a base de un estudio de las tres obras maestras del género." Ph.D. dissertation, Northwestern University, 1956.

Rand, Marguerite C. "Lazarillo de Tormes, Classic and Contemporary." *Hispania* 44 (1961): 222–29.

Randall, Dale B. J. "The Classical Ending of Quevedo's *Buscón.*" *Hispanic Review* 32 (1964): 101–8.

——. *The Golden Tapestry: A Critical Survey of Non-Chivalric Spanish Fiction in English Translation, 1543–1657.* Durham, N.C., 1963.

Ray, Gordon N. *Thackeray: The Uses of Adversity (1811–1846).* London, 1955.

Reilly, John M., ed. *Twentieth Century Interpretations of "Invisible Man."* Englewood Cliffs, N.J., 1970.

Reynier, Gustave. *Le roman réaliste au XVIIe siècle.* Paris, 1914.

Richetti, John J. *Popular Fiction before Richardson: Narrative Patterns, 1700–1739.* Oxford, 1969.

Rico, Francisco. *La novela picaresca española.* Barcelona, 1967.

——. *La novela picaresca y el punto de vista.* 2d ed. Barcelona, 1973.

Ritchie, J. M. "Grimmelshausen's *Simplicissimus* and *The Runagate Courage.*" In *Knaves and Swindlers: Essays on the Picaresque*

# Bibliography

*Novel in Europe*, edited by Christine J. Whitbourn. London, 1974.

Rodríguez Marín, Francisco. *Discursos leídos ante la Real Academia Española*. Madrid, 1907.

Rodríguez Moñino, Antonio. "Los manuscritos del *Buscón* de Quevedo." *Nueva Revista de Filología Hispánica* 7 (1953): 657–72.

Roland, Brother A. "La psicología de la novela picaresca." *Hispania* 36 (1953): 423–26.

Rosenberry, Edward H. *Melville and the Comic Spirit*. Cambridge, Mass., 1955.

――――. "Melville's Ship of Fools." *PMLA* 75 (1960): 604–8.

Rourke, Constance. *American Humor: A Study of the National Character*. New York, 1931.

Rudder, Robert S. Introduction to *Lazarillo of Tormes: His Fortunes and Misfortunes as Told by Himself*, translated by Robert S. Rudder. New York, 1973.

Russell, P. E. "*Don Quixote* as a Funny Book." *Modern Language Review* 64 (1969): 312–26.

――――. "English Seventeenth-Century Interpretations of Spanish Literature." *Atlante* 1 (1953): 65–77.

Sacy, S. de. "Le miroir sur la grande route: Les romans de Stendhal et le roman picaresque." *Mercure de France* 306 (1949): 64–80.

Salinas, Pedro. "El *Héroe* literario y la novela picaresca española: Sémantica e historia literaria." *Revista de la Universidad de Buenos Aires* 4 (1946): 75–84.

Salomon, Roger B. *Twain and the Image of History*. New Haven, 1961.

Sánchez y Escribano, Francisco. "La fórmula del Barroco literario presentida en un incidente del *Guzmán de Alfarache*." *Revista de Ideas Estéticas* 12 (1954): 137–42.

San Miguel, Angel. *Sentido y estructura del "Guzmán de Alfarache" de Mateo Alemán*. Madrid, 1971.

Scobie, Alexander. *Aspects of the Ancient Romance and Its Heritage: Essays on Apuleius, Petronius, and the Greek Romances*. Meisenheim am Glan, 1969.

Scott, Walter. *Lives of the Novelists*. The World's Classics. London, 1906.

Sealts, Merton M., Jr. "Melville's Reading: A Check-List of Books Owned and Borrowed." *Harvard Library Bulletin* 2

(1948): 141–63, 378–92; 3 (1949): 119–30, 268–77, 407–21; 4 (1950): 98–109; 6 (1952): 239–47.

Secord, Arthur Wellesley. "Studies in the Narrative Method of Defoe." *University of Illinois Studies in Language and Literature* 9 (1924): 3–248.

Sedgewick, William Ellery. *Herman Melville: The Tragedy of Mind*. Cambridge, Mass., 1945.

Seidlin, Oskar. "Picaresque Elements in Thomas Mann's Work." *Modern Language Quarterly* 12 (1951): 183–200.

Selig, Karl Ludwig. "Concerning Gogol's *Dead Souls* and *Lazarillo de Tormes*." *Symposium* 8 (1954): 138–40.

Seltzer, Leon F. "Camus's Absurd and the World of Melville's *Confidence-Man*." *PMLA* 82 (1967): 14–27.

Shroeder, John W. "Sources and Symbols for Melville's *Confidence-Man*." *PMLA* 66 (1951): 363–80.

Sicroff, Albert. *Les controverses des statuts de 'pureté de sang' en Espagne du XVe au XVIIe siècle*. Paris, 1960.

———. "Sobre el estilo de *Lazarillo de Tormes*." *Nueva Revista de Filología Hispánica* 11 (1957): 157–70.

Sims, Elmer R. "Four Seventeenth-Century Translations of *Lazarillo de Tormes*." *Hispanic Review* 5 (1937): 316–32.

Smith, Henry Nash. Introduction to *Adventures of Huckleberry Finn*, by Mark Twain. Boston, 1958.

———, ed. *Mark Twain: A Collection of Critical Essays*. Englewood Cliffs, N.J., 1963.

———. "A Sound Heart and a Deformed Conscience." In *Mark Twain: A Collection of Critical Essays*, edited by Henry Nash Smith. Englewood Cliffs, N.J., 1963.

———. *Virgin Land: The American West as Symbol and Myth*. New York, 1957.

Sobejano, Gonzalo. "De la intención y valor del *Guzmán de Alfarache*." *Romanische Forschungen* 71 (1959): 267–311.

Spivak, Bernard. *Shakespeare and the Allegory of Evil: The History of a Metaphor in Relation to His Major Villains*. New York, 1958.

Stamm, James R. "The Use and Types of Humor in the Picaresque Novel." *Hispania* 42 (1959): 482–87.

Stamm, Rudolf G. "Daniel Defoe: An Artist in the Puritan Tradition." *Philological Quarterly* 15 (1936): 225–46.

Stanford, W. B. *The Ulysses Theme: A Study in the Adaptability of a Traditional Hero*. Oxford, 1954.

Starr, George A. *Defoe and Spiritual Autobiography*. Princeton, 1965.

Stern, Milton R. *The Fine Hammered Steel of Herman Melville.* Urbana, Ill., 1957.

Stone, Albert E., Jr. *The Innocent Eye: Childhood in Mark Twain's Imagination.* New Haven, 1961.

Stonehouse, J. H., ed. *Catalog of the Library of Charles Dickens.* London, 1935.

Strugnell, A. R. "Diderot's *Neveu de Rameau*: Portrait of the Rogue in the French Enlightenment." In *Knaves and Swindlers: Essays on the Picaresque Novel in Europe*, edited by Christine J. Whitbourn. London, 1974.

Suárez, Mireya. *La novela picaresca y el pícaro en la literatura española.* Madrid, 1926.

Talon, Henri. *John Bunyan: The Man and His Works.* Translated by Barbara Wall. London, 1951.

Tarr, F. Courtney. "Literary and Artistic Unity in the *Lazarillo de Tormes.*" *PMLA* 42 (1927): 404–21.

Tawney, R. H. *Religion and the Rise of Capitalism.* London, 1926.

Thomas, Henry. "The English Translations of Quevedo's *La Vida del Buscón.*" *Revue Hispanique* 81 (1933): 282–99.

―――. *Spanish and Portuguese Romances of Chivalry.* Cambridge, 1920.

Thompson, Lawrance. *Melville's Quarrel with God.* Princeton, 1954.

Thompson, Stith. *Motif-Index of Folk Literature.* Rev. ed. 6 vols. Copenhagen, 1955–58.

Ticknor, George. *History of Spanish Literature.* 3 vols. London, 1849.

Tierno Galván, Enrique. *Sobre la novela picaresca y otros escritos.* Madrid, 1974.

Tilley, Arthur. *The Decline of the Age of Louis XIV, or French Literature, 1687–1715.* Cambridge, 1929.

Tillotson, Geoffrey. *Thackeray the Novelist.* Cambridge, 1954.

Tillyard, E. M. W. *The Epic Strain in the English Novel.* London, 1958.

Trenkner, Sophie. *The Greek Novella in the Classical Period.* Cambridge, 1958.

Trilling, Lionel. *The Liberal Imagination: Essays on Literature and Society.* London, 1951.

―――. *Sincerity and Authenticity.* Cambridge, Mass., 1971.

Troeltsch, Ernst. *The Social Teaching of the Christian Churches.* Translated by Olive Wyon. 2 vols. London, 1931.

# Bibliography

Turkevich, Ludmilla Buketoff. *Cervantes in Russia*. Princeton, 1950.

Tuveson, Ernest. "The Importance of Shaftesbury." *ELH* 20 (1953): 267–99.

Underhill, John Garrett. *Spanish Literature in the England of the Tudors*. New York, 1899.

Valbuena Prat, Angel. *Historia de la literatura española*. 2 vols. Barcelona, 1937.

————. Introducción to *La novela picaresca española*, by Angel Valbuena Prat. 2d. rev. ed. Madrid, 1946.

Van Ghent, Dorothy. *The English Novel: Form and Function*. New York, 1953.

Van Praag, J. A. "Sobre el sentido del *Guzmán de Alfarache*." *Estudios dedicados a Menéndez Pidal* 5 (1954): 283–306.

Vickery, John B., ed. *Myth and Literature: Contemporary Theory and Practice*. Lincoln, Neb., 1966.

Wagenknecht, Edward C. *Mark Twain, the Man and His Work*. Rev. ed. Norman, Okla., 1961.

Wagner, Charles Philip. Introduction to *The Life of Lazarillo de Tormes*, translated by Louis How. New York, 1917.

Warren, F. M. *History of the Novel Previous to the Seventeenth Century*. New York, 1895.

Wasiolek, Edward. "The Structure of Make-Believe: *Huckleberry Finn*." *University of Kansas City Review* 24 (1957): 97–101.

Watkin, E. I. *Catholic Art and Culture*. Rev. ed. London, 1947.

Watt, Ian. *The Rise of the Novel: Studies in Defoe, Richardson and Fielding*. London, 1957.

————. "*Robinson Crusoe* as a Myth." *Essays in Criticism* 1 (1951): 95–119.

Watts, Henry Edward. "Quevedo and His Works, with an Essay on the Picaresque Novel." In *Pablo de Segovia, the Spanish Sharper*, by Quevedo. London, 1927.

Weber, Max. *The Protestant Ethic and the Spirit of Capitalism*. Translated by Talcott Parsons. London, 1930.

Wellek, René, and Warren, Austin. *Theory of Literature*. London, 1949.

Wendt, Allan. "The Moral Allegory of *Jonathan Wild*." *ELH* 24 (1957): 306–20.

West, Rebecca. *The Court and the Castle: A Study of the Interactions of Political and Religious Ideas in Imaginative Literature*. London, 1958.

Wharey, James Blanton. "Bunyan's Mr. Badman and the Picaresque Novel." *University of Texas Studies in English*, 1924, pp. 49–61.

Whitbourn, Christine J., ed. *Knaves and Swindlers: Essays on the Picaresque Novel in Europe*. London, 1974.

White, John J. *Mythology in the Modern Novel: A Study in Prefigurative Techniques*. Princeton, 1971.

Willey, Basil. *The Eighteenth Century Background: Studies on the Idea of Nature in the Thought of the Period*. London, 1946.

———. *The Seventeenth-Century Background: Studies in the Thought of the Age in Relation to Poetry and Religion*. London, 1934.

Williams, Raymond. *Culture and Society, 1780–1950*. London, 1960.

Williams, Stanley T. *The Spanish Background of American Literature*. 2 vols. New Haven, 1955.

Willis, Raymond S. "Lazarillo and the Pardoner: The Artistic Necessity of the Fifth *Tratado*." *Hispanic Review* 27 (1959): 267–79.

Wilson, Edward M. "Cervantes and English Literature of the Seventeenth Century." *Bulletin Hispanique* 50 (1948): 27–52.

Wolkenfeld, Jack. *Joyce Cary: The Developing Style*. New York, 1968.

Wright, Nathalia. "The Confidence Men of Melville and Cooper: An American Indictment." *American Quarterly* 4 (1952): 266–68.

Wright, Richardson. *Hawkers & Walkers in Early America*. Philadelphia, 1927.

Yates, Norris W. *William T. Porter and the "Spirit of the Times": A Study of the Big Bear School of Humor*. Baton Rouge, La., 1957.

# Index

# Index

# Index

Reformation Spain, 60, 64, 66
Howells, William Dean: praises *Lazarillo*, 59, 230 (n. 7); and Mark Twain, 178–79
*Huckleberry Finn* (Clemens), 40, 116, 177–87. *See also* Picaro, psychology of

## I

*Invisible Man* (Ellison), 23, 208–10. *See also* Picaro, as invisible man

## J

James, Henry, 4, 85, 146, 165; distinguishes novel and romance, 94
*Jonathan Wild* [*The Life of Mr. Jonathan Wild the Great*] (Fielding), 101, 102, 111, 125–29
Joyce, James, 4, 6, 7, 28, 183, 203, 207, 209, 210

## L

La Bruyère, Jean de, 108, 112
*Lazarillo de Tormes* [*La vida de Lazarillo de Tormes y de sus fortunas y adversidades*], 4, 14, 15, 16, 19, 22, 23, 60, 66, 83, 91, 92, 100, 102, 103, 108, 120, 122, 124, 125, 128, 139, 143, 149, 157, 176, 177, 178, 185, 189, 195, 196, 197, 199, 201, 203, 204, 208, 213, 214, 215; parody and satire in, 12–13, 34–35, 38, 42–45, 47, 48, 54; trickster archetype in, 13, 26; autobiographical form of, 27–28, 32–33, 36, 45–49; text of, 28–29, 41, 45; authorship problem of, 29–32, 43, 48, 52, 55; date of, 30–32; as *Bildungsroman*, 37–42, 56; hunger motif in, 40–42; religious meaning in, 40, 44, 46, 51, 52, 55–57; compared with *Metamorphoses*, 51; critical reputation of, 58–59; compared with *Guzmán*, 68–71, 73, 78–80. *See also* Novel, modern; Picaresque novel; Picaro
Lesage, Alain-René, 23, 101, 102, 103, 201; as translator of *Guzmán*, 59–60, 115; as dramatist, 112–14. *See also* *Gil Blas*
*Leviathan* (Hobbes): myth of natural man in, 23, 93–97, 104, 106–8, 111; influences eighteenth-century novel, 107–8. *See also* Myth, of natural man and society
Loneliness. *See* Picaro, loneliness of
Love. *See* Myth, of unity and love

## M

Mann, Thomas, 16, 147, 148, 188, 201; idea of artist of, 193–95. *See also* *Felix Krull*
Melville, Herman, 147–55 passim, 179, 181, 186, 187, 188, 201, 205; visits West, 158; complex vision in, 158–62, 168; sense of history in, 177. *See also* *Confidence-Man*
*Metamorphoses* (Apuleius): compared with *Lazarillo*, 27–28, 51. *See also* Picaresque novel, autobiographical form of
Molière: *The Misanthrope*, 62, 112–14
*Moll Flanders* (Defoe), 24, 75, 100–101, 102
Myth: diversity of, 4–6; trickster archetype in, 6–7, 12–14, 25, 103, 111, 149–58, 180; as underlying narrative structure, 6–8, 102, 103, 111–12; as individual experience, 8–9; and genre, 16–17; of child-hero, 35; in *Lazarillo*, 57–58; of natural man and society, 93–97, 102, 103, 106–7, 109, 111–12, 121, 123, 125, 144; and the novel, 148, 163; of archetypal American, 152–61 passim, 168, 209; of Creation, 173–74; of unity and love, 192, 199–203, 205; of Hermes, 193, 199; of Faust, 194–95; Christianity as, 205–6; of conversion, 214–15. *See also* Picaresque novel; Picaro

## N

Nashe, Thomas: *The Unfortunate Traveller*, 99
Novel, modern: definition of, 3–4; birth of, in Spain, 4, 14–15, 203; perspective of, 11–12; realism in, 22, 85, 96, 148, 213; as quest, 26, 116–17, 159, 177, 206, 209, 215–16; history and poetry in, 67; of man-

# Index

141–42, 144, 148, 161; lack of, in Spanish picaresque masterpieces, 50–52, 85–86; and Cervantes, 68. *See also* Novel, modern; Picaresque novel, functional illusionism in

*Robinson Crusoe* (Defoe), 59, 79, 99–100

Rogue. *See* Picaro, misconceptions of

Rogue anatomies, 18, 19, 96, 111, 139, 141

Rojas, Fernando de, 155; life of, correlative to picaro's, 9–11; Petrarchanism of, 93. See also *Celestina*; *Converso* situation; Picaro, psychology of

Romances of chivalry: parodied in *Lazarillo*, 34–35. *See also* Picaresque novel, parody in

**S**

Shaftesbury. *See* Cooper, Anthony Ashley

Shakespeare, William, 11, 12, 16, 36, 54, 59, 93, 97, 131, 166, 169, 170, 172, 173, 212

Smollett, Tobias, 20, 23, 83, 98, 99, 101, 103, 110, 111, 139, 144, 201; didactic purpose in, 65; typical protagonists of, 132–34; inner conflict of, 135. See *Ferdinand Count Fathom*

Solórzano, Castillo, 100

Southwestern humor: picaro reborn in, 154–58; Mark Twain influenced by, 180–81. *See also* Hooper, Johnson Jones; Myth, of archetypal American

*Spirit of the Times*, 154–55, 233 (n. 26)

Stendhal. *See* Beyle, Marie Henri

Swift, Jonathan, 80–81, 120. See also *Gulliver's Travels*

**T**

Thackeray, William Makepeace, 23, 99, 102, 201. See also *Barry Lyndon*

Tragicomedy. *See* Picaresque novel, genre of

Trickster. *See* Myth, trickster archetype in

Twain, Mark. *See* Clemens, Samuel Langhorne

**U**

Ubeda, López de. See *Pícara Justina*

**V**

Vice, in allegory of evil, 14, 96–97, 99, 131. *See also* Picaro, as Vice or Satan

*The Author*

Alexander Blackburn is associate professor of English
at the University of Colorado at Colorado Springs.


*The Book*

*Typeface*
Mergenthaler V-I-P Bembo

*Design and composition*
The University of North Carolina Press

*Paper*
Sixty pound Olde Style by S. D. Warren

*Binding cloth*
Roxite B 53593 by Holliston Mills, Inc.

*Printer and binder*
Edwards Brothers


*Published by The University of North Carolina Press*